MANAGEMENT AND CULTURAL VALUES

MANAGEMENT AND CULTURAL VALUES

The Indigenization of Organizations in Asia

Editors

HENRY S.R. KAO
DURGANAND SINHA
BERNHARD WILPERT

Sage Publications
New Delhi/Thousand Oaks/London

First published in 1999 by

Sage Publications India Pvt Ltd
M–32 Market, Greater Kailash–I
New Delhi–110 048

Sage Publications Inc
2455 Teller Road
Thousand Oaks, California 91320

Sage Publications Ltd
6 Bonhill Street
London EC2A 4PU

Published by Tejeshwar Singh for Sage Publications India Pvt Ltd, typeset by Siva Math Setters, Chennai, and printed at Chaman Enterprises, Delhi.

Library of Congress Cataloging-in-Publication Data

Management and cultural values/the indigenization of organizations in Asia/editors, Henry S.R. Kao, Durganand Sinha, Bernhard Wilpert.
     p. cm. (cloth) (pbk.)
    Conference papers.
    Includes bibliographical references and index.
    1. Corporate culture—Asia—Congresses. 2. Management—Asia—Congresses. 3. Industrial management—Asia—Congresses. I. Kao, Henry S.R., 1940–. II. Sinha, Durganand. III. Wilpert, Bernhard, 1936–.
HD58.7.M345   658′.0095—dc21   1999   99–17242

ISBN: 0–7619–9318–5 (US-hb)   81–7036–783–2 (India-hb)
       0–7619–9319–3 (US-pb)   81–7036–784–0 (India-pb)

Sage Production Team: Aruna Ramachandran, R.A.M. Brown and
                 Santosh Rawat

Dedicated to
Professor Durganand Sinha
A Great Scholar, Humanist and Friend

(1922–1998)

CONTENTS

I

CONCEPTUAL ISSUES

II

WORK CULTURE

III

VALUES AND ORGANIZATIONS

IV

INDIGENOUS FACTORS IN MANAGERIAL LEADERSHIP

LIST OF TABLES

LIST OF FIGURES

LIST OF ABBREVIATIONS

A	Adult
APQC	American Productivity and Quality Center
BEL	Bharat Electronics Limited
CC	Compliant Child
CEO	Chief Executive Officer
CP	Controlling Parent
CPC	Communist Party of China
FC	Free Child
G & B	Godrej and Boyce
HCL	Hindustan Computers Limited
IAAP	International Association of Applied Psychology
IOC	Indian Oil Corporation
IPC	Influence–Power-sharing Continuum
IPCL	Indian Petrochemicals Corporation Limited
IR	Industrial Relations
IUPsyS	International Union of Psychological Science
IWE	Islamic Work Ethic
JDI	Job Description Index
JIT	Just-in-Time
MBO	Management by Objectives
METSA	Managerial Effectiveness Through Self Awareness
MUL	Maruti Udyog Limited
n-ach	need for achievement
NICs	Newly Industrialized Countries
NIIT	National Institute of Information Technology
NR	Nurturing Parent
NTL	Nurturant Task Leader
OB	Organizational Behaviour
OD	Organizational Development

PEM	Population–Ecology Model
PI	Pioneering Innovating (model)
QC	Quality Control
RC	Rebellious Child
SPIRO	Style Profile of Influence Role in Organization
SRF	Shri Ram Fibres
TA	Transactional Analysis
TELCO	Tata Engineering and Locomotive Company
TISCO	Tata Iron and Steel Company

PREFACE

Indigenous psychology in Southeast Asia has developed with the deep introspection of Asian psychologists, outgrowing its overwhelming dependence on the Western approach to studying and explaining human behaviour. The focus has shifted from merely adopting Western theories, conclusions and practices to one which cherishes the unique social and cultural factors influencing human behaviour and the applications of psychology for national development which are in considerable demand in the Southeast Asian context.

In the last two decades of the 20th century, psychologists from national organizations of forty-six countries under the International Union of Psychological Science (IUPsyS) have pursued the important interest of indigenous psychology by establishing an International Network of Centres of Research in Psychology in the Third World. The late Prof. Durganand Sinha, (Chairman of the IUPsyS International Network of Psychology and the Developing World), and Prof. Henry S.R. Kao (President of the Division of Psychology and National Development, International Association of Applied Psychology [IAAP]), organized the first international conference in the Department of Psychology at the University of Hong Kong, from 27 to 29 April 1987. The conference addressed how psychology could contribute to national development by understanding the shared beliefs and value systems of a culture. The papers presented at that conference were compiled in the first such volume, *Social Values and Development: Asian Perspectives* (Sinha and Kao, 1988, Sage). With such a promising beginning, this area of work has continued, with the support of colleagues from many developing and advanced economies, to promote the important theme of social and cultural factors in the development of indigenous psychology in both research and applications.

The International Symposium of Social Values and Effective Organizations (26–30 November 1988) was organized one year later at the National Central University, Chung-Li, Taiwan. Papers selected from this symposium were published in the second volume, *Effective Organizations and Social Values* (Kao, Sinha and Ng, 1995, Sage). With the positive reception and inspiration of the first two books, Prof. Kao and Prof. Sinha were encouraged to further enrich psychology literature especially within Asia. Hence, they undertook another joint project which resulted in their third publication, *Asian Perspectives on Psychology* (Kao and Sinha, 1996, Sage).

The third symposium, on 'Indigenous Behaviours in Effective Management and Organizations,' was organized during the Asian–Pacific Regional Conference of Psychology convened under the auspices of IUPsyS and co-sponsored by the IAAP and the International Association of Cross-cultural Psychology. It was held in Guangzhou, China, from 27 to 30 August 1995. This symposium was organized by Prof. Kao and Prof. Sinha together with Prof. Bernhard Wilpert (President of the IAAP) as co-convenors. The special agenda of this symposium was to exemplify the successful blending of traditional social values, attitudes and institutional norms and practices with the demand of techno-economic systems in Asian enterprises that has led to the emergence of characteristic patterns of management and organizational functioning that are distinct from those found in the West. Papers selected from that symposium have been included in the present volume. To fill certain gaps, several specially invited papers by scholars from Canada, India, Korea, Taiwan and Thailand have been added. The editors are beholden to all the participants of the symposium and the authors for sparing their valuable time and efforts to make their contributions.

We thank all the authors for contributing papers to this volume. Thanks are also due to Ms Leanne Chung Pui Ling and Violet Goan Ching Hui for their valuable help and assistance in the organization of the symposium. For secretarial assistance, we are thankful to Ms Cindy Li, Theresa Leung, Kendy Tse and Doris Fung. We are also grateful to Dr Prakash Nath Bhargava and Padmakar Tripathi for their patience and perseverance in the preparation of the final typescript. Lastly, without the facilities made available by the Department of Psychology of the University of Hong Kong, neither the organization of the symposium nor the preparation of the present volume would have been possible.

Finally, it is with deep sadness that we record the recent passing away of Prof. Durganand Sinha, who dedicated the whole of his academic life to the cultivation of psychology in the developing world. He has left an inheritance of achievements in the indigenous psychology of Southeast Asia that will be long remembered. We cherish the memory of his great contribution in this series of books, through not only his enthusiasm in the field of psychology but also his profound will and influence in promoting the emerging field of psychology and national development. We are proud to dedicate this book to the memory of Prof. Durganand Sinha, a great scholar, humanist and friend.

Hong Kong
June, 1998

Henry S.R. Kao
Bernhard Wilpert

INTRODUCTION: THE EMERGENCE
OF INDIGENIZATION

Durganand Sinha, Henry S.R. Kao
and Bernhard Wilpert

For long, countries in Asia, Africa and the developing world have
generally taken for granted that economic and industrial development
are possible only through the diffusion of modern technology from the
West, which inevitably necessitated the wholesale adoption of management practices, patterns of work organization and interpersonal relationships prevalent in industrially advanced countries. This paradigm has not
remained unchallenged. The question that naturally arises is: are management and organization theories based on Western experiences and tried
out in organizations in America and Europe applicable to employees in
Asian countries, each of which has a very distinct cultural heritage and
background? Instances of variations along cultural lines in the behaviour
of members of organizations are innumerable. To mention only a few,
it has been observed that while British managers rely mostly on formal communication, the Chinese communicate face to face or use the
grapevine, being more relationship-oriented. Again, the Chinese have
their own particular approach to the international trading network based
not on contract but on trust and family ties. It is, therefore, not surprising that an increasing number of behavioural scientists have begun
to have serious doubts about the universal applicability of single management techniques such as participation, incentive systems and job
enrichment.

There does not seem to be the 'one best way' in management. Not only
has the narrow concept of development of the 1950s and the 1960s been
seriously questioned and widened to include non-economic and human
dimensions, but factors considered 'universal' with regard to effective
management and organizational functioning are regarded as ethnocentric and applicable only within very specific socio-cultural conditions.
Management and work activities in an enterprise depend critically on
the social values of its members which are culture-bound. The cultural
embeddedness of industrial organizations has to be recognized. Although
the precise nature of the value–work interface is still inadequately understood, the recognition of 'cultural relativism' in people's social and work
values and in the management practices found to be effective in different countries is a corrective to the hegemonic yet optimistic assumption
implied by 'scientific management', by the Weberian 'bureaucratic' ideal
type, or even the enlightened human relations school, that there exists a
universal or monolithic prescription for the management of work organizations. Often cited is the case of Japan which has risen phoenix-like
from the ashes of World War II and become within a very short period one
of the foremost industrially advanced countries in the world, without having to cast off its traditional social values and cultural characteristics. In
fact, for several decades—particularly during the 1970s and 1980s—the
economic success of Japan and of some Asian NICs (Newly Industrialized Countries) of the Pacific rim were widely attributed to management
styles, work attitudes and values rooted in Confucian social philosophy,
familism, and institutional structures that are not by any means Euro-
American. Asian countries are 'experimenting' with a large variety of
management styles and organizational models which are indigenous in
that they are based on concepts and ideas embedded in their cultures,
philosophical systems and traditions that are in sharp contrast to those of
the West.

The mainstream literature on management and organizational
behaviour has since the beginning been fashioned predominantly from the
theoretical perspective which is rooted in the cultural contexts and socio-
industrial experience of Western societies. Although trendy notions in
acknowledging the 'culture' variable are conspicuous for their attempts
to emulate the Japanese practices and their underpinning logic, it remains
clear that the benchmark interpretations of key aspects of organizational
behaviour like leadership, motivation and decision-making are enmeshed
in Western tradition. Its concession to non-Western ideas has hitherto
been 'marginal'. Japanese, Chinese, Indian and other Asian experiences

have been captioned as 'special cases' and as 'exceptional', and the distinctively variant experiences of the East are kept at 'arm's length', thereby maintaining the Western theoretical framework undisturbed and intact.

Although recent economic problems in Asia have somewhat blurred the heroic image of Japan and of the 'Asian Tigers', their past economic progress has served to arouse Western-oriented theorists from their torpor. Indigenous developments have posed a serious challenge to the presumed universality of Western theoretical formulations. This may be somewhat disconcerting for a majority of us who have been fashioned by our background of a pre-eminently Western education and orientation. Knowledge in the field of management—and, for that matter, in the entire field of social sciences—has come to a point where what used to be taken for granted and was considered sacrosanct and imbued with pan-human verity has been found to be largely culture-bound. It has become essential in today's world to abandon a parochial and ethnocentric outlook and become sensitive to alternative formulations and approaches. Rather than transplanting and importing wholesale the management theories and models developed in the socio-cultural setting of the West, there is need to evolve these in the cultural contexts of Asian realities. It has now been conceded that the study of management practices and organizational behaviour has to be conducted with a broader perspective and a receptiveness to ideas and inspirations drawn from non-Western experiences in the workplace, especially from Japanese management and from the successes of the East Asian economies of China, Hong Kong, South Korea, Singapore and Taiwan.

The patterns of management and organization in evidence in East and South Asian countries as well as in many parts of other non-Western regions are often regarded as exemplifying what has often been called *indigenization*, i.e., a process by which organizations in their functioning are adapted to the socio-cultural soil of the host country so that the end-product is appropriate as well as unique. It is to be noted, however, that in most of the Asian countries, including the 'Dragon' and the 'Tigers', management practices and organizations contain many elements of Western practices. But it has rightly been remarked (see Adler et al., 1989) that Japanese and American management are 95 per cent the same, but differ in all important respects. In other words, the patterns that emerge display a kind of adaptation of the requirements of work and modern technology to specific elements of culture. They constitute a synergistic blend of traditional indigenous roots and modern techniques.

We do not intend here to define indigenization, nor to elaborate on the process and go into all its nuances. (For an in-depth discussion of these see D. Sinha [1997].) It would suffice here to point out that, by its very nature, indigenization is an integrative process. It is an interfacing of the exogenous with unique elements of the recipient culture. The basic values and behaviour patterns of indigenous culture are integrated with Western principles and practices, thereby evolving a system that is not only unique but also functional in a particular context. The contributions to the present volume provide specific examples of the process of indigenization in the fields of management and organization. They illustrate how the values, norms, perceptions and expectations generated by a culture are inter-woven in its managerial styles and organizational functioning. The chapters dealing with Thai leadership, the concept of corporate statesmanship and special features of corporate culture in Korean enterprises exemplify what Negandhi (1975) has termed the 'integrative model' of management.

Indigenization in management is a complex process. In some cases, it is largely endogenous, utilizing for management some of the basic tenets of Buddhism, Confucianism, Taoism and Hinduism as also the 'models' set by experiences in the family and other social institutions still powerful in many countries of Asia. But by and large, it is a process in which there is positive valence towards one's own traditions and cultural heritage as well towards the one that is 'foreign' and imported. It would be an over-simplification to consider the two as opposite and inimical, as pitted against each other—indigenous culture versus modern management—and regard the process of indigenization as representing a clash between tradition and modernity. In essence, indigenization implies that what are useful and valuable in the two systems in the contemporary context are retained and integrated to generate a synergic work culture that is not only congruent with socio-cultural realities but also functional and effective. It is an 'assimilative synthesis' of the two systems. As illustrated by the case of Korean corporate culture described in the present volume, it results from interaction between specific characteristics of organization (size, technology, human and material capital and organizational climate), task environment (consumers, government and labour market) and social environment (societal factors such as education and cultural dimensions). It does not in any way imply that the 'foreign' has to be rejected per se because the influence has come from outside, or that indigenous practices are good and are to be revived and retained simply because they are 'local' and rooted in the culture. In short, work organization and management practices are aligned with cultural values as well as with the needs and demands of modern technology (Sinha and Kao, 1988). The underlying processes involved have been discussed by Sinha in this volume.

In the context of the globalization of economy and business enterprises and the ceaseless onslaught of television and other mass media catering to Western values and lifestyles, a question that is automatically raised is whether, in years to come, the process of indigenization shall continue to have relevance or significance. The revolution brought about in international travel and communication by the marvels of science and technology has fostered intercultural contact at the global level on a scale undreamt of a few years ago. The world has shrunk and transformed itself into the proverbial 'global village'. This development has many important repercussions, both positive and negative, all of which need not be discussed here in detail. Only the implications in the context of indigenization are examined.

With the globalization of business and the jet-age of travel, individuals frequently move between cultures, and intermingle across national boundaries. People possessing divergent systems of values rub shoulders and work together. This is likely to foster the emergence of a common pattern of attitudes and behaviour in management and organizations all over the world. Further, people with diverse cultural backgrounds now work and closely interact in the same organization and share common organizational goals. Through organizational socialization and mutual interactions, they tend to acquire values and behaviour patterns that constitute the 'culture' of the organization. As a result, individual cultural proclivities are likely to be whittled down and rounded off. That being the case, individual behaviour is expected to conform progressively to universally prevalent norms and behaviour patterns. Such 'universalization' is likely to render the 'cultural factors' largely irrelevant and indigenization will cease to have much significance.

The fact of the matter, however, is that neither organizational socialization nor the intermingling of people of diverse cultures brings about complete uniformity of attitudes, values and behaviour dispositions. Similarities may appear in some superficial features, like dress, diction, manners and fashion. The experience of countries that have followed the 'melting pot' policy has shown that the basic cultural features of most ethnic groups tend to persist. What may be called the 'social traits' of groups, learned through generations of collective experience and having functional significance in their respective eco-cultural contexts, continue to linger. The process of indigenization thus remains important. Therefore, to function effectively in settings where people have divergent

perceptions, expectations and norms of superior–subordinate relationships, it is not only useful but also essential to be adequately sensitive to
the various cultural influences and their impact on employees' behaviour
both as individuals and collectively, and to the indigenous transformations
that take place in the functioning of organizations.

Exposure to electronic mass media and the consumerism they foster are serious matters. The influence of the media is so powerful and
widespread that the possibility of 'homogenization' erasing to a very large
extent the richness and uniqueness of different cultural groups cannot be
brushed aside. Without elaborating the point further, the question that
is pertinent in the present context is whether, if such cultural homogenization becomes a reality, indigenization of management—or, for that
matter, indigenization as such—will continue to have relevance. The
point can be debated endlessly. It would suffice here to point out that
even in countries which boast of rich and ancient cultural heritage and
continuity, many uniformities called 'modernity' are apparent. Western
management practices are increasingly being adopted. In the Chinese-
speaking world, the influence and importance of the family network in
business is no longer what it used to be. Confucian values and familism
in the functioning of work organizations are not as strong as they were
two or three decades ago. Need for autonomy, participation in decision-
making and many other values typical of work organizations in the West
are gradually becoming features of organizational functioning in many
Asian countries. To this extent, a kind of uniformity, if not universality,
is developing. In spite of this trend, one still observes much interesting diversity and uniqueness in managerial practices. It seems likely
that many of them will continue to exist especially due to their functional utility in particular contexts. Further, every culture has its inherent
strength and vitality not easily swept away by external influences. Mono-
tonic cultural homogenization is certainly a possibility, but is not likely to
turn into a reality given the strength and resilience of each culture. While
globalization may result in drastic reduction of diversities and emergence
of similarities at the surface level, the core elements of cultures would
prevail and influence the behaviour of individuals and work organizations, often in very subtle forms. Despite globalization and the forces of
homogenization, cultural proclivities would remain, and differences in
the hopes, beliefs, perceptions and expectations regarding the behaviour
of superiors and subordinates shall persist and continue to influence the
functioning of organizations. It is noteworthy that even European countries which belong to 'Western' culture, and to that extent are exposed

to very similar homogenizing influences, display very distinct 'intercultural' differences in the field of management. As has been observed in Komin's paper in this volume, sampled managers in countries like France and Italy tend to emphasize the importance of power motivation within the organization more than their counterparts in the United Kingdom, the Netherlands and Germany. Again, managers in France and Italy are seen as 'experts' who are expected to have answers to any problem, while those from the Netherlands and the United States are regarded as 'participative' problem-solvers. What is encouraged in one culture as 'participative management' is seen in another as managerial incompetence. These countries belong to Western culture and share Western values. Yet they display interesting basic differences. In other words, cultural differences seem to persist and affect managerial behaviour in spite of common homogenizing influences. Therefore, even in the context of globalization, awareness of the operation of cultural factors and insight into indigenization in organizational behaviour are going to remain effective tools for managers. The culture–technology interface will remain a significant feature of work organizations as long as complete homogenization does not come about—and this is quite unlikely. A look at the processes involved reveals, as Wilpert points out in his paper in this volume, that management and organizations are culture-specific and at the same time have tendencies towards universally valid characteristics.

The main thrust of the book is on indigenous practices in management and organizations. The chapters are organized in four sections. The first section, comprising three papers, focuses on conceptual and theoretical issues of indigenization in the work setting. The second section, also comprising four papers, relates to work culture and the way it is influenced by socio-cultural values and institutional characteristics. The third section deals specifically with the value–organization interface. It includes a chapter on the meaning of work in Islam and the contribution of Islamic civilization to the theory of management and organization—a perspective that is neglected in the 'mainstream' literature on management.

The five papers constituting the fourth and last section deal with the indigenous influences emerging from historical and cultural scenarios that affect the pattern of managerial leadership. Managerial styles that operate under specific cultural contexts and prove effective have the imprint of indigenous institutions, socialization and cultural behaviour. Divorced from their cultural moorings, some management practices may appear somewhat strange. But they have their roots in indigenous culture and many of them are found to be functional. The culturally transformed dimensions and styles of managerial leadership observed are blends of local indigenous factors and of supposedly universal technological requirements.

In general, the papers constituting this volume provide specific examples of the integrative processes in management and organizations in operation in the Asian context. They point to the fact that work behaviour is to be understood and interpreted not in terms of imported models, principles and theories, which is often the case, but reflects indigenous developments that require for their explanation culturally derived categories. In general, indigenization tends to make the organization appropriate and effective to a large extent. An analysis of the processes involved as reflected in the contributions reveals how in their industrial development Asian countries have tried to capitalize on the characteristics and strengths of local cultures.

I

CONCEPTUAL ISSUES

1

LEADERSHIP STYLES AND MANAGEMENT: UNIVERSALLY CONVERGENT OR CULTURE-BOUND?

Bernhard Wilpert

Some time ago Chinese and German managers, in the process of forming a German–Chinese joint venture, discussed their respective investment
shares. The Chinese side offered, among other assets, a somewhat aged
boiler of a steam generation plant to be included in their contribution. The
German managers protested on grounds that according to their usual rate of
depreciation the boiler would have been already written off as an investment
good. The Chinese side refused to budge from its position and the progress
of the negotiation was stalled on this single point for quite some time. The
Chinese managers insisted that the boiler was still of value since it still
functioned even though with limited capacity. And as long as something
works, it has value (Wilpert and Scharpf, 1990: 650).

The brief example illustrates a clash of managerial self concepts, of
different world-views, of managers from different countries and cultural traditions taking different things for granted. And it is the clash
of such implicit assumptions which creates friction and conflict in everyday encounters of managers who need to cooperate across cultural boundaries.

But it is not only in situations of direct personal contact within a
common enterprise such as a joint venture that these differences create

havoc and impede smooth economic progress. At a time when economic competition dramatically transcends national borders and becomes a truly international game, we are—for practical as well as theoretical matters— directly confronted with the question: are management and organizational leadership very specific to given cultures, or can we assume that they are convergent, i.e., tending to become similar?

I shall proceed in five steps. In the first section, I clarify the concepts of management and leadership. After briefly outlining certain received research approaches, I shall deal individually with the examples of Japan, USA, Germany and India. In the next section I shall discuss the findings of an earlier comparative study by Heller and Wilpert (1981). I conclude by answering the question posed at the outset of this paper, regarding the convergence or culture-boundedness of leadership and management practices.

CONCEPTS OF MANAGEMENT AND LEADERSHIP

Leadership has often been defined as the process of social interaction and influence by which an individual or a group of people is brought to pursue a given goal. The notion implies that the individual or group would not necessarily have pursued that goal on the basis of their own motivation or impetus, because if the specific goal is pursued without any additional social influence, no leadership is necessary. Hence, the notion of leadership often implies some hetero-determination. This is a very broad understanding of the concept of leadership which applies to formal organizations as well as to informal groups, families, and peer and friendship relations.

The concept of management, in contrast, is usually understood in more limited ways as pertaining to formal organizations. The functions of management are considered to be six-fold (Staehle, 1996): 'creating, planning, organizing, motivating, communicating, controlling'.

Creating is the activity of relating previously unrelated things for purposes of achieving a task in better ways.

Planning relates to setting goals and determining the ways in which these goals ought to be reached.

Organizing covers the sequencing of activities and the distribution of responsibilities among various actors for the most efficient achievement of goals.

Motivating is the activity which insures through incentive or punishment that organization members act in the desired direction, It often entails making sure that individual needs and expectations and organizational objectives become congruent.

Communicating constitutes the manager's task of giving meaning to members and organizational activities and is thus instrumental to providing proper motivation.

Controlling, finally, is directly related to the planning process, because it refers to the evaluation of success and failure of planning, and to correcting any deviations from the plan.

We may therefore say that leadership is the more general or comprehensive notion, and management the organizational form of exercising leadership. 'Acting in their managerial capacity, presidents, department heads, foremen, supervisors, college deans...(clergymen), and heads of government agencies all do the same thing' (Koontz and O'Donnell, 1964: 45). In that sense management functions are indeed universal. The question is, however, whether their implementation is universal too.

RECEIVED RESEARCH APPROACHES

This question, whether management is culture-specific or whether the managerial task of creating a concerted, goal-directed, efficient organizational activity follows its own, and therefore universal, logic, has stimulated whole libraries of research literature. The eminent Indian organizational theorist Anant R. Negandhi, whose untimely death has shocked the scientific community, had already in 1975 attempted to summarize the four main lines of relevant research and theorizing with regard to the relationship of culture and management. He distinguished among:

ECONOMIC DEVELOPMENT ORIENTATION

This approach is linked to the seminal work of Harbison and Myers (1959) who postulated a specific 'logic of industrialization' which, independently of a given cultural setting, induces a convergence of management styles: 'the logic of industrial development calls for an increasing managerial decentralization as enterprises grow in size and complexity' (ibid.: 44–45). According to Harbison and Myers, the style of managerial leadership changes from traditional, culture-bound styles to constitutional ones and ultimately to a participative style based on professional competence.

ENVIRONMENTAL APPROACH

Farmer and Richman (1964; 1965) attempted to identify the so-called ecological factors presumed to impact managerial style. These factors were thought to include the socio-cultural, economic, legal and educational characteristics surrounding the enterprise. Their central focus was on the importance of these factors for the role of hierarchic authority and the role of subordinates' behaviour and their relevance for efficient management.

BEHAVIOURAL APPROACH

This third approach covers many studies on the significance of attitudes, value and need hierarchies for managerial practice (especially England, 1975; Haire et al., 1966). If we understand culture as 'collective programming of minds' (Hofstede, 1980a) we have here an approach which stresses culture-specific conditions for management.

OPEN SYSTEMS APPROACH

Negandhi (1975) in turn favoured an 'integrative model' which he believed would allow us to scrutinize the interaction between organization-specific characteristics (size, technology, organization climate, human and material capital), task environment (consumers, governments, labour market etc.) and societal environment (covering societal factors such as education as well as more strictly speaking cultural dimensions).

We shall come back to these different approaches in our conclusions.

SOME SELECTED EXAMPLES

It seems to me that it is an exercise in futility to generalize about 'the' American, 'the' Japanese, 'the' German or 'the' Indian management, because we are dealing here with large continents or countries with a great variety of enterprises, industries and people. The best we can do is to identify a few particular characteristics of management in these regions. And generally, we will have to focus on relatively large enterprises, because small businesses follow their own logic. Besides, it would take an almost superhuman mind to cover adequately such a large variety.

USA

The man who more than anyone else has influenced American managerial practice (and indeed, managerial practice in the whole world) was an engineer, F.W. Taylor. In his booklet *Principles of Scientific Management* (1911) he tried to design work and work organizations on a scientific basis. His main principles were:

1. Workers are mainly interested to increase their personal, individual remuneration (cultural value: individualism).
2. Time and motion studies of small, partialized work activities will allow us to find the one best way through which work can be distributed among the most able workers (organizational principle of horizontal division of work).
3. This means that we must select workers systematically according to their gifts and competences and give them those tasks they can perform best (principle of scientific selection).
4. Workers themselves cannot analyze and distribute their own work. This is the task of management; in other words: we must divide thinking and executing, dispositive and executing functions (principle of vertical division of labour).
5. There is a fundamental harmony of interests among workers and management, because both are interested to maximize their income (principle of harmony).

These principles had important consequences:

- drastic increase in productivity
- partialization of work into small units which reduced learning time for workers
- easy replacement of workers
- extremely strong position of management in firms
- fostering of individual rivalry and competition among workers, thus further increasing individualistic attitudes and a high mobility of labour

Henry Ford, using Taylor's principles and by introducing the transmission belt, raised productivity to even higher levels. All these originally American practices are still very much in use today the world over.

However, in the early 1930s began a new wave of so-called human relations in industry. Elton Mayo, an Australian social psychologist at Harvard University, attempted to improve productivity in the Hawthorne factory of General Electrics through better lighting and the granting of short breaks. In the course of his experiments, however, he discovered that irrespective of lighting and breaks the productivity of women workers improved. He attributed this to the social attention of management given to workers and the improved social climate among workers. Hence, he concluded, if you want to improve productivity, you must improve work climate and allow informal relations among workers. In other words: pay attention to the social needs of workers.

Like Taylorism, the human relations wave also spilled over to other continents. In the 1960s and 1970s managers the world over were trained in this tradition. Participative management became the key word, thus apparently demonstrating the general transferability of these models which seems to prove the thesis of a logic of industrial development.

GERMANY

Although many aspects of Taylorism, Fordism and the human relations tradition were introduced in Germany and can still be found there, some aspects of German managerial reality are specific.

Meistersystem

Traditional German industry developed a particular feature, the role of 'meister' (master craftsman) which is much more than that of a foreman in other countries. Becoming a 'meister' requires nine years of formal schooling plus three-and-a-half years of apprenticeship, then passing an examination to become a so-called skilled worker, and two or three years of additional specific training to pass another examination as 'meister'. These fifteen years of industry-specific training produce technically highly qualified middle managers who know their job from bottom up. Their power position in the hierarchy is often extremely high. Top management could not do without them. Here is an example of a societal characteristic—the vocational education system—which is highly specific to German management.

Co-determination

Another particularity of the German management system is based on its specific industrial relations system, the features of which I am obliged to simplify somewhat for brevity's sake. Its intellectual tradition reaches back more than 100 years when Bismarck introduced in Germany a social security system which taught the labour movement that something can be gained through influencing work life by way of national laws. This led in the 1920s to the introduction of laws requiring companies to enable workers to elect so-called works councils. Works councils are bodies elected by workers to represent their interests vis-à-vis management with rights such as participation in organizing work and hiring personnel. Furthermore, the laws provided legal bases for the election of workers' representatives to management boards which influence company policies.

The German system of co-determination thus provides a basis for legal employee rights and legal claims to participate. It is more than participative management where participation is a benevolent gift, offered to workers by management, which can always be claimed back. This situation has had a definite impact on the relationship between trade unions and employers' associations. In contrast to many European countries, Germany enjoys a relatively harmonious relationship among employers and trade unions. Class struggle notions are virtually absent from collective bargaining.

New Production Methods

In recent years, a third particularity of the German management system has been observed. The dramatic increase in the capital intensity of workplaces due to the widespread introduction of new technologies and the rising level of general education in German society has generated a need to include workers more intensively in decision-making processes. This is due, first, to the emerging need to rely on responsible and reliable work habits of workers, whose potential to impede the production process has increased as a consequence of the fragility of technological devices. Second, the higher level of general education has increased aspirations to participate in organizational decision-making. By an ironic twist of history, technical innovations, meant to increase control over the work process and make it more independent of the whims of workers, are working towards increasing the significance of human work.

The meistersystem, historical developments towards co-determination and technological trends (in other words, mainly societal aspects) have set the specific present conditions for German management.

JAPAN

Japanese management can best be understood by looking more closely at historical and cultural factors (Misumi, 1983). 'Ie', the Japanese word for the traditional agrarian household, still seems to have significance, even for large companies. The term conveys clear rules for the inclusion or exclusion of members belonging to the 'ie', clear status differences with a household head at the apex, and the strong inclination of all members to share responsibility for the joint 'ie'. It is permeated by a strong feeling of group belongingness ('groupism'). Working in a group is not only a method of carrying out work, but makes work meaningful.

Religious Shintoist (search for the new and pure) and Buddhist (devotion to work) traditions coupled with specific historical experiences seem to form the basis for modern Japanese patterns of management. Losing World War II came as a shock to Japan, seeming to be proof of its relative inferiority. Added to this was Japan's post-war experience, when Japanese products were considered by many to be second-rate. It thus became almost a national programme for Japanese companies to copy Western products and to improve them as much as possible. Within two decades Japan succeeded in reaching and surpassing international quality standards and generated successful innovations in many domains.

We find here a creative linking of old cultural and religious traditions with conscious effort to open up to new ideas and challenges. The old traditions included the way of reaching decisions—a combination of bottom–up (*ringi*) and top–down (*nemawashi*) decision-making—as well as the benevolent paternalism of the 'ie' concept. The new practices included the relentless determination to learn, through the formal system of education, but also through in-company training. Its result was the 'company man', the employee who is totally devoted to his/her enterprise. Further, the determination to make it to the top in the world economy was also new.

Yet another new strain comprised the conscious application of modern social science. A case in point is the nation-wide drive towards quality. A case study I undertook in 1983 may serve as an example. The Sumikin Shipping Co. was founded in 1957 as a subsidiary of Sumitomo Metal

Industry Corp. Ltd, one of Japan's largest steel manufacturers. In 1972, Sumikin Shipping was almost bankrupt when Teiji Sato became its Chief Executive Officer (CEO). He introduced a new leadership style, the Performance plus Maintenance (people and group) orientation developed by Misumi (1985), and organized the 1,100 employees in 129 quality circles. Furthermore, Sato-san introduced a new system of inciting employees to submit as many improvement proposals as possible. Each proposal, whether later implemented or not, was rewarded by 500 yen. The results were, among others:

- about 23–25,000 improvement proposals per year (the number was still growing in subsequent years!),
- savings of the magnitude of 7.7 million yen/year, and
- reduction of the accident rate to 1/20 within twelve years.

INDIA

Never having had the privilege myself of conducting studies in India, I must rely on published sources. Sinha and Sinha (1990) summarize the main factors which seem to determine the boundaries for Indian managers:

1. The traditional differentiation of hierarchical relationships in Indian companies with the notion of 'check with the boss' as the 'crux of the majority of decision-making which naturally shifts the locus of control into the highest position in the organization' (ibid.: 708). This tendency would certainly have consequences for the mode of organizing in Indian organizations.
2. The power play, with 'affective reciprocity' among superiors and subordinates on the one hand, and danger of manipulative behaviour on the other. It seems evident that communication patterns will be affected by power-play patterns.
3. A preference for personalized relationships within organizations which contrasts with the more contractual relationships in Western countries. In consequence, we might expect controlling criteria to co-vary with such preferences: face-saving would dominate over hard-nosed checking of contractual, impersonalized agreements on goal achievement.
4. Social networking through own–other (we–they) orientations, where family members are more often consulted in job-related problems 'than superiors and co-workers on family-related matters'

(ibid.: 710). Such familism may sometimes result in a dilution of organizational norms, and thus affect planning.

5. A collectivist orientation which facilitates motivation of personnel to loyal and committed work, but also generates conflicts between newcomers, such as professionals at higher levels, and the 'old' personnel who refuse to give up old ways of doing things.

The literature thus shows that what counts is again the creation of that synergetic mix between traditional indigenous roots and modern techniques which increases the efficiency of Indian enterprises (Tripathi, 1990).

By way of a preliminary summary: the four cases show that we can observe a great variety of local conditions likely to affect emerging patterns of conduct in managerial functions. Such conditions can be identified not only along dimensions of cultural and religious traditions, but also on the level of societal constraints and opportunities such as education and learning from historical experience.

COMPARATIVE MANAGERIAL BEHAVIOUR RESEARCH

Some time ago, we published the results of an eight-country study on managerial behaviour (Heller and Wilpert, 1981). At that time we were interested in finding out whether there existed any significant behavioural differences between American and European managers. The starting point for our research was the debate in the 1970s over whether the relative success of American multinational companies was due to the more participative leadership style of American managers compared to their European colleagues. That difference in participation, so it was claimed (Servan-Schreiber, 1967), explained the presumed differences in creativity, mobilization of competence and motivation which gave American companies the edge over European ones.

We defined participation as the process whereby a superior allowed his immediate subordinate to participate in making decisions. The different leadership styles ranged over five degrees of participativeness in the superior's decision behaviour, which we called the Influence–Power-sharing Continuum (IPC):

I   Own decision of superior without explanation
II Own decision of superior with prior explanation
III Prior consultation with subordinate
IV Joint decision-making with subordinate
V   Delegation of decision to subordinate

Figure 1.1
Decision-making Styles of Managers (Total Sample)

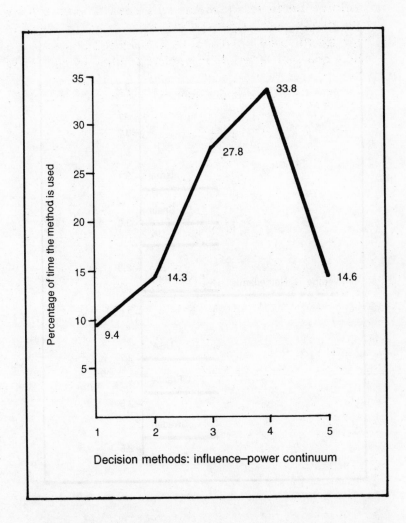

More than 1,600 managers from 129 matching companies in eight countries (France, Germany, Israel, the Netherlands, Spain, Sweden, UK and USA) participated in the research. The managers came from the two top levels below the CEO of large companies. We looked at twelve decisions which must be made occasionally by any average company.

Figure 1.2
Decision-making Styles of Managers Per Country (Averages)

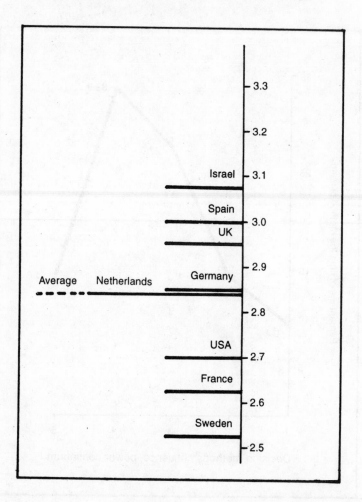

Here are two of our main findings:

1. Average decision-making behaviour: as Figure 1.1 illustrates, the overall decision-making of our 1,600 managers from the eight industrialized countries can be described as 'consultative–participative': 75 per cent of the decisions reached are made either

after consultation or jointly with subordinates or are delegated to subordinates.

2. Country differences: When we order country averages along our IPC (Figure 1.2; high scores indicate centralized, authoritarian decision-making), we see that differences exist, but they are statistically not significant except for the difference between the two extremes: Swedish and Israeli managers. American managers are found near the average. Hence, we concluded that no Atlantic gap existed with regard to participation.

Thus, our results seemed to indicate that there indeed exists a relative homogeneity (convergence) in leadership styles of managers in industrialized countries.

CONCLUSIONS

Given the contradictory evidence of the national cases reported earlier which suggest considerable differences in management styles, and the results from our eight-country study which indicate considerable similarities, how should we answer our question about the convergence or culture-boundedness of leadership and management?

My answer is: leadership and management are both culture-specific and tending towards universally valid characteristics. Why this should be so is best explained in terms of Negandhi's (1975) interactive open systems model. As already pointed out, his model postulates the interaction of three main sets of variables: *organizational characteristics* (technology, size, educational level of employees and their expectations etc.), *task environment* (industrial sector, competitors, consumers etc.) and *sociocultural environment*. In line with this approach, Hui (1990: 204) points out the culture-boundedness of work attitudes, leadership styles and managerial behaviour in different cultures: 'The cultural environment is a primary agent for the formation of managers' own values and beliefs, which, in turn, influence their choice of management styles.' In that sense, organizations (their members, methods, processes, characteristics) are shaped in the image of their surrounding cultures. On the other hand, I would surmise that the competitive world-wide task environment and technological developments tend to produce forces in the direction of universal homogeneity and convergence of structures and processes in organizations.

Thus, our seemingly contradictory evidence from the case studies and the international comparisons can be understood as resulting from similar dynamic interactions of the three factors mentioned: given the similar task environments, organizational characteristics (size, technology) and even relatively similar socio-cultural backgrounds of the 129 organizations of our eight-country study, we would have to expect similarities in managerial practice. Given the drastically different socio-cultural conditions evidenced in our four-country cases, we might expect larger discrepancies in management styles.

There, remains the question of the comparative efficiency of different styles. Here I would again evoke a principle of general systems theory, the principle of *equifinality*, which means that given objectives can be reached by different means. What seems important then is to find the optimal fit between managerial style on the one hand and the characteristics of organizations, task and socio-cultural environments on the other. This is what constitutes the fundamental problem for every enterprise in search of efficiency.

2

APPROACHES TO INDIGENOUS MANAGEMENT

Durganand Sinha

The influence of the West on ideas and practices in non-Western countries has been strong. It is patently reflected in their adoption of Western norms and practices in different spheres of human activity. The same is true of the development of organizations and management. Rather than evolving their own unique patterns, imitation and replication seem to characterize work and work organizations in developing countries. Overwhelmed by the level of industrialization and economic prosperity in the West, and in the anxiety to catch up, non-Western countries have adopted almost wholesale the patterns of management and organizations that prevail in the West. These patterns are regarded as universal, and as the *only* path to economic development and industrialization. The basic assumption is that development is possible only through the diffusion of modern technology from the West, which in turn requires adoption of Western management practices, work organizations and interpersonal relationships. Management theorists and practitioners have turned a blind eye to the role of culture and indigenous belief systems, values, attitudes and institutions in shaping the functioning of organizations. In their uncritical emulation of and extrapolation from the experience of industrially advanced countries, they have greatly disregarded the influence of basic differences in culture, local conditions and circumstances. Underlying this has been the assumption that the pattern of effective organization and management is universal and applicable in every context, conditioned only by the nature and level of technology.

Humanistic approaches like participative management and job enrichment (Herzberg, 1966; Likert, 1967a; 1967b; McGregor, 1960), despite their recognition of the key role of human interests and needs, are no exception. For example, McClelland and his associates (McClelland, 1961; McClelland and Winter, 1969) have emphasized the inculcation of the need for achievement in entrepreneurs for boosting economic activity and development as a panacea for every country, irrespective of cultural divergences. The fact that in many cultures the meaning of success and achievement is different has been ignored. Achievement is not always considered in individualistic and egoistic terms—as it seems to have done in most Western cultures—but constitutes a strong social concern, rather than a matter of individual striving and competition (Agarwal and Misra, 1986; Misra and Agarwal, 1985). Assertion of the signal importance accorded to attitudinal modernity (Inkeles and Smith, 1974) is another instance of the universalistic approach. Dichotomizing the attitudinal characteristics of traditional and modern societies, Triandis (1973) has identified a syndrome of features considered vital for the full utilization of modern technology. Again, modernity has been equated with the values, attitudes and belief systems of people in the West. The possibility of its having somewhat different dimensions in other cultures has been disregarded. Models like need for achievement and modernity are ethnocentric in that the pattern of motivation and set of attitudes that characterize the West and have produced good results have been considered basic universal conditions for the proper utilization of modern technology, and consequently for industrialization and rapid economic development.

I shall not go in any detail into the consequences of positing a universalistic model and the resulting policy of replication that has inevitably produced a 'mismatch' between implanted management practices and the cultural proclivities and demands of the indigenous workforce. Nor is it necessary to go into the controversy over whether the pattern of effective management is universal or conditioned by factors specific to a culture. It would suffice here to refer to the pertinent observation by Kanungo and Jaeger (1990: 1) that 'uncritical transfer of management theories and techniques based on western ideologies and value systems has in many ways contributed in organizational inefficiency and ineffectiveness in the developing country context.'

NEED FOR INDIGENIZATION

Three factors have been mainly responsible for putting in doubt the universal applicability of single management techniques, and for the need to look for situational and cultural factors that limit the operation of borrowed elements. These are:

1. Mismatch between the implanted management practices and the cultural values, needs and basic behaviour dispositions of the indigenous workforce (D. Sinha, 1988), and the consequences—often dysfunctional—of such a mismatch.
2. Inconsistent and often conflicting findings obtained in different cultural contexts on theories and models imported from the West. Graves (1972) has shown that differences in the background of employees create the need for different kinds of organizational, management and supervisory styles. Greater participation and enriched jobs with responsibility and decision-making are effective only for those employees who place high value on autonomy and participation (Kanungo, 1980: 122). Findings such as these that do not conform to the 'borrowed' models have generally been regarded as 'exceptions' leaving the theoretical framework intact. The situation has changed. Now, in the face of 'inconsistent' findings, scholars have begun to examine the cultural assumptions of such models. As a result, the effectiveness of job enrichment, incentive systems and participation under different conditions has been challenged. This has generated the need for a search for 'alternative' forms of management styles and organizations appropriate to particular cultural settings (J.B.P. Sinha, 1980; 1993a).
3. The phenomenal economic success of Japan, and more recently of the four 'Asian Tigers', which has exploded the myth not only of the superiority of Western management but also of its universality. These highly successful countries of the Pacific Rim have adopted development strategies that utilize the socio-cultural features of a society for overall managerial and organizational effectiveness. This indicates that alternative styles of management tempered by cultural factors are not only feasible but successful.

Hofstede's (1988) analysis of McGregor's theory in the context of Southeast Asia brings out the point clearly. While examining the basic assumptions of the model of man inherent in McGregor's theory, Hofstede asserts that they do not apply to Southeast Asia. He contends that

Theory X and Theory Y stem from the culture of an individualistic and 'masculine' society (i.e., USA.) and as such are not relevant to the Southeast Asian setting. In that context, McGregor's categories will not be considered mutually exclusive opposites, but complementary to each other. Hofstede emphasizes that the system of management must respect continuity with old values and traditions, and that sound management development should take into cognizance cultural differences, or else it will become irrelevant. To quote Hofstede (1988: 313), 'foreign theories could be used as sources of inspiration, but should be tested for their underlying basic assumptions where these are different. If necessary, they should be reconceptualized according to the best of the local traditions'. This underlines the need for indigenization and the development of indigenous management taking due account of cultural realities. As Kanungo and Jaeger (1990: 2) point out, 'there is need to develop indigenous management theories and practices for use in the developing country context.'

NATURE OF INDIGENIZATION

In the field of management, as in most spheres of human endeavour, indigenization is an integrative process. In terms of Berry's (1986) model of intercultural interactions, indigenization is a position in which people have positive valence towards their own cultural and traditional systems as well as towards the one that is imported. It would be an oversimplification to pit one against the other—modern management versus indigenous culture—and regard the process of indigenization as a clash between tradition and modernity. In essence, indigenization implies that what are valuable and useful in the two are retained and integrated to generate a synergetic work culture and organization that is functional and congruent with the socio-cultural realities. The interface produces, to use Prof. Radhakrishnan's expression (Gopal, 1989: 120), a kind of 'assimilative synthesis' of two systems, in which what has been valuable in the past is retained and the old is re-stated in new forms adapted to the present needs. The best and the most appropriate of both the old and the new are accepted and integrated. This does not imply that the 'borrowed' is rejected because it is foreign, or that there is blind and uncritical idolization of the indigenous. Work organization and management practices are sought to be aligned with cultural values and social realities (see Sinha and Kao, 1988). The kind of interface visualized is reflected in the work organizations in Japan, and in the 'Confucian League' of

Hong Kong, Korea, Singapore and Taiwan, and to some extent even in countries like India, Indonesia and Thailand. The trend is visible in the Islamic world as well, as evidenced in studies by Ali and Azim (1994) and Khadra (1990).

TWO APPROACHES TO INDIGENIZING MANAGEMENT

There are two distinct but interrelated approaches to indigenizing management. In the first, traditional and indigenous values and attitudes are reinterpreted in the light of contemporary needs, reinforcing those characteristics likely to be functional (Sinha and Kao, 1988: 19). In the second approach, if the foreign model of management and indigenous cultural characteristics are not in harmony, there is need to modify and reconceptualize the former by taking into account the best in the local culture, thereby realigning the two. The two approaches are discussed here by providing appropriate examples.

REINTERPRETING THE INDIGENOUS IN THE CONTEXT OF CONTEMPORARY NEEDS

Not everything that is culturally rooted and derived from tradition is relevant in the contemporary situation. In fact, analysts have shown that many aspects of Hindu religion, Indian values and traditional practices have no significance for modern life. On the contrary, many basic Hindu concepts like *sanyas* (renunciation), *maya* (illusion) and *karma* (action), and traditional social institutions like the joint family and the caste system, are seen as the main barriers to economic development (see Kapp, 1963; D. Sinha, 1988; for a detailed discussion). In the context of work, it has been observed that culturally determined value factors frequently compromise technological requirements and job demands leading to 'soft management' styles. The professed goals of the organization are diluted by social habits, values and other extraneous considerations (J.B.P. Sinha and D. Sinha, 1994). It has however been shown that some managers are able to utilize existing values for fulfilling the goals they set themselves, or for the work forms they establish (ibid.: 166). Existing social values like dependency, strong relational orientations, in-group feeling, personalized relationships and preference for hierarchical ordering usually found to be dysfunctional in the efficient working of modern organizations have been utilized for generating a synergetic work culture. An insightful manager can skilfully utilize indigenous values and dispositions towards

developing a vibrant work culture with high productivity and greater stability. What is required is to channelize indigenous urges to serve the
needs of modern organizations.

Triandis' (1988) discussion of individualism and collectivism provides
another excellent illustration of this approach. Individualism–Collectivism
constitutes an important axis of cultural variation in work-related values
across the world. It has been argued on good evidence that individualism is associated with a high level of economic development, while
collectivism, which characterizes most developing countries, seems to be
negatively correlated with Gross National Product (Hofstede, 1980a).

Elaborating on the nature of collectivism, Triandis (1988) analyzes
some of its aspects that are counterproductive to the efficient functioning
of modern organizations. Intense involvement in in-groups, relationship-
rather than task-orientation, emphasis on harmony, obedience etc., are
features of collectivism that often hinder organizational functioning.
Triandis argues that these features could be modified so that they no more
constitute obstacles to efficiency. However, exclusive emphasis on either
individualism or collectivism is not desirable. In its extreme form, individualism also has many adverse consequences. It is associated with forms
of social pathology, such as high rates of crime, divorce, child abuse,
alienation, emotional stress and mental illness. Collectivism, on the other
hand, does not seem to suffer from such consequences. Some transformation is therefore desirable in both orientations. It has been argued
that while individualistic cultures need to be more sensitive to personal
relationships, collectivistic cultures require greater sensitivity to tasks.

This indicates that the obvious approach is not to discard traditional
and cultural influences and proclivities because they have often proved
obstacles to the functioning of modern organizations. They need rather to
be analyzed in the contemporary context. Aspects that are dysfunctional
require to be reinterpreted and modified to bring them in line with the
requirements of modern organizations. In this process of indigenization,
traditional cultural elements are not rejected outright. Aspects that are
likely to be functional are retained and others are modified and utilized
for the furtherance of organizational goals.

RECONCEPTUALIZING FOREIGN MODELS TO ALIGN THEM WITH THE INDIGENOUS

In the first strategy, internal elements are modified to harmonize them with
modern needs. In the second approach, the external or the exogenous is

transformed so that it is in tune with cultural realities. We have already referred to Hofstede's contention that McGregor's theory—or, for that matter, foreign theories and models of management—be reformulated and reconceptualized to take into account the cultural characteristics of the region. This, in essence, is the second strategy adopted in indigenizing management.

The Nurturant Task Leader (NTL) style advocated by J.B.P. Sinha (1980) is an excellent example. The participative/democratic style of leadership, which has generally been found effective in the West, is commonly suggested as ideal for management in non-Western cultures. However, as indicated earlier, the pattern has not always, yielded the desired outcome. Finding the two extremes of autocratic and participative leadership styles inappropriate to the Indian cultural setting, J.B.P. Sinha proposed the NTL model that incorporates the basic cultural values of affection, affiliation, dependency, need for personalized relationships and strong authority patterns with large power distances and hierarchy, and the nurturance and assertiveness of a father-figure—features that characterize the Indian socio-cultural setting. The NTL model has been found to be more congruent with Indian cultural values and behaviour dispositions. It has been found more effective in work organizations during the phase of economic transition in the country. The style is essentially paternalistic, drawing heavily on the patterns of interaction typifying family dynamics in India. In this style of management, while the boss cares for his subordinates, shows affection, and takes a personal interest in their well-being, he is above all committed to the group goal, and is therefore task-oriented. Subordinates who meet his expectations are reinforced by nurturance. As they develop and grow in confidence and properly manage their work, the dependency is reduced, and in course of time they are given more responsibility. As a result, the paternalistic style is gradually replaced and the relationship becomes more participative. The NTL model is considered an indigenous management style more appropriate to the cultural context of developing countries (J.B.P. Sinha, 1993b). The model is a blend of the exogenous and the indogenous, in which the 'implanted' is sought to be modified taking cultural characteristics into account so that the outcome is not only congruent but more effective in the existing work situation.

Management practices in Japan and the countries that share Confucian values also provide examples of the two approaches to indigenization. While they share many of the features of American management, they have integrated the basic values and behaviour patterns of their cultures with Western principles and have evolved styles and practices that are unique in many ways. Culture-specific features are integrated with modern technological requirements. As Fujisawa, the co-founder of Honda Motor Company, is reported to have remarked, 'Japanese and American management are 95 per cent the same, and differ in all important respects' (quoted in Adler et al., 1989). Various studies point out certain features that differentiate Japanese management from Western practices. Japanese workers and managers have been found to display a sense of identity with their work groups, an ethic of cooperativeness, a high dependence on their organization, a strong sensitivity to status, and an active respect for the interests of individuals and for each individual as a person. Three factors underlying the heart of Japanese management are: a long-range planning horizon, commitment to lifetime employment and collective responsibility—all rooted in Japanese culture (Keys and Miller, 1984). Individuals in Japanese corporations are evaluated on the basis of their contribution to the team rather than how far they can push ahead of their colleagues (Moghaddam et al., 1993). American managers are more 'segmented' while the Japanese are simultaneously segmented and 'holistic' (Ouchi, 1981). Another important feature of Japanese management is the central importance of the group in the decision-making process. Grouping implies not simply 'affiliation' but a sense of interrelatedness among all natural elements which results in strong cohesion.

Chinese management also exemplifies the two approaches to indigenization very clearly. It shares many of its characteristics with Japanese management and is embedded in the Confucian traditional ethos. It is paternalistic and rooted in normative values of trust, subtlety and loyalty. Chinese work organization is also characterized by personalism and particularism in economic relationships. Derived from the agrarian past, some of the values cherished in Chinese management are paternalistic authority, loyalty, familism, familial cohesion and mutual dependence (C.F. Yang, 1988a), altruism, rule of seniority and respect for the wisdom of elders (Chao, 1990: 585). These are amply reflected in the contemporary management and organizational functioning said to underlie the industrial and economic advancement of Taiwan, South Korea, Hong Kong and Mainland China.

INDIGENIZATION IN MANAGEMENT TRAINING

Indigenization can also be seen in another aspect of management, namely, management training. The validity of training modelled entirely on

Western practices is questioned, and traditional sources are proposed to be utilized for providing training modules for enhancing managerial performance. Training has by and large been modelled on Western practices such as sensitivity training, management by objectives, socio-technical analysis, structural interventions, institution-building and so on. Training materials also frequently consist of well-known games and exercises of alien origin. They are interesting to indulge in but poor in their relevance (Chakraborty, 1987; 20). Training of individuals isolated from the cultural milieu is likely to be ineffective.

Chakraborty's approach (1987; 1991; 1993) is illustrative of indigenization in this sphere of management. A new perspective is advanced which refers to religio-philosophical literature relating to the Indian view of an effective person, which is very different from what generally obtains in the West (Chakraborty, 1987; Singh, 1990). In the Western approach to training, the emphasis is on acquiring skills, knowledge and motivation to develop systems and organize resources (both human and material) in order to realize targets set by the organization, as well as to develop individuals themselves by being integrated into the organization. The stress has been on managing and organizing others.

On the other hand, the emphasis of the Indian approach has been on the 'purity' of the individual's mind (Chakraborty, 1987). The individual is considered the central force, and work a duty meant for self-purification. The goal of training is to develop managers who, instead of being analytic and technical, should function as synthetic and spiritual systems. For this purpose, Chakraborty (1987, 1991) advocated yoga and meditation as the techniques for experiential training. The keynote of his programme is *chittasuddhi* (purification of mind/heart) through providing in modules materials derived from Hindu and Buddhist philosophy and the writings of Sri Aurobindo.

The approach has been tried out in some industrial organizations, and the feedback received from the participants seems to be positive. Despite the evidence, the approach is still open to further examination. Its effectiveness in stress management is more conclusive than in other areas of managerial functioning. In any case, it exemplifies indigenization in that the traditional is sought to be blended with modern management practices to attain more effectively the goals of work organization. As the chairperson of the Godrej group of companies, where this training project was recently tried out, says in his foreword to Chakraborty's book (Chakraborty, 1993), it is a 'case for workable synthesis of Indian Ethos– Western Technology', which demonstrates that the classical wisdom of

India can be utilized in secular organizations for total quality improvement. The approach provides a new direction in management training.

A glance at the managerial scenario in Asia reveals that the universality of Western models and practices is no longer uncritically accepted. As Adair (1989) has observed with respect to psychology in India, there is a trend towards the blending of foreign models, theories and methods with indigenous ones to make them culturally appropriate. Similar trends are observable in the field of management and work. Two interrelated approaches to indigenization, besides training modules based on cultural values and ideals, have evolved. Though the process of indigenization has been slow, it is increasingly becoming more articulate. In the years to come, appropriate patterns of management and work organization are likely to develop in most Asian countries that utilize and integrate their unique cultural elements with the best features of Western practices.

3

ENTREPRENEURSHIP DEVELOPMENT: CONCEPT AND CONTEXT

Suresh Balakrishnan, K. Gopakumar
and Rabindra N. Kanungo

Development in India, with its emphasis on expanding the domain of market-oriented action, places its rural communities on the threshold of a new revolution. The transition from a subsistence-oriented, tightly integrated, inward-looking local community to one of surplus-seeking, market-led, outward orientation calls for rapid emergence of a multitude of 'enterprises' in all walks of life. This would be possible only with the build-up of a wider base of population capable of entrepreneurial behaviour. Historically, the initial build-up of entrepreneurial activity took place in urban centres. This was followed by a trickle-down effect to rural communities over time. Development strategy today, however, seeks a more proactive and immediate change in India. While much of policy-making in this regard treats enterprise creation as a function of appropriate economic conditions (made possible through institutional and economic interventions), others have emphasized attitudinal change as the vital element in the process. However, all these interventions derive their content from the conceptualization of case-based administrative experience and macro-economic research, rather than from systematic observation and research into the process through which rural entrepreneurship emerges and sustains itself. Hence, there is a need to develop comprehensive conceptual models of entrepreneurship for future research and practice in the field.

Enterprises and entrepreneurs have been at the centre-stage of modernization since the days of the Industrial Revolution. Their ubiquity, variety and mutability have made theorization on entrepreneurship complex and ridden with controversy. Economists, sociologists, psychologists and anthropologists have studied this concept, usually within the frontiers of their respective disciplines. This has led to more divergence than convergence in moving towards the goal of practical conceptualization of entrepreneurship.

Models of entrepreneurship and research associated with them have been critically examined in recent years. Such examination has identified several major issues, such as vagueness in definition, conceptualizing of entrepreneurship as a trait, significance of innovation in entrepreneurship, meaning of activities in the post–enterprise creation stage, validity of measures of entrepreneurial propensity, and significance of demographic factors. Contemporary efforts towards entrepreneurship development have been criticized for being poorly conceptualized, and not being able to focus on critical issues (see, e.g., Oza, 1988). Given the wide range of conceptual issues, any effort to conduct research on rural entrepreneurship would have to begin with taking a position on the key issues confronting the theme. Only then can one get down to examining the specific constraints in rural communities that affect creation of rural enterprises. This broad-based understanding would provide a sound background for designing interventions and training programmes for facilitating the creation of rural enterprises.

This paper presents a conceptual analysis of entrepreneurship. At the outset, it seeks to present a glimpse of the various theoretical approaches adopted and expositions made over time and across disciplines to capture the phenomenon of entrepreneurship. After familiarizing oneself with the 'conceptual map', an attempt is made to project a 'paradigm shift' whereby the entrepreneur is recast in a pragmatic mode, keeping in perspective the need to intervene for augmenting and developing entrepreneurial potential. For analytical convenience, we proceed along four themes. Theme I traces the evolution of the concept of entrepreneurship in economics, its place in the frontiers of development, divergence in treatment and conceptual stagnation. Theme II attempts an overview of the alternative approaches in conceptualizing the concept. Theme III delineates the emergent and dominant trends in explaining the concept of entrepreneurship, and provides a critique of the prevalent trends. Finally, Theme IV proposes an integrated framework for conceptualizing the development of entrepreneurship in behavioural terms. Within this framework, entrepreneurship is related to other constructs such as leadership and managership, and to the life cycle of the enterprise.

THEME I: EVOLUTION, FRONTIERS, DIVERGENCE AND STAGNATION

For a long time there was no equivalent for the term 'entrepreneur' in the English language. Three words were commonly used to connote the sense the French term carried: adventurer, undertaker and projector; these were used interchangeably and lacked the precision and characteristics of a scientific expression (Gopakumar, 1995). Thus, the term 'entrepreneur' did not find any prominence in the history of economic thought. The earliest attempt to invest the concept with some economic content may be traced to the works of an 18th century French writer, Bernard F. de Belidor, who defines entrepreneurship as buying labour and materials at uncertain prices and selling the resultant output at contracted prices. Entrepreneurship as a concept gathered space in economic literature mainly through the writings of Richard Cantillon (1680–1734), who gave the concept some analytical treatment and assigned the entrepreneur an economic role by emphasizing 'risk' as a prominent entrepreneurial function (Gopakumar, 1995).

The classical and neo-classical economists assigned the entrepreneur a practically non-operative part in the process of economic growth and development, because of their obsession with the 'equilibrium' of the economy rather than with the entrepreneural activity that breaks the status quo. There were, however, a few exceptions, notably J.B. Say and J.H. von Thunen. Jean Baptiste Say (1767–1832), the French political economist, assigned the entrepreneur a crucial role—coordination—and made a distinction between the entrepreneur and the capitalist (Say, 1967). This distinction was also made in Germany by J.H. von Thunen (1783–1850) (Hebert and Link, 1982). This type of work did not however provide any framework for an integrated theory.

A dynamic theory of entrepreneurship was first advocated by Schumpeter (1949), who considered entrepreneurship the catalyst that disrupts the stationary circular flow of the economy, and thereby initiates and sustains the process of development. Embarking upon the process of 'new combinations' of the factors of production—which Schumpeter succinctly terms innovation—the entrepreneur activates the economy to a new level of development. The concept of innovation and its corollary, development, embraces five functions: (a) introduction of a new good; (b) introduction of a new method of production; (c) opening of a new market; (d) conquest of a new source of supply of raw materials; and (e) carrying out a new organization of any industry. Schumpeter presents a synthesis of different notions of entrepreneurship. His concept of innovation includes the elements of risk-taking, superintendence and coordination. However, Schumpeter stresses the fact that these attributes, unaccompanied by the ability to innovate, would not be sufficient to account for entrepreneurship (Gopakumar, 1995).

Although the Schumpeterian perspective had its critics (Hebert and Link, 1982; Solo, 1951), Schumpeter 'stood at the cradle of modern entrepreneurial explorations' (Greshenkron, 1968). Post-Schumpeterian developments have proceeded along two different themes—the Harvard tradition and the neo-Austrian school; the former is portrayed as an extension of the Schumpeterian view, while the latter is represented as an alternative (Hebert and Link, 1982).

According to the Harvard school (Cole, 1949), entrepreneurship comprises any purposeful activity that initiates, maintains or develops a profit-oriented business in interaction with the internal situation of the business or with the economic, political and social circumstances surrounding the business. This approach emphasizes two types of activities: the organization or coordination activity, and sensitivity to environmental characteristics that affect decision-making. Another exposition of the Harvard tradition is that of Leibenstein (1968) who emphasized activities such as searching for and evaluating economic opportunities, mobilizing resources necessary for the production process, connecting different markets and creating or expanding the firm.

Despite its stress on the human factor in the production system, the Harvard tradition never explicitly challenged the equilibrium-obsessed orthodox economic theory. This was challenged by the neo-Austrian school which argued that disequilibrium, rather than equilibrium, was the likely scenario and that as such, entrepreneurs operate under fairly uncertain circumstances. The essence of entrepreneurship consists in the alertness of market participants to profit opportunities. A typical entrepreneur, according to Kirzner (1973), is the arbitrageur, the person who seizes the opportunity to buy at low prices and sells the same items at high prices because of intertemporal and interspatial demands.

To sum up, the major theories and expositions from Cantillon's to Kirzner's view the entrepreneur as performing various functional roles as *risk-taker, decision-maker, organizer or coordinator, innovator, employer of factors of production, gap-seeker and input-completer, arbitrageur* etc. In spite of the diverse roles portrayed, certain common themes may be identified. All the theories ascribe a functional role to the entrepreneur in the productive process and explain entrepreneurial reward by the degree of success attained by fulfilling that function, rather than by a purely proprietary claim on income by virtue of mere asset ownership (Hebert and Link, 1982). Again, all the theories have been framed against the backdrop of a capitalist society, and as a result the functional roles performed by the entrepreneur are determined within the capitalist paradigms of production and distribution.

The classical and neo-classical writers, barring a few French and German contributions, offered little in terms of a meaningful position to entrepreneurship in the development process. Only during the brief Schumpetarian interregnum did the entrepreneur occupy centre-stage in the theory of economic development. Subsequent contributions amount to little more than expanding Schumpeter's schema or cutting and pruning, refining or modifying it (Gopakumar, 1995). A possible explanation for this conceptual stagnation could be that by the end of the Schumpetarian era, the focus had started shifting from merely explaining entrepreneurship to developing it. By the mid-1950s, the supply of entrepreneurial capabilities had come to be recognized as one of the critical factors in economic development (UN, 1955).

THEME II: ALTERNATIVE APPROACHES

Attempts to comprehend and theoretically analyze the vexing issue of 'who is an entrepreneur?' have been made in various disciplines. The major contributions will be examined under two subthemes: socio-cultural and psychological.

SOCIO-CULTURAL APPROACHES

Some scholars have stressed the importance of the socio-cultural milieu in entrepreneurship development (Cochran, 1949; Cole, 1949; Lamb, 1952; Williamson, 1966). Jenks (1949) and Cochran (1949) suggested that socio-cultural history accounts for the performance of entrepreneurial functions by a large number of individuals. Gregory and Neu (1952) adopted an inductive approach to examining the social characteristics of the entrepreneur. Questioning the stereotype of 'rags to riches' American entrepreneurs, they delineated certain social characteristics that distinguish entrepreneurs from commoners. These include an academic education well above the average, an early urban environment and a background of relatively high social standing.

Several writers used a comparative framework to highlight the ways in which different societies, with differing interests, attitudes, systems of stratification etc., operate to produce different kinds of businessmen and different patterns of entrepreneurial behaviour (Swayer, 1952). Weber (1930) suggested that the Protestant faith, particularly Calvinism which emphasizes the duty to be diligent, thrifty, prudent and sober, entails increased well-being of the individual (Reynolds, 1991). Cochran (1949) held that culture differentials must be considered in the formulation of universal historical analogies and general economic laws. Though cultural and social variables have been used to explain entrepreneurial behaviour, most studies undertaken under this rubric fail to answer the questions: 'what constitutes entrepreneurial behaviour?' and/or 'who is an entrepreneur?'

PSYCHOLOGICAL APPROACHES

The focus shifted from the act to the actors (Shaver and Scott, 1991) in the work of McClelland (1961). According to McClelland and Winter (1969), the need for achievement (n-ach) is responsible for economic development. The greater the development of n-ach during the early socialization of people, the more likely it is that economic development will be achieved. A society with a generally high level of n-ach will produce more rapid economic growth. Achievement motivation could be inculcated through training in self-reliance, rewarding hard work and persistence in goal achievement, and creating interest in excellence. Education and child-rearing practices that emphasize such values are significant in creating a foundation for a strong n-ach society. In spite of criticism (Schatz, 1971; Smelser, 1976), McClelland's (1987) analysis has triggered off the 'trait approach' to comprehending entrepreneurial behaviour.

In another psycho-social theory, Hagen (1962) relegates economic variables to a relatively minor role and emphasizes certain aspects of the personality. More recently, several other psychological approaches to entrepreneurship have been suggested. Hisrich (1990) identifies several characteristics of entrepreneurs, in terms of (a) conditions that make entrepreneurship desirable and possible; (b) the childhood family background; (c) level of education, personal values and motivation; and (d) role-modelling effects and other support systems. Bird (1989) also examines entrepreneurial behaviour by focusing on work and family background, personal values and motivation.

THEME III: THE CONTEMPORARY FOCUS

The two most common approaches used in researching the characteristics of entrepreneurs have been the trait approach and the demographic approach (Robinson et al., 1991). In the trait approach, the entrepreneur is assumed to be a particular personality type whose characteristics are key to explaining entrepreneurship as a phenomenon (Gartner, 1988; 1989). Following McClelland (1961; 1987), many other researchers have explored areas such as achievement motive, locus of control, risk-taking and innovation (Brockhaus, 1975; Brockhaus and Horwitz, 1986; Collins and Moore, 1970; J.A. Hornaday and Aboud, 1971; Palmer, 1971; Shapero, 1975; Swayne and Tucker, 1973). The trait approach has been criticized on four grounds (Robinson et al., 1991). First, the research methodologies for identifying personality traits were not developed for or specifically intended to be used in the study of entrepreneurial behaviour. The instruments were borrowed from psychology and applied to the field of entrepreneurship, sometimes inappropriately and often ineffectively (R.H. Hornaday, 1987; R.H. Hornaday and Nunnally, 1987). Second, the different instruments that aim to examine the concept actually correlate poorly; that is, they lack convergent validity. Third, since personality theories are intended for use across a broad spectrum of situations for measuring general tendencies, they lose their efficacy when applied to a specific domain such as entrepreneurship. Finally, the trait approach fails to explain how traits both influence and are influenced by activities in the environment.

In the demographic approach, demographic information is used to arrive at a profile of a typical entrepreneur assuming that people with similar backgrounds possess similar underlying stable characteristics. This approach presumes that by identifying the demographic characteristics of known entrepreneurs it will be possible to predict entrepreneurship in unknown populations (Robinson et al., 1991). The demographic variables usually examined are family background, birth order, role model, marital status, age, education level of parents and self, socio-economic status, previous work experience and work habits (Brockhaus, 1982; Cohen,

1980; Gasse, 1985; Hisrich, 1986; Sexton and Auken, 1982; Swayne and Tucker, 1973). Three major drawbacks of the demographic approach have been identified (Robinson et al., 1991). First, the approach assumes that human behaviour is strongly influenced by demographic characteristics such as sex, race, or birth order. However, as psychologists point out, it is not so much the demographics as the conclusions drawn from life experiences that influence the future actions of entrepreneurs (Rychlak, 1981). Second, the practice of using demographic characteristics as surrogates for personality characteristics is not appropriate. There is also a lack of empirical evidence in this regard (Ernst and Angst, 1983). Third, the approach does not help predict who will or will not be an entrepreneur on the basis of knowledge of birth order, level of education or parental heritage. Besides, demographic characteristics, being static in nature, cannot explain a dynamic multifaceted phenomenon like entrepreneurship.

Apart from these two approaches, Hannan and Freeman (1977) use the population–ecology model (PEM) to analyze the concept of entrepreneurship. The PEM seeks to predict the probability of births and deaths within a population of firms within a given industry niche, conferring on the environment rather than on the person the status of key entity in determining organizational survival. Recent research following this approach has focused on the presence and characteristics of and changes in a population of organizations in the ecological context provided by the host society (Reynolds, 1991). The deficiencies of this model have been pointed out by Bygrave and Hofer (1991). These models, while making statistical predictions at the population level, fail to predict the fate of specific firms. Again, like pre-Fisherian statistics, these models deal with averages, whereas the most interesting entrepreneurial events are to be found in variances; thus, they would fail to capture the Schumpeterian innovator phenomenon. The PEM, due to its overemphasis on environmental determinism, does not provide any role for human volition—a cardinal concept for any entrepreneurial behaviour. It also lacks rigour in empiricism, since there has been no instance where population ecologists have made accurate predictions about future births and deaths in an industry. All tests of the theory to date have been on historical data sets.

THEME IV: ENTREPRENEURSHIP: AN INTEGRATIVE BEHAVIOURAL FRAMEWORK

This framework for understanding entrepreneurship begins with differentiating between the act of enterprise creation and the larger phenomenon of entrepreneurial behaviour (Vesper, 1980). While the creation of an enterprise represents a point of culmination, much of the behaviour that is associated with this event would have been in operation well before the actual birth of the enterprise and could continue into the period of enterprise growth and regeneration. Therefore, the event of enterprise creation can be seen as the consequence of a congruence between environmental conditions and the entrepreneurial behaviour of individuals (Robinson et al., 1991). Both these contributing factors can be studied separately. Hence, interventions to develop individuals for creating enterprises would have to build on perceived behavioural dispositions that directly relate to the repertoire of what constitutes entrepreneurial behaviour.

In our view, the effort to augment and strengthen entrepreneurial disposition needs to be grounded in a logical framework that can be tested empirically. It is necessary to build a framework that relates the significance of particular dispositions to the process of enterprise creation. Given the stage of development of the theory of entrepreneurship, with its tendency to borrow on traits and behaviour observed in other fields and in general situations, we have attempted to put together a repertoire of dispositions in the process of enterprise creation; most elements of this repertoire have been studied in the past as entrepreneurial traits. The key elements identified are Personal Resourcefulness, Achievement-orientation, Strategic Vision, Opportunity-seeking and Innovativeness.

PERSONAL RESOURCEFULNESS

The roots of the entrepreneurial process can be traced to the initiative taken by some individuals to go beyond the existing way of life; the emphasis is on initiative rather than reaction, although events in the environment may have triggered off the person's desire to express that initiative. This aspect seems to have been subsumed within 'innovation', which has been studied more as the 'change' or 'newness' associated with the term rather 'proactiveness'. The tendency to take initiative has been approached from different angles at various stages in the development of theory in entrepreneurship. For instance, when Bygrave and Hofer (1991) talk of the importance of human volition, Carland et al., (1984) define an entrepreneur as one who 'establishes' an organization, and Schumpeter (1949) talks of the agent who consciously disturbs the stationary process to take it in a new direction, they all reflect on the primacy of individual initiative. Studies of entrepreneurial traits related to this aspect of behaviour, such as internal locus of control (Brockhaus,

1982), ability to take personal risks (Gasse, 1985) and a positive approach to work and problems without excessive fear of failure stemming from strong belief in a favourable future (Kuratko and Hodgetts, 1989), all emphasize the strong sense of personal resourcefulness (Kanungo and Misra, 1992) through which entrepreneurs take up and deal with non-routine tasks and situations. Hence, 'personal resourcefulness' in the context of this paper is the belief in one's own capability for initiating actions directed towards creation and growth of enterprises. Such initiative requires cognitively mediated self-regulation of internal emotions, thoughts and actions (ibid.).

ACHIEVEMENT ORIENTATION

While personal initiative and purposeful behaviour can be viewed as good starting points for entrepreneurial effort, many such initiatives fail. The archetypal successful entrepreneur is supposed to epitomize achievement motivation (McClelland, 1961) which facilitates the creation and development of enterprises in competitive environments. While critics have raised serious questions regarding the unique or overarching significance of n-ach in the emergence of entrepreneurship (Smelser, 1976), this element of personality has persisted in the mainstream of entrepreneurship theory (Shaver and Scott, 1991). People with high n-ach are known to seek and assume a high degree of personal responsibility, to set challenging but realistic goals, work with concrete feedback, research their environment and choose partners with expertise in their work (Kanungo and Bhatnagar, 1978); this contributes to the successful completion of tasks that such people venture to take up. Hence, we see achievement orientation as a set of cognitive and behavioural tendencies oriented towards ensuring that outcomes such as enterprise creation, survival and growth are realized.

STRATEGIC VISION

Unlike routine tasks for which structures and processes provide a frame of reference, the creation of enterprises involves unmet needs and gaps (Leibenstein, 1968) that are relevant in the present and the future, and around which both competitive forces and uncertainty operate. Mitton (1989) suggests that entrepreneurs have a knack for looking at the usual and finding the unusual. This entails what is commonly referred to as entrepreneurial vision (Kuratko and Hodgetts, 1989), based on a very clear perception of environmental opportunities and constraints (McClelland, 1987), that inspires the individual and his team to embark, with a sense of direction, upon gap-filling or innovation even before its effectiveness has been established. This bears strong resemblance to leadership behaviour of the kind described in the operationalization of Charismatic Leadership (Conger and Kanungo, 1994). We therefore describe strategic vision in this context as future-oriented goal setting, based on environmental analysis, for determining the content of enterprise action.

OPPORTUNITY-SEEKING

The context in which an individual brings to bear her/his initiative, achievement-orientation and visioning has a strong bearing on what they produce; when these forces are directed towards realizing surplus or value in a market environment over a period of time, we see the creation of enterprises. This perspective of the entrepreneur as a merchant adventurer who, in Cantillon's view, balances out imperfections in the market (Gopakumar, 1995) in pursuit of what Bentham terms wealth, provided the historical basis for the development of entrepreneurship. Wealth is seen as the reward of the entrepreneurial individual for the risk taken or exercise of judgement where there is greater possibility of error; this distinguishes between certain return from wage labour, and return from risk-oriented production for the market. Schumpeter (1949) gave this gain more respectability, by defining profit as the reward for the innovative combination of factors of production. Human beings are not only calculating agents but also alert to opportunities. Typically, they assess spatial and temporal gaps (Leibenstein, 1968), and operate as arbitrageurs (Kirzner, 1973); such operations may be limited to one-shot operations like a middleman in a single-period operation, or a multi-period market operation requiring imagination and creativity associated with the classical entrepreneur. Hence 'opportunity-seeking' would include the 'ability to see situations in terms of unmet needs', identifying markets or gaps for which product concepts are to be evolved, and the search for creating and maintaining a competitive advantage to derive benefits on a sustained basis.

INNOVATIVENESS

The role of capital in the creation of enterprises, and the consequent importance of the capitalist, has cast its long shadow on the conceptualization of entrepreneurship. While the capitalist seeks a market return

on the capital he invests, an entrepreneur invests skills, assumes responsibilities and controls the activities of the enterprise (Gopakumar, 1995),
and seeks residual surplus for the 'human industry' and 'coordination'
he puts in for the creation and survival of the enterprise (Say, 1967).
Schumpeter (1949) conceptualized entrepreneurs as persons who are not
necessarily capitalists or those having command over resources, but individuals who create new combinations of the factors of production and
of factors in the market to derive profit. This focus on new combinations has been operationalized in terms of discontinuity and change of
state in the environment (Bygrave and Hofer, 1991), and the starting of
more than one venture (Robinson et al., 1991). However, Gartner (1989)
raises the question of identifying which firms are innovative and therefore
entrepreneurial; in simpler terms, he asks whether the very first firm in an
industry alone qualifies to be called innovative, while other 'me too enterprises' would be merely small businesses. The extent of innovativeness
employed is thus not only a function of the discontinuity generated in the
situation, but also of where and when it takes place. We conclude that
innovativeness, in the context of this paper, refers to the creation of new
products, markets, product–market combinations, methods of production and organization etc., that enable the enterprise to gain competitive
advantage in the market.

It is evident that each of these dispositions may be found in all types
of individuals (entrepreneurs and non-entrepreneurs). How then can we
relate these dispositions to entrepreneurship? We propose that the convergence of these five elements at high intensities in non-restrictive environments is likely to give rise to enterprise formation. One may therefore
find individuals who have created enterprises in the past now becoming
weak because they are no longer proactive enterprise creators; they may
instead be content to play the role of managers in their stable businesses,
or turn to community leadership, and so on. Hence, this perspective lends
to a process view of entrepreneurship.

Entrepreneurship is more a process of becoming than a steady state or
event. In line with this perspective, one can see that some elements in
the repertoire of entrepreneurial behaviour may be weak while others
are strong; so also, the extent of strength may change over time, or
across significantly different situations (Shaver and Scott, 1991). Therefore, the nature or intensity of entrepreneurship would depend on the
intensity of the complete set of behavioural dispositions related to being
an entrepreneur (Carland et al., 1984). For example, a person with
a relatively lower level of achievement motivation but a high level of

opportunity-seeking behaviour would be happy carrying out trading in a stable market, with a small margin but large volume; another person with strong innovativeness but a low level of opportunity-seeking behaviour would persevere with projects that have a long gestation period, till they take off. This suggests that variations in the combination of behavioural dispositions could be used for developing entrepreneurial typologies (Vesper, 1980) or placing them along a continuum (Carland et al., 1984).

If one were to extend this behavioural perspective further, the different roles assumed by a person as her/his enterprise goes through its life cycle could be viewed as extensions of the entrepreneurial role; changes in role would be consistent with changes in the intensities of the different components in the repertoire of entrepreneurial dispositions. Gartner (1989) strongly objects to this view, and insists that 'entrepreneurship ends when the creation stage of the organization ends'. The major drawback in this view is the high level of mortality one observes just before ventures are launched and immediately after the stage of enterprise creation; hence, even at the risk of complexity, it would be more appropriate to visualize entrepreneurial dispositions as the building-blocks of a process, in which the point of enterprise creation is a milestone. This would also make it possible to use the construct to explain variations in the growth of enterprises, and the intrapreneurial role played by enterprise creators while continuing their association through roles as managers and chief executives. It would also explain why some experienced enterprise owners may show weak entrepreneurial dispositions when they start managing enterprises after creating them.

Extending this point of view, we present here a simple model of how entrepreneurial dispositions could vary across different stages of the life cycle of a small enterprise (see Table 3.1). At the start-up stage, when the entrepreneur is in action, one would expect the five behavioural dispositions to be in operation with reasonable intensity. However, it is more likely that a person without experience in setting up enterprises will express a greater degree of initiative (resourcefulness), opportunistic behaviour and innovativeness and a greater degree of risk-taking than would a mature achievement-oriented person, and be limited in vision to prospects the enterprise would enjoy soon after its creation. After going through the initial start-up process, the key objective shifts from creation to stabilizing the firm's internal operations; successful entrepreneurs are likely to continue intense direct involvement to realize the expected results on a day-to-day basis, without trying to radically alter or innovate, and only seeking opportunities that mesh with the enterprise's on-going

Table 3.1
Entrepreneurial Dispositions in Enterprise Life Cycle

Entrepreneurial Dispositions	Enterprise Life Cycle		
	Start-up	Stabilization	Diversification
Resourcefulness	High	High	Medium
Achievement orientation	Medium	High	High
Visioning	Medium	Low	High
Opportunity-seeking	High	Medium	High
Innovativeness	High	Low	Medium

operations. Once assured of the enterprise's survival, entrepreneurs may seek a return to the mode of action in the start-up stage, to expand or diversify their businesses, which often involves setting up new firms. We see this stage as one in which the person draws on a strong vision reinforced by experience, which is linked to well-directed scanning of the environment and emphasis on continuously achieving realistic goals; he also brings to bear greater delegation or incorporates external resources, but limits innovativeness to areas related to previous experience.

If we compare enterprises that have remained small businesses over long periods of time with those that have grown over time, the simple conceptual model described here could provide some explanations. If an entrepreneur's response to competition at the start-up stage are contraction of visioning and/or reluctance to seek opportunities, the growth or continuation of entrepreneurial action would be unlikely; rather, the commitment to overcoming immediate problems will completely tap the resourcefulness of the person, and the target of achievement will be restricted to that which can be achieved in the current situation. In contrast, persons who respond through vigorous opportunity-seeking, strong orientation towards success and achievement and visioning would be able to transcend the situation and grow.

While the strength or weakness of the five behavioural dimensions would explain the likelihood of a person successfully setting up an enterprise, it would be a mistake to assume that these attributes would automatically result in a person becoming an entrepreneur. Shaver and Scott (1991) suggest that individuals express a specific choice when they take up entrepreneurship, and that it depends on their subjective perception of capacity to be effective and successful in achieving what they want. Many of the earlier described environmental variables proposed by sociologists and economists and the attractiveness of other opportunities open to the individual would affect this choice. Changes in the socio-economic environment would also have a bearing on the propensity to expand/diversify or set up new enterprises.

ENTREPRENEURSHIP, MANAGERSHIP AND LEADERSHIP

It would be appropriate to examine our reformulation of entrepreneurship vis-à-vis two closely related constructs in organizational behaviour, namely, leadership and managership. This becomes very important because entrepreneurs perform several roles that lie in the domain of these two constructs.

The distinction between leadership and managership has been based on two different criteria. The first criterion refers to the type of roles played by leaders and managers in organizations. The manager plays the role of caretaker or system stabilizer responsible for day-to-day routine maintenance, supervision and administration of the status quo or the existing system of operation. Leaders, however, play the role of change agents responsible for effectively bringing about changes or transformations in the existing system and its members (Kanungo and Conger, 1995). The second criterion for distinguishing leadership from managership is based on the nature of influence on the organization and its members. Managers in their supervisory and administrative roles use various rewards and sanctions to induce compliance in others. This manner of influencing others' behaviour is known as 'transactional influence'. Leaders, on the other hand, use 'transformational influence' to bring about changes in others' attitudes, values and behaviour. This is done essentially through effectively articulating future goals or visions and empowering others to work toward the achievement of these goals (Kanungo and Mendonca, 1994).

In view of this distinction, it becomes apparent that entrepreneurs play the roles of both managership and leadership. The managerial role is exhibited by entrepreneurs in their capacity as heads of the enterprise, procuring and allocating resources to manage the enterprise. They also play the leadership role when driven by their own vision to innovate or to bring about a change in the manner events take place. The relationship between the three constructs, entrepreneurship, managership and leadership, can be examined in terms of their task demands in three areas: major goals, time frame and arenas of action. The comparison also examines five dimensions of entrepreneurial behaviour resulting from the personal dispositions conceptualized earlier (see Table 3.2).

Table 3.2
Contrasting Leadership, Managership and Entrepreneurship

	Leadership	Managership	Entrepreneurship
Task demands			
Major goal	Change	Efficiency	Profit
Time frame	Future	Short run	Short and long run
Arena	Social systems	Enterprises	Enterprises and markets
Personal dispositions			
Resourcefulness	Medium	High	High
Achievement orientation	Medium	High	Medium
Visioning	High	Low	Medium
Opportunity-seeking	Low	Medium	High
Innovativeness	Medium	Low	High

Leadership behaviour has usually been visualized in the context of change; change may be driven by environmental pressures or the values of the leader, but is often related to a vision of a more desirable future state shared by leaders and followers. The arena for leadership action is, in the conventional sense, not bound by formal boundaries; it is seen as having relevance to larger issues, but may be operationalized with reference to the arena in which the leader operates, and this could be within an organization. The strong emphasis on the intrinsic value of the goal addressed by the leader makes it possible for him to perform without paying too much attention to mundane activities connected with task completion; rather, the eloquence of the vision often places the process beyond the scope of the immediate results characteristic of achievement-orientation. The identification and emotional involvement of the leader with his vision and his passionate advocacy of that vision may sometimes make him a dreamer without a specific action plan. In this regard, he may be somewhat less innovative, resourceful and opportunistic than an entrepreneur.

The manager's role, in contrast, is directed towards ensuring efficiency in the organizational arena; while most of the results are visible on a day-to-day basis, other outputs are related to short-run performance indicators. In order to ensure that routines are not upset, managers are required to exhibit a high degree of personal resourcefulness and achievement orientation; but their role requires little visioning. The need to generate superior output in the short run also gives rise to a degree of opportunity-seeking behaviour, but leaves little room for the type of inno-vativeness that is expressed by entrepreneurs in the start-up stage.

Finally, an entrepreneur engages in visioning with a practical bent of mind. A leader's vision is often idealized, whereas an entrepreneur's vision is more pragmatic and deeply rooted in the environmental realities representing constraints and opportunities. He is therefore highly resourceful and innovative, always seeking opportunities to materialize his vision.

CONCLUSION

The behavioural framework presented here identifies several key components of entrepreneurs and distinguishes entrepreneurship from both leadership and managership in terms of these components. It also indicates how these components play differential roles in three stages of the life cycle of the enterprise. The framework integrates the environmental factors and behavioural dispositions that facilitate the creation, maintenance and growth of enterprises. The type of analyses presented in this framework can help us design appropriate training programmes for entrepreneurship development with a view to meeting the specific needs of enterprises at different stages of their life cycles.

II

WORK CULTURE

4

'BUSHIDO': THE GUIDING PRINCIPLE OF NEW JAPAN

John Fukuda

Since its bubble economy burst in the early 1990s, Japan has been struggling to cope with its worst post-war economic recession at home and a steady decline in business competitiveness around the globe. After more than four decades of rapid economic growth, the world economic superpower is now in deep trouble. With their self-confidence somewhat shattered of late by a series of economic woes, the Japanese are now telling themselves, 'Change or Perish!' and turning in every direction for sources of light and strength. While many recognize that big changes are indeed necessary for Japan to get back on the track, the strong feeling of cultural uniqueness persists as an enduring characteristic of Japanese society. At the root of its culture is the Japanese Spirit. And it has long served as a constant force guiding and driving Japan toward what it is today. The Spirit evolved from 'bushido' (The Way of the Samurai-Warrior), which began to develop more than 800 years ago as the unwritten code of conduct among the ruling military class in feudal Japan. Although its influence may be on the wane, 'bushido' could well be the guiding principle that will help the Japanese regain their self-confidence and strength, much needed to surmount a great many problems they now face.

JAPAN IN TROUBLE

Throughout the first half of the 1990s, Japan was plagued by the worst economic recession in the post-war period. By the end of the first quarter of 1995, the nation's official unemployment rate rose to 3.2 per cent—the highest level in four decades. However, it should be noted that Japanese firms then had a total of 1.4 million excess workers (or more than 2 per cent of the national workforce) on payrolls, with no real work for them, according to the Sumitomo-Life Research Institute. Job opportunities for new university graduates fell by 22 per cent from the previous year, and were expected to decline by a further 9 per cent in 1996. Thus, while the unemployment rate among heads of families or main wage earners stood at just over 2 per cent in March 1995, nearly 6 per cent of young people aged between 15 and 24 were officially registered out of work (C. Smith, 1995). In spite of a gradual improvement in the economy, the overall unemployment rate rose to 3.4 per cent in January 1996, with the figure for the 15–24 age group also rising to 6.5 per cent (Kobayashi, 1996).

In the spring of 1995, the Japanese yen rose to a historic high of below 80 yen to US $1, before coming down to a 105-yen level later in the year. With the Bank of Japan's study estimating that only a third of all Japanese firms could make profit at a yen-to-dollar exchange rate of between 105 and 110, many firms reported a sharp drop in profits. The year 1995 was indeed marked by the shocking retreat of some of Japan's biggest and best-known firms, which had acquired large US firms during the heyday of their overseas investment from the late 1980s to the early 1990s. Sony, which paid US $3.4 billion in 1989 to purchase Columbia Pictures, wrote off more than $3 billion for the movie-maker's operations. Likewise, Matsushita sold MCA (the owner of Universal Studios) to Canada's Seagram at $5.7 billion—nearly $400 million less than the price it had paid in 1990. And Mitsubishi Estate, which had paid $846 million in 1990 to buy an 80 per cent stake in New York's Rockefeller Center, was forced to give up the property when the twelve-building complex filed for bankruptcy.

The rapid rise in the value of the yen made Japanese products more expensive abroad, resulting in steady decline in Japan's business competitiveness around the globe. According to the World Economic Forum, which has been tracking the competitiveness of a nation in business relative to its competitors since 1980, Japan replaced the long-time title holder, the US, as the world's most competitive nation in the mid-1980s. However, the US regained top position in 1993. The Forum's report published in 1995 placed Japan in fourth position behind the US, Singapore, and Hong Kong. In spite of the general decline in its business competitiveness, Japan, in 1994, was still placed at the top in science & technology and management—two of the eight factors used by the World Economic Forum to determine a nation's overall competitiveness. However, even the effectiveness of its long-enshrined style of management is now being questioned.

In particular, as Japanese firms continue to expand their overseas operations, the weaknesses of their management are increasingly exposed by mass media. In September 1995, Toshihide Iguchi, the executive vice-president holding the third-ranking job at Daiwa Bank's New York office, was arrested by US federal authorities on charges of falsifying records and concealing a US $1.1 billion bond trading loss. Bank analysts were shocked by the Daiwa management's cover-up of the loss and, moreover, by the fact that Japan's finance ministry knew about the bank's problem but did not inform the US banking regulators until just before Iguchi's arrest. The aspect of the Daiwa affair that most impressed analysts was the company's apparent lack of any system for monitoring the bond trading activities of a senior employee who had caused Daiwa the single biggest loss in banking history. Following the company's tradition that discouraged employees from taking long holidays, Iguchi rarely took a day off from work and, as a result, there was no substitute trader to monitor his deals. The problem was compounded by the company's practice of posting senior Japanese employees to run its overseas operations for relatively short periods. In fact, the top two men in Daiwa's New York office were posted there for a stint of less than five years.

While some of the inherent weaknesses of Japanese management are coming to light, the once-cozy relationships between government and business are also blamed for the nation's current economic problems. For example, housing-loan companies, brought into being by the Ministry of Finance during the economic boom of the bubble economy which lasted through the latter half of the 1980s into the very early 1990s, were alleged to have been created as nice landing spots for the ministry's top officials upon retirement. And these retired officials, many without any management experience or ability, did not adequately check whom they were lending money to. For one, companies related to the Yakuza (Japan's organized crime syndicate) are said to owe billions of dollars that they borrowed to finance real-estate deals before the market crashed in the early 1990s. As the government wrestles with ways of liquidating the housing-loan companies that hold much of this bad debt, critics allege that bank officers are simply too afraid to collect debt from the Yakuza. They also allege that gang involvement is prolonging Japan's recession (*Newsweek*, 1996).

In his recent book, *Megatrends Asia*, John Naisbitt notes a shift in the global axis of influence from the West to the East. But he argues that Japan's economic dominance has reached its apex, and that its relative economic position in Asia and the world is on a long downward slide, giving way to the dynamic collaboration of the Chinese network (Naisbitt, 1995). In fact, the recent series of economic woes, coupled with the 'Great Quake' in Kobe, the poison gas attack in Tokyo's subway, and the outbreak of epidemic in Osaka, have shattered the self-confidence of the Japanese. In his inaugural speech in January 1996, Japan's new prime minister Ryutaro Hashimoto, whose sudden rise to the top was itself largely attributed to the continuing turmoil in Japanese politics, painted a picture of the nation as facing serious social, economic and political problems.

Stressing the rebuilding of the economy as the most urgent task for his government, Prime Minister Hashimoto promised to introduce a number of measures to lay strong foundations for a dynamic economy by the year 2000. He also proposed the introduction of reforms in the nation's antiquated education system to make young people think more for themselves. In addition, he advocated a proactive foreign policy, rather than a reactive one that simply responds to 'gaiatsu' or pressure from outside. In short, the prime minister challenged his fellow countrymen with a clear message—'Change or Perish!' How can the Japanese meet this challenge to build a dynamic economy and a more innovative society, which can truly play an active leadership role in world politics as well? To begin with, they must change the way in which they think and behave. But they do need an underlying principle that will guide them in making painful yet necessary changes. One such principle may be found in the very root of their traditional culture—the Japanese Spirit.

JAPANESE SPIRIT: THE ROOT OF JAPANESE CULTURE

The Japanese are very proud of their distinct cultural heritage, which they believe distinguishes them from everybody else in the world. Many Japanese are convinced that no matter how hard they try, foreigners can never really understand their unique way of life. They also say that one cannot be regarded as a 'real' Japanese unless one was born of Japanese parents and raised as a Japanese in Japan. This strong feeling of cultural uniqueness persists as an enduring characteristic of Japanese society. Yet, the fact of the matter is that the Japanese culture was actually created through the interactions of a deeply rooted national ethos with doctrines imported from abroad.

Archaeological evidence suggests that the first identifiable native culture appeared in Japan in about 8000 B.C. By the year A.D. 300, despite their mixed ethnic origins, the habitants were unified in culture and in language. Sometime between A.D. 200 and A.D. 500, Japan began to be permeated by influences from the Asian continent. Especially, the discovery of an advanced culture in China and the importation of Chinese ideographs had an immediate effect on Japan. What followed was the world's first programme of study abroad as Japanese youths went off to China to study art, science, philosophy, architecture, law and administration. The Japanese soon revealed a passion for learning, adopting, and adapting foreign ideas to their own use. It was a matter of conscious, organized study and catching up—a path that was to be followed for many centuries since.

At the heart of its societal development to date is Japan's readiness to borrow anything that can serve its purposes, from anyone and anywhere. This is well reflected in Japanese national slogans. Beginning in the middle of the 7th century and effectively for twelve centuries, Japan was under the overwhelming Chinese influence. Though interspersed with a period of Christian influence (1549–1638) and seclusion under the Tokugawa shogunate (1603–1867), 'Japanese Spirit plus Chinese Experience' largely remained the national slogan during this whole period. The Meiji Restoration in 1868 and with it the assertion of Western influence led Japan to adopt a new national slogan, 'Japanese Spirit plus Western Technologies'. However, by the early 1970s, after a century of borrowing from the West, Japan caught up with the West and became the world's second largest economy. And the national slogan became 'Japanese Spirit plus Japanese Technology'. It is to be noted that while the national slogan changed over the years, the Japanese Spirit remained its important and constant component.

Throughout its transformation, from being a collection of primitive tribes centuries ago into a modern nation-family, Japan did not turn its back on its roots. The Japanese made a clear distinction between borrowed and native elements. They threw away nothing. Japan is the admixture of a strong indigenous non-absorbent core of Japanese culture, which is like igneous rock, and external layers of alien cultures which are like sedimentary deposit (Burks, 1981). At the root of Japanese culture is the Japanese Spirit, the original and the unique. In fact, long before the advent of the overwhelming Chinese influence in the 7th century, Japan went through a vital foundation period of developing its own national ethos, as represented by the Japanese Spirit. The Spirit began to be further refined and crystallized more than 800 years ago during the Kamakura era (1185–1333). This era coincided with the emergence of feudalism and the samurai-warriors ('bushi'). The samurai developed the unwritten code of moral principles, known as 'bushido', to govern their lives and conduct. It started as the ideal of this military class that came to rule feudal Japan, then became an aspiration and inspiration to the nation at large, and eventually evolved into the solid foundation of the Japanese Spirit.

'BUSHIDO': THE UNDERPINNING OF JAPANESE SPIRIT

Originally, 'bushido' was a synthesis of borrowings from three main sources—Buddhism, Taoism and Confucianism, which were all imported from China in the 7th century. Buddhism taught the value of continual refinement toward enlightenment. In the late 12th century, Zen was introduced into Japan as an attempt to return to the original rigour of Buddhism. Although Zen means meditation, it came to mean more than mere contemplation in feudal Japan. The ultimate goal pursued by Zen is to attain the essence of the real, as summed up in its simple proposition: 'What is, is' (Randon, 1987). It is to apprehend the situation clearly and see it for what it is, and not for what we think it is. It also signifies that everything already exists in ourselves, and that if only we can get rid of all the things that mist over true knowledge, then we can renew our contact with that knowledge and see the reality. To put it in another way, the goal of Zen is to realize one's own potential. With its emphasis on self-reliance, self-discipline and self-perfection, this new, practically Japanese form of Buddhism became a fundamental ethic of the samurai. It furnished a sense of calm trust in fate, a quiet submission to the inevitable, a stoic endurance and composure in the face of danger or calamity, and a scorn for suffering and death.

Taoism was a mystical religion, which was later transformed to become Japan's state creed—Shintoism. What Buddhism failed to give, Shintoism offered in abundance. Such loyalty to the sovereign, such reverence for ancestral memory, and such filial piety as are not taught by any other creed, were stressed in Shinto doctrines. Shintoism served to impart passivity and femininity to the otherwise aggressive and masculine character of the samurai. The tenets of Shintoism cover two predominating features of the emotional life of the Japanese—loyalty and patriotism. Shintoism thoroughly imbued the samurai with loyalty to the sovereign and love for the country. Accordingly, the ideal samurai was a man who would remain loyal to one master, in whose service he was always willing to sacrifice even his life.

If we consider ethical doctrines, Confucianism was the most prolific source of 'bushido'. It taught five virtues that should be observed by the rulers of society to justify their power—'jen' (benevolence), 'i' (righteousness), 'li' (propriety), 'chih' (wisdom), and 'hsin' (loyalty). The teachings of Confucius served as confirmation of what the Japanese instinct had recognized long before his writings were introduced from China, and they were particularly well suited to the samurai. In his book *Bushido: The Soul of Japan*, first published in 1905, Inazo Nitobe explains 'bushido' as an ethical system constituted by the five Confucian virtues and three other related moral principles—courage, sincerity and truthfulness, and honour (Nitobe, 1969).

'Bushido' begins with righteousness or justice, that is, to know what is right. Courage is the outward manifestation of righteousness; it is to do what is right. Benevolence is a tender virtue, with the gentleness of feminine nature, as against the stern virtue of righteousness with the uprightness of masculine nature; it represents tender feelings toward the sensibility of others, especially those weaker and distressed. Propriety or politeness is the outward manifestation of benevolence, i.e., the act of expressing a high regard for the feelings of others. Sincerity and truthfulness are what make a polite man truly polite and a courageous man truly courageous. In other words, without sincerity, politeness is simply a farce and a show; and without truthfulness, one can only be a coward. Honour implies a vivid consciousness of personal dignity and worth; not being truthful or lying is denounced as the dishonourable and shameful act of cowardice. Loyalty is a virtue implying homage and fealty to a superior; a samurai's life was regarded as the means whereby to serve his master. However, 'bushido' did not require the samurai to make their conscience the slave of their lord; a man who sacrificed his own conscience to the capricious will of the master was accorded a low place.

In short, 'bushido' dictates that: (*a*) loyalty assumes paramount importance in the code of honour; but (*b*) that one must remain truthful to be an honourable and courageous man, who knows and actually does what is right; and (*c*) that one must be a benevolent man, who expresses his respect

for others' feelings through politeness with sincerity. The whole education and training of the samurai were conducted with the ideal being set
upon these moral principles. Philosophy and literature formed the main
part of pedagogics. Though considered indispensable to a man of culture,
the pursuit of wisdom or intellectual superiority was regarded basically
as necessary rather than essential to samurai training. As the great warrior
Miyamoto Musashi noted some 400 years ago in *The Book of Five Rings*
('Gorin-no-Sho'), a samurai was essentially a man of action (Miyamoto,
1982). In fact, besides intellectual training, 'bushido' stressed constant
physical training to maintain and improve the technique of swordsman-
ship. The technique must be mastered by practising so often that it would
be internalized; only then could one use it without any effort. Mastering
the technique is 'Mind over Body'—the mind forcing the body to accept
the pain and utter exhaustion of constant practice, until the body learns.
Using the technique is 'Body over Mind'—the body just doing what it
has already learned by heart, without even thinking. In other words, to
know and to act were regarded as one and the same—knowing without
acting is labour lost, and acting without knowing is perilous. It was with
this practical end in view that education and training were conducted.

The samurai took advantage of the teachings of Buddhism, Shintoism
and Confucianism in so far as they concerned their profession of arms.
Buddhism taught them self-discipline to develop the character, the confidence, and inner self-control needed to face an opponent's blade to death
without flinching. Shintoism imbued them with loyalty to one master and
the willingness to sacrifice even their life without a moment's hesitation.
And Confucianism helped them refine their native and traditional virtues
to govern their life and conduct as members of the ruling class. Put
together, these religious and ethical doctrines that formed the foundation
of 'bushido' taught a samurai to be a man of justice, benevolence, courage,
propriety, sincerity, honour, loyalty and wisdom, and to act accordingly.

JAPAN'S CULTURAL ORIENTATION

Fundamentally, Japanese culture is characterized by its strong orientation
to learn from others (Rohlen, 1992). It is often said that Japan behaves like
a 'black hole', which in astrophysics represents an imploding star whose
energy and force of gravity are so dense that it sucks in all that comes
within reach. Indeed, throughout its history, Japan has always shown a
keen interest in scanning its external environment for knowledge. The
Japanese have also demonstrated a strong talent for sucking in and then

changing useful knowledge to fit their own needs. But what they did was not plain borrowing, much less was it blind imitation. Rather, it was a matter of creative borrowing and conscious, organized learning. The Chinese did not force-feed Japan their ideas, nor did the West force its technologies upon Japan. The Japanese chose to borrow and learn from others on their own initiative.

By the early 1970s, Japan finally caught up with the West in a number of key industries. In fact, in the actual application of certain technologies to commercial production, Japan has surpassed the industrialized Western nations. Although it was still a net importer of technologies from the US and Europe, amounting to 170 billion yen or US $1.6 billion (at the exchange rate of 105 yen to US $1) in 1993 (*Weekly Post*, 1996), Japan is now masterminding the transfer of its expertise to the West. Nowhere is this more notable than in the production of memory chips used in computers, televisions and other high-technology products. Japan's dominant position in this particular technology, which is obviously vital for future industrial and economic development, is prompting the US and European countries to worry about their increasing dependence on a single country for the supply of memory chips. The former US secretary of state Henry Kissinger even predicted that Japan might become a military superpower because of its potential ability to control the supply of the most advanced semiconductors that would be used to drive all high-technology weapons in the future (Morita and Ishihara, 1989). In short, the pupil has become the teacher and is well on its way to becoming the master.

In the field of management, the period prior to 1970 saw an extraordinary enthusiasm among the Japanese to learn what they considered superior to their own, i.e., American theories and practices. In this period, management scholars were very critical of Japanese-style management, often calling it backward and irrational. Some scholars even warned that unless basic and vital changes were forthcoming, Japan was destined to fall behind in the ranks of modern industrialized nations (Harbison, 1959; Yoshino, 1968). However, despite all the well-intended criticism and warning, Japanese managers as a group went ahead to make the self-conscious decision to stick to their own traditional way of management, albeit with some modifications (Dunphy, 1986). This decision made in the late 1960s reflected the then growing confidence in what they were doing, as well as a renewed awareness of their cultural uniqueness.

Among others, the lifetime employment system and the seniority-based promotion/pay system, consciously invented after World War II as Japan's answer to the Western labour regime, have long stayed the two main pillars of Japanese management. Japanese firms generally hold a unitary notion of management, which sees as identical the interests of the manager and the managed (Dore, 1973). Though there are signs that this notion is now giving way to a more pluralistic one, it still persists in Japan today, at least as the ideal. Thus, even in hard times, Japanese firms find it difficult to rationalize their operations as American and European firms do, by disposing of excess labour. What they do instead is offload excess workers to subsidiaries or reduce staff by attrition. However, an increasing number of observers inside and outside Japan believe that this practice should be changed to tackle social and economic changes. Even some trade union officials are now saying that this tradition should not be discussed emotionally at a time when Japan is struggling to get out of the prolonged recession.

With prospects of slower economic growth in coming years, many Japanese firms see that they can no longer afford the lifetime employment and seniority systems. A study by Japan's institute of Labour Administration shows that more firms now reward an individual's performance over years of service. At the beginning of the 1990s, Japanese firms were already applying equal weight to merit and seniority in rewarding their employees; by 1995, the weight given to merit rose to roughly 60 per cent. For example, as early as 1989, Toyota Motor—Japan's largest and the world's third largest industrial company, with nearly 150,000 employees and a revenue of US $111 billion in 1995—introduced a sweeping corporate restructuring programme which would in effect cast aside decades of hierarchical, group-oriented tradition in favour of individual creativity and initiative. Matsushita Electric Industrial—the world's largest consumer electronics maker, with 265,000 employees and $70 billion in revenues in 1995—is also seriously considering providing its employees freedom in deciding whether they want a fixed-term contract or some other terms of employment, and how they want to receive their salaries and benefits. The introduction of these corporate moves has resulted in, or rather resulted from, the change in people's work ethics itself.

There is, in fact, a growing realization, especially among young workers, that the time has come to set and pursue one's own individual life goals outside the workplace. When asked to name the things they admired about America, the Japanese polled in a Time/CNN survey selected freedom of expression (89 per cent), leisure time available to workers (88 per cent), respect for family life (87 per cent) and the variety of lifestyles (86 per cent) as the most admirable aspects of American society they should perhaps emulate (Morrow, 1992). In fact, a study by the

Hakuhodo Institute of Life and Living, a private think-tank, revealed that in 1990, nearly a half of Japanese men in their 20s sought to be promoted in the company; but by 1994, that dropped to about 35 per cent, with the remainder preferring to take it easy and enjoy life rather than being promoted to a responsible position. Moreover, in a country where companies once commanded the total loyalty of employees, job-hopping is becoming increasingly common. A recent government survey found that 60 per cent of working adults would not rule out switching companies (Takayama, 1996). To cope with the on-going economic and social changes, Japanese firms are making headway toward becoming leaner and meaner organizations. Though they have not jettisoned the ideals of lifetime employment or seniority system, they are in the process of reshaping these ideals, becoming increasingly American-style companies.

CONCLUSION: JAPAN IN TRANSITION

In 1870, feudalism was formally abolished after seven centuries of absolute power. In spite of all the revolutionary reforms and societal changes that followed, 'bushido', developed and refined by the samurai in feudal Japan, has not vanished altogether. Yet there are indications that its standing as the underlying moral principle is waning, as demonstrated by the findings from a survey of more than 200 high school students in Japan aged between 15 and 18 (Fukuda, 1996). While roughly a half of the respondents perceived the Japanese as kind and benevolent people, less than 10 per cent said that the Japanese have the courage to do what they consider right. Nearly 70 per cent regarded themselves as polite people; but with only about 10 per cent stating that the Japanese are truthful and sincere, this often stereotyped characteristic of the Japanese may be regarded as simply a farce. Although 'bushido' considers loyalty to superiors and groups as a must for winning personal honour, only one-third of those polled in the survey agreed that the Japanese are loyal. In sum, the survey findings seemed to suggest that the traditional code of moral principles is not necessarily governing the lives and conducts of the Japanese today.

Nevertheless, the pursuit of wisdom or intellectual superiority stressed by 'bushido' is still regarded very important. An overwhelming majority (86 per cent) of the respondents said that the Japanese are hardworking; over 60 per cent considered them intelligent as well. With its practical outlook and strong emphasis on education and training, Japan continues to adopt and adapt the choicest the world has to offer. One might say that this has been the main determinant of Japan's industrial and economic success to date. Lorriman and Kenjo (1994) note three elements almost invariably present in Japanese firms, but rarely in Western firms: (a) well-educated individuals capable of learning new skills; (b) managers committed to continuously training their staff; and (c) organizations providing an environment conducive to learning and training. Calling them 'Japan's three winning margins', they argue that Japan's success is still only in its infancy and, as the Japanese saying goes, 'mada-mada korekara-da,' which roughly translated means 'You haven't seen everything yet.'

With momentum on its side, Lester Thurow of the Massachussetts Institute of Technology argues, Japan could well be the favourite to win the economic honour of owing the 21st century. But he makes this bet with some reservation, casting doubt upon Japan's taking over technological leadership from the West before the turn of the century (Thurow, 1993). He points out that in the 19th century, Americans were famous for taking British inventions and making them work better than the British—much as the Japanese have been doing with American inventions for the last twenty-five years. After America caught up with Britain at the end of the 19th century, it eventually learned to be inventive in the 20th century. But it took half a century to do this. Likewise, it may take Japan at least another twenty-five years to become the world's technological leader. As reflected in its current national slogan, 'Japanese Spirit plus Japanese Technology', Japan is indeed determined to develop innovative technologies on its own. In 1993, the country spent 13.7 trillion yen or just under US $130 billion on research and development (R&D), as against the US $230 billion spent by the US. On a per capita basis, this placed Japan ahead of the US, Germany, France and Britain, as the biggest spender on R&D (Weekly Post, 1996). With nearly 580,000 people engaged in R&D, Japan's per capita scientific and engineering workforce is also the largest in the world—47 per 10,000 as against 37 for the US.

Over the years, many people outside Japan attributed the nation's post-war success in industrial and economic development almost entirely to its political and economic systems. In recent years, however, this was replaced with the view that this success is largely accounted for by cultural factors, in effect promoting the practice of Japanese-style management. In fact, a survey conducted in the late 1980s showed that more than 70 per cent of the Japanese executives polled regarded their culture and personality as the most important determinant of Japan's success, with only a quarter citing economic and political factors as the main reason (Coates, 1988). However, the present young generation of Japanese who admire many aspects of American culture do not exactly see themselves as gate-keepers of the traditional cultural values as represented by 'bushido'. Besides, the humility brought by the severe economic recession of the 1990s is changing the long-held image of Japan as a juggernaut. It has also humbled the Japanese, making them even more determined to learn from others. The traditional Japanese way of management, for one, is being increasingly replaced with a more American style of management. Japanese firms are displaying a US-inspired anxiety about profitability and rates of return, and not just about increase in sales and market share, and have begun to apply more weight to merit than to seniority in rewarding their employees.

It is quite clear that Japan is now at a historical crossroads. The strong feeling of cultural uniqueness however persists as an enduring characteristic of Japanese society. There are many who still believe that 'bushido' could and should remain their society's guiding principle and source of strength. The 'bushido' spirit of self-reliance, self-perfection, self-discipline and self-sacrifice will no doubt be necessary for the nation to lay strong foundations for the 21st century. It was both the maker and the product of 'old Japan', and it could well be the formative force of 'new Japan'. The real question is whether it can survive and thrive once again in Japan, hard pressed as it is today by all the changes imposed from within and outside the country. The answer may determine whether or not Japan can actually win the honour of owning the next century.

5

DETERMINANTS AND CHARACTERISTICS OF THE CORPORATE CULTURE OF KOREAN ENTERPRISES

Son-Ung Kim

THE GROWTH OF KOREAN BUSINESS ENTERPRISES

The GNP of Korea increased from US $1.9 billion in 1960, to US $60.6 billion in 1980, US $251.8 billion in 1990 and US $451.7 billion in 1995. This rapid growth of the Korean economy has been largely attributed to the rapid increase in exports as a result of quick industrialization. Since the 1990s, however, with the slowing down of the increase in exports and increasing trade deficit due mainly to the decline of competitiveness in both price and quality of products in international trade, the Korean economy has been experiencing difficulties. Nonetheless, the Korean experience of rapid economic growth has become a development model both among Third World countries and in the erstwhile socialist planned economies including Russia and socialist China.

The history of capital formation by Korean businessmen and the development of business enterprises in Korea is fairly short. There were virtually no business enterprises owned and operated by Korean nationals under Japanese colonial rule, and most existing industrial facilities were devastated during the Korean War. Of the older, large business enterprises, those which had close and reciprocal relationships with the political influentials were able to establish their enterprises, mainly on the basis of the favourable transfer of state properties owned and operated by the colonial government to private ownership, or through favourable allocation of foreign aid during both the post-Liberation and post–Korean War periods of the late 1940s and 1950s. They also received special favours from the government in the allocation of foreign aid, facilities for foreign loans, bank loans, and tax reductions. With these incentives, the business enterprises grew rapidly.

The development of big business enterprises began in 1962 with the export-drive policies of the First Five-Year Economic Development Plan. The Korean government adopted export-orientation and rapid industrialization as its development strategies. This led to the rapid expansion of big business enterprises which played a leading role in national economic growth. In the initial phase of industrialization, these export industries were concentrated largely in the sector of light processing industries like garments, leather, shoes and toys which were low-tech and labour-intensive, and based on low wages. They absorbed the vast pool of urban unemployed. Over a period of three decades, Korean workers have become known for their diligence and strong motivation to achieve.

The government's strongly growth-oriented economic policy has led to the rapid development of big business enterprises. In the 1970s, some of these large enterprises formed themselves into big business conglomerations called *Chaebul* by establishing 'the integrated trade company' (*zong he shang she*) with various special favours under the government's export-drive policy. With the construction boom in the Middle East, they grew rapidly.

These *Chaebul* groups also adopted the diversification strategy by expanding into every possible business sector. Consequently, the top five are known to own on an average over thirty companies unrelated to each other. Such a strategy is usually compared in Korea to the 'octopus style of management'. These big business groups have prospered due to favourable international business conditions, i.e., the so-called 'three low-rates' including the low price of oil, the low interest rate on foreign loans, and the low value of foreign exchange rates throughout the 1980s, which provided Korean exporters with favourable conditions for price competitiveness in international markets.

With the rapid growth of business corporations and the national economy, Korea's industrial structure began to shift from labour-intensive light industries to heavy industries such as petrochemicals and steel, including semiconductors, computers and so on. The role of big business groups as the driving force behind rapid economic growth cannot be denied. Since the 1990s, however, the Korean economy has been experiencing various domestic and external difficulties. The domestic difficulties include inflation, soaring wage levels, manpower shortage and chronic labour disputes. As for the external difficulties, Korea is currently sandwiched between the challenges emerging from competition from developing countries with low wages, the pressures of market liberalization, and the rising protectionism of industrially advanced countries.

The positive aspects of Korea's economic success are reflected in the expansion of job opportunities, improvement in the level of living and welfare standards through increased income, and the provision of necessary goods and services. On the other hand, its negative aspects include the structural distortion of income distribution with extreme concentration of economic resources and wealth in the big business groups, weakening of small and medium industries, and the problems of relative deprivation and social conflict between the rich and the poor.

The strategy and style of Korean management and the subculture of Korean workers has resulted in a distinct kind of corporate culture. The main objective of this paper is to identify the characteristics of the corporate culture of Korean business enterprises and indicate their impact on job performance. It also discusses at some length the factors affecting the corporate culture of Korean enterprises.

CORPORATE CULTURE AND ITS COMPONENTS

Before going into the details of the corporate culture of Korean business enterprises, its nature and components are briefly outlined. Being more specific than the concept of organizational climate and organizational culture, corporate culture is defined as the sum total of values, beliefs, habits, traditions and norms shared by the members of an organization, as also their knowledge and skills. Thus, it not only influences employee behaviour and the functioning of the organization, but reflects the organization's characteristics as well. Corporate culture influences the employees' manner of doing things and their ways of thinking. As such, it has an impact on the extent of job commitment, work motivation, sense of affiliation and loyalty to the organization, group morale, collective consciousness and group solidarity.

The components of corporate culture can be categorized at three levels, namely, at the level of consciousness, the institutional level and the attitudinal level. The values and beliefs shared by both managers and employees, their respective norms, and the awareness of members of an organization about common interests constitute the components of corporate culture at the level of consciousness. Formal aspects of the organizational system like its structure, management strategy, procedural standards, business methods and communication pattern comprise the institutional components. The behavioural-level components include both informal and attitudinal aspects of interpersonal relationships among the members of work groups as well as between management and employees. In short, corporate culture is embedded in the first instance in the general culture and social environment of the country and, more proximately, jointly determined by the management system, infrastructure and technology of the organization, the orgnizational system in general, government policies and the characteristics of employees. In turn, corporate culture has a strong influence on job performance and organizational effectiveness. To understand the nature of corporate culture, it is essential to view it in the context of the culture of the country as such and the government policy at the time.

GENERAL FACTORS AFFECTING CORPORATE CULTURE IN KOREA

To understand Korean corporate culture, it is necessary to view it against the general cultural, economic and business scenario of the country. Corporate culture as an organizational subculture is broadly affected by two groups of factors, external and internal. The external factors comprise structural and institutional characteristics influencing individual business organizations. They include cultural traditions, government policies and political influences, the manpower situation, changing market conditions and changes in the tastes and needs of consumers. The internal factors on the other hand include the management system, the nature of infrastructure, the type of industrial sector, and the characteristics of the organizational system and the employment structure. Social values and cultural factors have also operated in the rapid industrial growth of Korea. Korean social values were formed under the influence of three major sources, namely, Confucian thought, the patriarchal system of extended large families and the collective community system. First, the heritage of Confucian thought is still deeply rooted in the social values of Korean people. Confucianism emphasizes virtuous human character in terms of generosity (*ren*), righteousness (*yi*), etiquette (*li*), wisdom (*zhi*) and trust (*xin*). It also advises people to take the middle path (*zhong yong*) in dealing with tasks or problems, avoiding extreme measures.

A person is judged usually by his/her overall character or personality, and not by manifest ability and/or short-term achievements. This Confucian heritage is believed to influence the criteria for both evaluation and recruitment of personnel in the business organization. As a result, in matters of recruitment and promotion, the quality of personnel is judged largely in terms of overall character and personality and not necessarily by specialization or ability.

Second, the modal personality of Korean people has been characterized by nepotism, particularism and informalism, believed to be derived from the patriarchal large family system. Korean society, like many others, is characterized by the extended large family system, where the majority of members live together, including both grandparents and members of married brothers' families. The extended family system is patriarchal in that it emphasizes the principles of strict hierarchical order and Confucian filial piety in father–son relationships.

In the patriarchal family system, children are expected to be obedient to their parents and to pay them respect. In return, the father, as the chief head of the family, is expected to be benevolent to family members by caring for their welfare. Thus, large partriarchal families are authoritarian, with strict hierarchical orientation and at the same time benevolent paternalism in organizational life. Because large families were traditionally cohesive and self-sufficient 'in-groups' with a common destiny, their social values and interpersonal relationships tended to be oriented to and charaterized by nepotism, particularism and informalism in terms of blood ties, residence, school backgrounds, etc.

Third, Western and Asian people differ in their value orientations. While in the West people are generally oriented to individualism, in the East they are oriented to collectivism. The collective orientation of the Koreans is said to be attibutable to the characteristics of their traditional rural communities. Like many other societies, Korea consisted of typical agrarian rural communities which were relatively closed and self-sufficient, requiring cooperative effort among community members for production, consumption and various social events. Such cooperative efforts were basically voluntary.

In the folk culture of Korean communities, there were three kinds of collectivized cooperative customs: *Kye, Dure*, and *Pumatshi. Kye* refers to the association for mutual help for ceremonial occasions such as marriage and funerals, or for financial needs, or just for friendly goodwill. The *Kye* is still widely practised even in urban areas, especially among schoolmates, members of the same workplaces and even among those with the same hobbies. Both *Dure* and *Pumatshi* are like manpower banks created through cooperative effort for serving mutual needs in farming activities. The effect of such customs and folk culture has been to foster group unity and cooperative spirit which are highly valued. Together with collective orientation, the Koreans have traditionally been very conscious of reputation and face-saving in terms of social role and status in the community.

Fourth, Koreans are generally considered *this-worldly* in orientation. Though they follow different religions, one thing common to all Koreans is their wish to attain worldly success in this life rather than bliss in the after-life. Having experienced conditions of destitution until the early 1960s, wealth and fame have become their life-goals. Koreans are materialistic in orientation with strong motivation to achieve success within a short period. As a result, they are much more concerned with outcomes than with the processes and means adopted.

The growth-oriented policy of rapid industrialization, as reflected by the First Five-Year Economic Development Plan launched after the military coup d'etat by the Park regime, also constitutes an important factor influencing Korean corporate culture. The basic policy of the government's economic development plan was 'distribution after economic growth'. The government indirectly encouraged big business enterprises dealing with export industries to expand and diversify. With the additional advantage of abundant supply of unemployed and underemployed manpower at low wage levels, these big business organizations gained price competitiveness in the international market. Thus, they grew rapidly, and so did the Korean economy. The big enterprises at the same time maintained a very close relationship with influential politicians and agencies.

Although industries faced an acute manpower shortage in the 1960s, there was a serious urban unemployment problem with the oversupply of off-farm migrants from rural areas which were overpopulated due to the high fertility rate especially among the 'post (Korean) War baby-boom' generation. Such massive off-farm migration to metropolitan areas was attributed not to the pull factor of job opportunities in the urban areas, but largely to the push factor of economic burden in the rural areas. The oversupply of unemployed or underemployed people in urban areas was responsible for the low wage level. Competition was high among job-seekers, thereby restricting the mobility of workers. Thus, labour in general was docile and obedient to superiors in business organizations.

The success of a business enterprise is essentially dependent upon how effectively the organization is able to adapt to changes in the external environment and market conditions. These include the manpower situation, the extent and characteristics of competition among business organizations and the changes in consumers' needs and preferences. When the export-drive policy was adopted as the major development strategy, the level of technology in export industries was relatively low. However, they were able to gain price competitiveness by keeping wages low. Besides, they had few competitive counterparts in the international markets in the 1960s and 1970s. However, the conditions have changed drastically in recent years. As the standard of living has improved, wages have also rapidly increased. At the same time, young industrial workers now tend to avoid the so-called '3-D' jobs (*difficult, dirty* and *dangerous* jobs) in manufacturing industries. As a consequence, the price competitiveness of labour-intensive industries could no longer be maintained.

Manpower shortage is particularly noticeable in the small and medium industries. Jobs in these sectors are considered to belong largely to the '3-D' category avoided by young job-seekers. Besides, industries are also suffering from the frequent scouting for skilled manpower by big business enterprises. As a result of all this, managerial attitudes and management styles have begun to change from being owner- and manager-centred to being employee-centred. Due mainly to the sharp rise in wage level and the shortage of needed manpower, a substantial number of labour-intensive industries are moving out to countries where cheap labour is available. There has also been an increase in the import of foreign labour from low wage countries.

The nature of the market has changed from domination by suppliers to domination by consumers' demands. During the time of shortage, whatever products were supplied were sold out and consumed. With a substantial improvement in the level of living, however, individual consumers have become highly selective about their purchases. Furthermore, their needs and tastes have changed rapidly due largely to rapid changes in fashion. Instead of the mass production of a few items, the production of diversified items in smaller quantities is required to cater to these changing needs and tastes. Accordingly, marketing strategy has shifted from the supplier's standpoint to consumers' concerns. The client is considered the 'king' and after-service is emphasized.

The management system, the characteristics of the business sector, employee characteristics and the organizational system broadly constitute the internal factors influencing Korean corporate culture. Of these, the management system is the most important factor in the formation of the basic characteristics of corporate culture, and usually reflects the ideology of the business establishment. Korean business enterprises usually follow the owner-manager system. The owner-manager usually exercises absolute power in all internal matters of the enterprise. The management style of owner-managers is characterized by paternalism under the general influence of Confucian values and the extended family system. Such familial paternalism puts more emphasis on vertical relationships based on obedience and unity than on functional and role relationships based on cooperation and unity.

Corporate culture varies with the type of business sector and industrial characteristics. For instance, the organizational climate of the construction industry is different from that of the high-tech electronic manufacturing industry. While the corporate culture of the former emphasizes aggressiveness, the electronic industry puts high value on creativity and innovative effort.

The organizational system also influences corporate culture. It comprises the structural aspects of organizations such as division of labour and allocation of work, chain of command and internal communication structure. In general, communication in Korean organizations is vertically oriented with top–down flow, and lacks horizontal interaction as well as bottom–up flow. The organizational structure is usually pyramidal with the chain of command based on a strict hierarchical order with absolute power at the top.

Corporate culture is also based on socio-demographic features, the level of education and other personal characteristics of the labour force. Most Koreans display high aspirations for education and children are under strong parental pressure for the same. As a consequence, the average level of education among workers is high. Further, with the majority of Koreans having experienced military service due to conscription, the labour force in organizations is usually well-disciplined and motivated. The middle-ranking executives are generally war veterans who have undergone rigorous and hard training. The effect of all this is visible in the corporate culture of Korean organizations.

CHARACTERISTICS OF CORPORATE CULTURE OF KOREAN ENTERPRISES

In spite of a certain degree of universality in the structural and functional characteristics of organizations, corporate culture varies significantly across societies and cultures. Three important differences between the West and the East that provide an insight into Korean corporate culture may be noted. First, corporate culture in the West is generally individualistic in orientation, based on rules of fair competition and the importance of its outcome. On the other hand, corporate culture in the East is collectivistic with emphasis on order and harmony among group members. As a result, work preferences and evaluation systems vary sharply. While workers in the West tend to prefer specific work assignments on an individual basis, and are evaluated and rewarded in terms of individual achievement, workers in the East feel more comfortable with team-work assignments and a reward system based on seniority.

Second, autonomy and equity are emphasized in the West more than order and consolidation, whereas the East places high value on hierarchical order, loyalty to the membership group, collective consciousness and group cohesion. The young are expected to show respect and obedience to the elders. The latter in return display benevolence and generosity and paternalistic care for the younger members.

Third, Western management is task-centred. Specialized division of labour is emphasized on grounds of both autonomy and the assessment system which is based on individual achievement. Relatively speaking, Western management is based more on rational principles than its Eastern counterpart. On the other hand, corporate culture in organizations in the East is more person-centred (relational), rooted in familism and personal trust. In general, both managers and employees tend to regard the work organization as an extension of the family.

The features just outlined are shared by the corporate culture of organizations in all Asian countries. However, the values, group norms, symbols, customs and specific socio-cultural features of a country also mould its corporate culture. The main characteristics of the corporate culture of Korean business enterprises are described against this backdrop.

Managerial subculture is a major component of corporate culture. Its value aspect is represented by business goals and management ideology. Separation between ownership and management is not sharp in Korean business organizations which generally started as small self-employed family enterprises and developed in the course of time into

Figure 5.1
Typology of Management Subculture

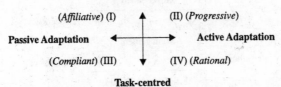

large-scale organizations. Their business goals are characterized by externally 'growth-oriented ideology' with short-term achievement goals. This has been influenced and implicitly encouraged by the economic policy of achieving rapid economic development as reflected in the five-year economic development plans of the 1960s and the 1970s.

Owner-managers generally emphasize internal harmony and integration among members. The emphasis on internal harmony is influenced by both Confucian thought and the traditional paternalistic family system. The owner-manager system generally adopts a person-centred rather than task-centred management approach. The former is relation-oriented and based on personal trust.

From a conceptual point of view, a typology of management subculture can be made in terms of two criteria: (*a*) the management approach; and (*b*) the nature of adaptation mode. The management approach is either *person-centred* or *task-centred*, and the mode of adaptation is either *passive* or *active*. Management characteristics can be classified into four types (see Figure 5.1).

Type I or the *affiliative* type is more person-centred than task-centred, and is at the same time passive in its adaptation to environmental constraints. Its emphasis on mutual trust and cooperation results in greater group cohesion and collective consciousness. Type II or the *progressive* type, though person-centred, is active in its adaptation to the changing environment. It is risk-taking and attempts innovative action. In its goal, it is growth-oriented. Type III, the *compliant* type, is characterized by a task-centred approach with passive adaptation to environmental constraints. It is more concerned with orgnizational stability than with growth or change. It is thus bureaucratic in its functioning and hierarchical in structure. Lastly, Type IV, called the *rational* type, is task-centred and active in its adaptation to changing environment. It stresses efficiency and practicability under realistic goals and planning. It may be observed

Figure 5.2
Tripartite Relationship among Labour, Management and Government in Korea

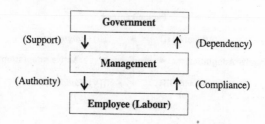

that growth-oriented Korean organizations are considered to be generally of the *progressive* type in this typology.

Three other important characteristics of the Korean managerial leadership system are to be noted. First, in its authority structure there is a high concentration of decision-making power at the top level, especially in the owner-manager. Delegation of authority or empowerment to the middle and lower levels of management is low. Second, communication within the organization displays a vertical pattern. Official communication is largely one-way, 'top–down' through designated chains of command with little voluntary feedback from below. Third, the processes at the operational level exhibit two contradictory aspects. While the formal processes are highly bureaucratic and regulative, the informal aspects display efficiency and flexibility in terms of particularism, and are characterized by nepotic relationships.

The employee subculture among Korean business organizations is to be understood in terms of a tripartite relationship among the employee organization (labour union), the management and the government. As illustrated in Figure 5.2, the tripartite relationship is an interpolative vertical relationship in terms of authority and power. The relationship between employee and manager is generally characterized by the compliance of the employee with the authority of management. The relationship between government and management is a relationship with government's support to management and management's dependency on government. Thus, labour issues in Korea are not only dealt with by the management but are also influenced and regulated by the government. The autonomy of employees in Korea has been limited largely by the management and indirectly by the government.

Personnel and labour management practices in Korean business organizations have customarily followed a mixed system of seniority and

Figure 5.3
Typology of Employee Subculture Patterns (Management–Labour Relationship)

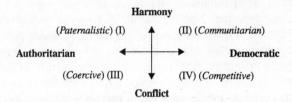

Harmony

(*Paternalistic*) (I)   (II) (*Communitarian*)

Authoritarian ⟵—————⟶ **Democratic**

(*Coercive*) (III)   (IV) (*Competitive*)

Conflict

merit. Promotion and/or rewards have been frequently determined by discriminatory personal relationships. Such discriminatory criteria are usually based on nepotism and particularism which result in favouritism and factionalism. Much of the labour conflict in Korea is attributed to such discriminatory treatment by and the authoritarian attitude of managers rather than to issues of class interest. Therefore, in dealing with industrial conflict, Korean workers tend to display emotionally charged responses in group actions which often result in violent collective behaviour, rather than rational responses by means of institutionalized procedures.

Employee subculture is shaped by the interaction of management style with the orientation of human relationships among members of the organization, as illustrated in Figure 5.3. Management style can be either authoritarian or democratic. Further, there can be two contrasting orientations to human relationships, viz., harmonious and conflictual. Thus, employee subculture can be categorized into four types in terms of management style and relationship orientation. Type I may be named *paternalistic* subculture, which stresses harmony among employees under the authoritarian management style. In this type, the owner-manager tends to treat employees as family members and displays a benevolent attitude towards them, and employees, in return, are expected to regard their owner-manager as the family head responsible for taking care of them.

Type II can be labelled *communitarian* subculture, in which the common interests of labour and management are harmoniously sought by means of rational procedures on the basis of the democratic principle for organizational intergration. Major organizational issues are discussed and decisions are taken with the participation of the members of the organization. This type of employee subculture implies industrial democracy as prevails in north-western Europe. Type III can be called *coercive* subculture, in which the members of an organization are in a state of conflict with the owner-manager who is authoritarian and wields absolute power. The terms of employment are generally unequal and in favour of management. In consequence, employees are largely exploited. This is a transitional type found during the initial stages of industrialization. Type IV can be labelled *competitive* subculture, in which both labour and management pursue their own interests independently on the basis of democratic principles. Although in this type the interests of individual employees are sought, this is attempted through the formation of trade unions. The relationship between labour and management is maintained through collective bargaining on an equal and competitive basis. This type of subculture is found generally in the UK and the United States.

From the conceptual point of view, the *paternalistic* type represents the employee subculture of Korean organizations. According to a survey conducted in 1991, over half (50.3 per cent) of the 207 Korean business organizations studied were found to belong to Type I, i.e., *paternalistic* subculture, and about a quarter (24.6 per cent) to the *communitarian* type of subculture. Only 14.5 per cent and 10.6 per cent respectively were found to be of *coercive* and *competitive* types (Shin, 1992: 620).

The three major characteristics of the corporate culture of Korean business corporations are highlighted in Figure 5.4. The work organization, with employees displaying collective orientation in a strict hierarchical structure under paternalistic management, is typical. The familistic nature of Korean corporate culture is rooted in the tradition of the extended large family system and in Confucianism. As has already been observed, the majority of Korean business corporations started as self-employed family businesses, and members tended to regard their company as a second home and an extension of the family. Further, Korean management tends to value personal and personality aspects more than the aspects of rationality and efficiency. It is believed that though efficiency and working ability can be improved through education and job training, the qualitative aspects of personality cannot be changed. Of the companies sampled, over 75 per cent were found to have precepts and slogans that emphasized moral aspects of the personality such as honesty, responsibility, diligence, patience, cooperation and harmonious relations (KCCI, 1991). Thus, it is not surprising that personnel management practices including recruitment, reward allocation and promotion are more person-oriented than task-oriented.

A few other features of Korean business corporations are outlined here. According to their annual manpower plan, large organizations recruit the entire amount of needed manpower annually at the same time and allocate

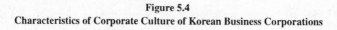

Figure 5.4
Characteristics of Corporate Culture of Korean Business Corporations

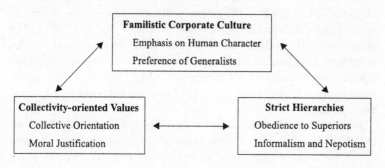

job placements for the entire group of member companies. The job applicants go through various screening processes of recruiting criteria. In the selection process, the personal interview by the managerial groups is particularly devised to assess the personality aspect of the job applicants which is considered more important than aspects like job speciality and work ability. Through such personal interviews, applicants are examined in terms of their fitness and suitability to the corporate culture of the company. It has been a general practice among Korean business corporations, as in Japanese ones, that the new recruits must undergo a compulsory and thorough training programme for acculturation to the corporate culture. For this purpose, some corporations have recently adopted the internship programme as a part of the selection process.

In the evaluation of merits and promotion, 65 per cent of the personnel managers emphasized character and personality; 30 per cent preferred working ability and only 5 per cent emphasized job achievement (KCCI, 1991). The managers preferred generalists to specialists. The majority of business corporations in Korea practised job rotations on a periodical basis. According to the survey, 67 per cent of the employees preferred job rotation for generalist purposes rather than for specialized jobs (ibid.). Through job rotation, the employee becomes a generalist acquiring a wide range of experience and knowledge which enhances her/his adaptive ability. Most business corporations also have periodical training and education programmes for different levels of employees which focus largely on spiritual education and human relationships rather than on specific techniques of business. The employees as generalists with a wide perspective and flexibility are expected to be able to manage internal conflicts and to adapt to rapidly changing environments.

As indicated earlier, members of organizations are collectivity-oriented with regard to their values and organizational behaviour. Collectivism is characterized by the prioritization of collective interest over individual interest through cooperation, harmonious relations and unity. It is to be noted that about two-thirds of the sampled employees were found to prefer team-work to individual job assignments (KCCI, 1991). Quality control (QC) activities in small work groups were widely practised. Even in off-job situations, Korean employees prefer drinking with their colleagues to drinking alone.

Job performance is influenced by the effect of 'face-saving'. Thus, the individual is very sensitive to the expectations, attitudes and perceptions of others. Korean employees seem to prefer ritualistic formality and moral justification to practical effect and self-interest. According to the survey, 82 per cent of the respondents preferred others' recognition to monetary reward, and about 90 per cent wanted to be treated humanely as one of the in-group members rather than be paid with higher wages (KCCI, 1991).

Organizational behaviour in Korea is status-oriented, based on the hierarchical status ranks in an organization. Younger employees and those at lower levels are expected to respect and be obedient to officers with superior status and older senior people. On the other hand, those with superior status in turn treat their subordinates in a benevolent and generous manner. This kind of reciprocity between superiors and subordinates has been influenced by Confucianism and is believed to contribute towards the maintenance of social order and organizational stability.

Informal personal and primary group relationships strongly influence organizational effectiveness. The majority of Korean business corporations are still run by the owner-manager system. In such corporations, decision-making power is highly concentrated in the hands of the owner-manager with low empowerment at lower levels. The inner core group revolves around the owner-manager and always develops informal personal relationships as an alternative route to formal channels. Such relationships are usually developed along the lines of blood ties, home-town backgrounds and school alumni, which become sufficient conditions for mutual trust. This enhances group cohesion, smooth communication and flexibility. However, it also often results in nepotism, favouritism and corruption, which frequently give rise to factionalism thereby hampering organizational integration.

In conclusion, it may be observed that the Korean corporate culture outline here has deep socio-cultural and historical roots. It has been a powerful factor in human mobilization and the success of business enterprises. It would, however, be wrong to think that this corporate culture has remained static and inflexible over the years. In spite of being normative in nature, it has undergone changes to meet the exigencies of the rapidly changing environment. With changes in technology, government policies, the needs, values and expectations of people and market conditions, adjustive changes have been taking place constantly making possible the survival and effective functioning of Korean business enterprises.

6

THE TRULY FAMILIAL WORK ORGANIZATION: EXTENDING THE ORGANIZATIONAL BOUNDARY TO INCLUDE EMPLOYEES' FAMILIES IN THE INDIAN CONTEXT

Rajen K. Gupta

I

The family is the first and longest-surviving human social organization. On the other hand, industrial organization is young and still in its formative stages. There is an uneasy and dynamic relationship between these two social forms of human coexistence. Business firms in the West have fluctuated in their attitudes to employees' families since the beginning of the Industrial Revolution. In the East, however, familism has stronger roots. The industrial success of Japan is partly attributable to its own kind of familism. In India also, which is seen as an emerging economic power, a proper appreciation of familism is crucial for creating internationally competitive organizations. The family-mode organization relationship in India is discussed against the background of the situation in other parts of the world.

This paper very briefly summarizes the dominant ideas about the relationship between industrial organizations and employees' families in the West over the last couple of centuries. In the section that follows, the role of Japanese familism is discussed in the context of its successful industrialization, and a comparison made between Indian familism vis-à-vis the Japanese version. This comparison poses some unprecedented challenges for business organizations in India. A reconceptualization of the boundary between family and business organization is proposed, and the concept is substantiated by the examples of some successful Indian organizations. It is concluded that the reconceptualized boundary be applied in organizations all around the world, after taking account of cultural variations in the form and functions of family in different countries.

II

As Britain moved from feudal to capitalistic agriculture to capitalistic industrialization, the initial phase in the attitude of owner-managers to employees and their families provided fodder to Karl Marx's tirade against capitalism itself. The key features of this period were exploitation of labour and its resulting alienation. Working hours were long, working conditions appalling, child labour was rampant, and family benefits unheard of. It gave rise to militant collectivization of labour, a legacy which still haunts Britain. E.P. Thompson (1963: 416) describes the effect of industrialization on the family: 'Each stage in industrial differentiation and specialization struck also at the family economy, disturbing customary relations between man and wife, parents and children, and differentiating more sharply "work" and "life". . . . Meanwhile the family was roughly torn apart each morning by the factory bell.'

The imperial phase brought prosperity in Europe as well as in the Americas. This gave rise to the notion of 'welfare capitalism' and the concomitant corporate paternalism in industry in the last quarter of the 19th century. A number of major American corporations introduced a variety of employee welfare programmes (Hareven, 1982: 38). Though many focused on the Taylorist line of efficiency, there were others who created kindergartens for workers' children, boarding-houses for the 'mill-girls', clubs and other facilities for recreation, and some even tried to create architecturally pleasant industrial towns. The creation of 'ideal' towns like the one constructed by Amoskeag Corporation in New England 'provided the moral justification for the new industrial order', while avoiding 'the horrors associated with industrialism in Britain' (ibid.: 53–54). As the nature of the labour force changed from local girls to immigrant families in the early 20th century, changes were made in welfare provisions. But the spirit of paternalism continued.

Such corporate welfarism peaked during the 1920s in USA, 'a decade of prosperity, levelling out during the latter half of the decade' (Kamerman, 1983: 4). The explanations for this decline range from Depression, to the availability of alternate services, to the growing employee resentment of employer paternalism. Corporate welfarism re-emerged in the USA in a less paternalistic form after World War II, but acquired a bad reputation and began to be contrasted with professionalism in management.

For our purposes, Bailyn's (1992) summary of cultural assumptions in the USA taken from Auerbach (1988) is pertinent. To quote:

1. Families/children are in the private domain.
2. Children/elder care, i.e., nurturance—is rightfully the province of women, either because they do it better or because it is somehow their specific job.
3. In an individualistic, achieving society, balance in life, i.e., between work and personal life—is not seen as a high priority goal, career and work success are more important.

The analysis of Indian familism later in this paper clearly shows that at least the first and third of these assumptions are untrue in the Indian cultural context.

From the vantage point of management practice and preaching in India, Britain and USA have a special place. While Britain initiated the process of industrialization in India in the 19th century, management ideas from America have been the guiding force especially since India's independence in 1947. Educated professional managers still swear by these ideas, though they have slowly started looking towards Japan as well. In order to provoke culturally relevant innovation in India, it is essential to deconstruct the cultural roots of the attitudes of business organizations towards employees' families in both American and British models of management which are emulated by Indian managers in their thinking. The main conclusion drawn from this overview of British and American attitudes is that, apart from a period of welfare capitalism in the early 20th century, business organization has kept itself at arm's length from employees' families—a stance that fits well with the strong individualistic streak in these cultures. Extraordinary affluence has also helped this individualistic orientation.

III

A major contribution of cross-cultural psychology in specifying the differences between East and West (specially North Europe and North America, or the Anglo-Saxon West) is through the concept of individualism versus collectivism (Triandis, 1988). The roots of this dimension are also seen in child-rearing practices and early socialization. Collectivist cultures show stronger familism than those which are individualistic. Accordingly, both India and Japan are collectivist societies with strong familial orientation. However, while Japanese culture is considered to be one of the main factors in Japan's successful industrialization, in the case of India its culture is seen as a major impediment. How do we resolve this paradox? The answer lies in identifying finer distinctions between collectivism in the two countries.

'Japan Inc.' may be the most appropriate phrase for characterizing Japanese society in the context of industrialization. Except for a few pockets of minorities and outcastes, Japan is a densely homogenous culture. Even when forced out of historical isolation and despite forceful efforts to Westernize it during occupation, Japanese society absorbed only a number of useful ideas from the West, and did not lose its unique character. Instances of close cooperation between government and industry are legion. The networks within Japanese industry are only now beginning to be understood. The paternalism of its large industries is also well-documented in terms of lifelong employment and continuous training and development. Employees' contribution to organizations is fairly well known, especially in terms of their industriousness and useful innovations to improve quality and performance. However, much less is popularly known about the linkages between the organization and the family of the employee. This invisibility of the family is partly because Western researchers and other writers have had a cultural blind spot for the family. But, more importantly, it is because the Japanese mother nurtures her son and prods him to perform well, after which the wife takes on the full burden of managing the family and nurturing the next generation, while the adult male dedicates almost all of his waking life to the organization he works for. So, from the organizational viewpoint, the family is in the background while the business organization is in the limelight. It is only recently that educated young wives have begun to resist the subordination of the family to the organization, while throughout the period of industrial development the family played only a secondary role.

The practice of 'tsukiai' which involves four or five hours of social-izing between employees every day after work is an illustration of the importance of work organizations. The group may go to a bar or two, then a restaurant, and finally to a coffee shop or another bar. ' "Tsukiai" is an indispensable technique designed to make affairs of the firm run more smoothly' (R.J. Smith, 1983: 65). 'His family may worry if he comes home from work early on week days' (ibid.: 67). The other side of the coin is that 'A traditional [Japanese] company will arrange mar-riages, housing, holidays and even funerals for its workers, in some cases buying plots in the cemetery so that their unity will not be disturbed even after death' (Wilson, 1986: 149). According to Chie (1988: 9), 'The characteristics of Japanese enterprise as a social group are, first that the group is itself family like and, second, that it pervades even the private lives of its employees, for each family joins extensively in the enterprise. These characteristics have been encouraged consistently by managers and administrators since the Meiji period. And the truth is that this encour-agement has always succeeded and reaped rewards.'

Anthropologist Rodney Clark (1988) traces the historical development of familism as an element in the nationalistic ideology of industrialization. He points out how initially, in the second half of the 19th century, the first industry—i.e., textiles—cared little about the employees, not unlike the British. It was around the turn of the century that some employers decided to be paternalistic in the face of labour shortage and to follow the example of America. That, however, did not prove sufficient for metal-working and engineering industries. There was labour unrest and demand for labour legislation. Clark observed that:

> the rise of the union movement and the imminence of labour legislation evoked a range of similar reactions among industrialists. A few gave more or less limited approval to the new developments. Others professed to wel-come them in principle but argued that it was too early to allow them full practical expression, usually because having unions and labour laws would cost industry too much money and make Japanese business uncompeti-tive. But a common reaction was to assert that the unique circumstances of Japan made western imports like unions and labour laws unnecessary (ibid.: 105).

In Japan, the relations between managers and employees and between capital and labour were essentially harmonious. Employees loved their masters, and masters preserved their traditionally benevolent attitudes towards those who worked for them. Industry was provided by a spirit (to which union and laws would surely prove inimical) of mutual understanding, peace and solitude, 'so much so that it was possible to assimilate the factory to the family' (ibid.). The reason was that 'the idea of familism, the epitome of Japanese uniqueness, arose with apparent naturalness out of the circumstances of the time and was, for that reason, a powerfully persuasive doctrine.' The metaphor of the family was perfectly adapted to interpreting employment practices forced on employers by the labour market. The notion of the firm as family was also consistent with one of the political concepts of the Meiji period—a concept widely supposed to have remote historical antecedents, but one which was in fact a new garment of old threads—that 'the Japanese nation was a gigantic family with emperor at the head' (ibid.).

It can be safely stated that under the umbrella of the nation as a family, the families of employees committed themselves to the business organization, which too has been culturally predisposed to taking care of them. The combination, then, created the 'Japan Inc.' Changes have of course taken place in Japan over the fifty years since World War II. 'The Japanese family itself has changed and no longer constitutes a single pattern for conduct. There remains, however, an influential idea of harmony and cooperation in relations among employees and between employees and their firms' (Clark, 1988: 105).

IV

The cultural reality of familism is also a feature of the Indian scene. Compared with Japan, there are differences at the intra-family level as well as at the level of the relationship between the employee's family and the business organization. Alan Roland's (1988) *In Search of Self in India and Japan: Towards a Cross-cultural Psychology* is a useful source for identifying the differences which R.K. Gupta (1991) has summarized. Roland contends that while the Japanese self can be characterized as familial-group self, the Indian self is to be characterized as familial-*jati* self. The familial nature of the self in both the countries is reiterated. However, while the Japanese extend or transfer their identification with and loyalty to the family to the work group and work organization, Indians do not do so spontaneously. The Indian self is consistent with the much-studied characteristic of Indian society—the caste system. For an Indian, familial loyalty extends to the extended family and then to the caste community (*jati*). Though not so very well studied by organizational psychologists in India, social anthropologists have studied the extension of caste or

regional groupings in business organizations. Bahl (1995) shows the existence of Bihari and Bengali groups in TISCO in Bihar; Uma Ramaswamy
(1983) illustrates it in the context of the Coimbatore textile industry in
Tamil Nadu; Sheth (1968) shows the existence of caste preferences in a
factory in Gujarat; Baviskar (1982) found caste to be very important in a
cooperative in Maharashtra. The social legitimacy of such preferences is
questionable within universalistic norms such as those enshrined in the
Constitution of India, but at the ground level of cultural reality it is far
from so, as illustrated by the following statement made by a worker in the
factory studies by Sheth (1968: 90): 'There is nothing wrong in the top
officials favouring their relatives and castemen. Every Hindu must do so.
If your relatives and caste-fellows do not benefit from the authority you
possess, what use are you to your society?'

Such *jati*-based preferences pose a very difficult challenge to the management of organizations in India. A fascinating but unstudied example
of community-based groupings exists in the Indian army, in which lowest-
level groupings of soldiers have been based on homogenous communities.
Such an option, however, is not available to business organizations due
to the law of the land and the skill requirements of modern industry.

Along with the group versus *jati* difference between Japanese and
Indian psyches, which can be explained by the much greater heterogeneity of Indian society, there also exist crucial differences in intra-family
dynamics and early childhood socialization. First, while an intimate and
indulgent relationship between mother and child is common to both countries, the Japanese mother is much more demanding during later childhood and pushes the child towards achievement. This is not the case in an
average Indian family, though educated urban middle-class mothers are
beginning to be concerned about their children's performance at school.
Therefore, the average Indian would appear to be less achievement-
oriented. Second, while the Japanese individual would suppress her/his
desires and only hope for the others to sense them, the Indian is much
more conscious and vocal about his desires. This has very challenging
connotations for managing the Indian subordinate. He may, to a considerable extent, contain his expression within the family due to his deference
to the familial role structure and hierarchy, but outside the family such
self-restraint becomes weakened. He also becomes very unsure of the
affection of his superiors at the workplace. Lack of identity with the
work group also releases a sibling-like rivalry for the superior's favour.
As a result, focus on the task is submerged in anxiety. The superiors, at
least at the middle levels, also come to the workplace with familial-*jati*

strings attached, and are more concerned about their relationship with their own superiors, emotionally neglecting their subordinates. At best, there develop multiple patronage systems across the organizational hierarchy (Virmani and Guptan, 1991). Thus, we end up with an organizational setting which is rarely well enough integrated to perform complex and interdependent tasks optimally. Third, if an Indian subordinate feels that he is unlikely to be in the good books of his superiors, his aggression is likely to be directed not against task achievement, but towards organizational sabotage. Joining a group of disaffected people becomes a convenient and useful avenue for expressing such aggression. More often than not, this arouses the anger of paternalistic top management and the organization ends up with a disharmonious employee–management relationship which adversely affects quality, productivity and organizational change necessary in the increasingly competitive market environment.

In short, given their psycho-cultural predispositions, neither Indian managers nor junior employees feel optimal identification with the work organization, and may end up reinforcing a negative spiral of alienation from organizational goals. This is a formidable challenge in managing organizations in India.

Both conceptual and empirical studies have been conducted on the special challenge of motivating Indian employees. J.B.P. Sinha (1980) proposed the concept of Nurturant Task Leadership, which has been backed up by the researches of his associates (e.g., Hassan and Singh, 1990). Kanungo (1990) has also developed a comprehensive model of work alienation in the Indian context, and proposed a framework for performance management (Mendonca and Kanungo, 1990).

Though culturally sensitive, these contributions suffer from an Anglo-Saxon bias in their portrayal of the nature of linkage between business organization and employees' families. Attempts at conceptualizing the fine-tuning of managerial leadership to cultural realities are confined to the day-to-day relationship with employees. This represents the same atomistic assumption prevalent in Britain and America in which the boundary of belongingness to the organization is coterminous with the legal contract of employment. Empirical research, however, indicates that an Indian does not see a clear separation of his work from his family, and in that he is different from Canadians (S. Misra et al., 1990). Researches on Indian samples indicate similar characteristics (Kalra, 1981; J.B.P. Sinha, 1990). Kalra (1981) gives the example of clerks in a bank accepting promotions not for the sake of their careers, but to get a better match for a daughter, or for the pride it would bring to their children and wives. However, these sporadic findings have not led to any significant shift towards reframing the relationship of employees' families with the organization. Major research and conceptualization in Japan has also tended to overemphasize intra-organizational practices to the neglect of the role of employees' families.

Mention must be made of a new interest in Western management litera-ture. The adverse impact on productivity of problems faced by employees in their families is now recognized, e.g., the spillover of stress from family to work. The problems of caring for children and elderly specially in dual career families is now demanding attention. Some companies (though the number is small) are beginning to respond to the new challenges (Gonyea and Googins, 1992). While sacrificing family needs appears to be the only way of dealing with career ambitions and global competition, Hall (1990: 11–12) conjectures that this may be counterproductive in the long run because it leads to burnout and high turnover. 'The appropriate focus of corporate pressure should be end results, not employee time or effort. In fact, some of the most productive, best managed firms—such as Dupont, IBM, Eli Lilly, and Johnson & Johnson—are taking the lead in legitimizing work/family boundaries.'

Management literature classifies such concerns in 'work–family issues', and looks at the benefits offered as 'family-friendly benefits'. It is a welcome trend, though still far from allowing for a conceptual integration of the family with the organization. In the West, these are seen as concerns of a developed, affluent economy. In India, they may be essential preconditions for optimal business development.

India faces an important challenge in this regard. Family is important as the cradle of every society. However, societies differ significantly in developing psychological identification with the family vis-à-vis with the employing organization. In Indian society, identification with the family is higher than in America or Japan. The family cannot thus be ignored while conceptualizing effective organization and management. In reconceptualizing its role, it may be necessary to break the existing legal contractual boundary of the business corporation and find a place for employees' families. This amounts to a radical critique of organization theory. Over the years, the number of beneficiaries sharing the gains of an organization has multiplied, from the entrepreneur or owner-manager as sole beneficiary, to other partners and shareholders who invest their wealth. Workers fought a long and hard battle to claim a right over profits through the institution of bonus payments. In due course, even suppliers and customers came into this orbit. It is only with the long-term economic logic of Japanese relational contracting (Whitley, 1992) that suppliers are gaining some emotional leverage, and more and more customized mass production has given a new status to the customer. All these new additions to organizational 'membership' are justified by a clear logic of economics. How can the family of the employee enter the boundaries of this logic?

As indicated in the previous section, the imperative of including employees' families has a strong cultural basis in the Indian context. For an Indian employee, the family is not secondary to business or career achievements as for the Western employee; nor does the family spontaneously subjugate itself to the employing work organization, as occurs among the Japanese. The Indian employee demands more, and there might be a primordial wisdom in that.

This cultural logic in the Indian context is not governed by a purely materialistic ethic of demanding a proportionate share in the profit. It is a remainder of Granovetter's excellent argument regarding the embeddedness of economic transactions in wider social relations (Granovetter, 1985). In the Indian context, meaningful emotional linkages have primacy. Dominique Lapierre, author of the popular book on life in the slums of Calcutta, *The City of Joy*, said that 'People in India have assimilated cultural values, retained family ties and maintained traditions, which is what makes them so warm, caring, with immense capacity to celebrate life, in sharp contrast to people in the West, who more often than not live uprooted lives' (*The Hindustan Times*, New Delhi, 20 May, 1995, p. 20). Wealth is useful, but not the only or the most important yardstick for social status. In fact, it becomes a reason of derision or is considered devoid of a spirit of sharing and giving (McClelland, 1975). Modesty and simplicity are still common, notwithstanding the more visible conspicuous consumption and greed. Therefore, the proposition for developing linkages between the business organization and employees' families deserves a wider social interpretation than a narrow short-term economic one.

Giddens' theory of structuration is useful here (Giddens, 1984). It divides the problem of societal order and integration into two: social integration and system integration. For Giddens, 'Social integration' means 'reciprocity between actors in contexts of co-presence' (ibid.: 28), which refers to the face-to-face and day-to-day interactions between persons. In the context of business organizations it is exemplified by the frequent face-to-face interaction between superiors and subordinates and amongst subordinates. The creative concept of Nurturant Task Leadership (J.B.P. Sinha, 1980) addresses this concern in the Indian context. System integration, on the other hand, means 'reciprocity between actors or collectivities across extended time-space' (ibid.: 28). 'The mechanisms of system integration certainly presuppose those of social integration, but such mechanisms are also distinct in some key aspects from those involved in relations of co-presence' (ibid.: 28). The concept of system integration demands that we seriously take note of collectivities which bear upon the effectiveness of the collectivity known as the business organization. The most well-recognized collectivity of this kind is the state apparatus. The role which MITI played in Japan's process of industrialization challenged the American notion of the separation between state and business. Recognition of the importance of networks of business firms is another instance of system integration. But the question which has not been asked is whether employees' families also form important collectivities for the integration of a business system. The presumed answer in organization theory has so far been in the negative. Organizations in India would accept that answer at their own cost. But the employees know that their family's survival depends on their continued employment. Accordingly, they would invest the minimum necessary effort at work to ensure employment. This is consistent with a number of studies indicating that the caste system in India has not come in the way of industrialization (e.g., Sheth, 1981). However, as Gupta (1991) has observed, such a contingent attitude on the part of employees cannot create global leadership in business. Thus, the necessity arises of examining and encouraging system integration between the two types of collectivities in the Indian context.

V

Such an imperative makes it worthwhile to take a fresh look at some successful organizations in India which show sensitivity towards employees' families. As this concept is being proposed for the first time, there is no available study which explicitly focuses on it. However, to provide the initial empirical base, evidence is culled from published case studies and this author's interactions with employees conducted for varying purposes. Since the purpose is to illustrate possible Indian models for family–organization linkage rather than to establish a definite model, the choice of cases is purposive. In case the model appears sound, systematic research may be undertaken on it.

Two models of differing degrees of inclusion of employees' families by the work organization in Indian organizations are considered. The first involves inclusion based on and contingent upon loyalty. It is a model which implies a very selective inclusion. Because of its covert political nature no formal systematic studies of such organizations are available. No researcher has used innovative and demanding methods like those of Dalton (1959) or Kamata (1982) to circumvent formal permission which would not be forthcoming. However, the stereotype is well known and professional management graduates from top-level institutions shun it. They call these organizations 'Lala type' organizations. (Lala in Hindi stands for a traditional trader/industrialist especially in north India.) The Marwari community, which after independence took over business from the British especially in the eastern part of India, also falls in this category.

In this model, the owner-managers clearly recognize the familial orientation of Indian employees. However, they do not see the necessity of responding to every single need of employees. In fact, the extremely negative view towards workers in general was stated by a personnel manager of such an organization: 'My management believes that the stomach of workers should never be allowed to be full. As soon as it is full they begin to create trouble.'

The owner-managers of such organizations believe that by cultivating a few employees at each level they can control organizational functioning to their advantage. At the most senior level these are relatives of the owner-manager, or belong to the same or similar communities. While conducting training programmes for such an organization the author was told that you have to be an 'M.Com.', i.e., belong to the Marwari Community, to rise in the organization. At lower levels people are identified for their willingness to be personally loyal to the owners and to become informers against their colleagues. In return for such personal loyalty, the management provides their families extra benefits which are not a part of any formal organizational policy. The employees in general are cogs in the wheel and can be bought at market rates. Many such organizations are immensely successful in terms of their financial performance. It is not therefore an unattractive model, though all the details of the management systems of such organizations are not known; however, we do know something about their tight financial control system (Khandwalla, 1980). A major drawback of this model seems to be that it may become less functional in the face of higher levels of technology and fiercer competition, conditions in which the commitment and involvement of most of the employees are imperative.

In the second model, the inclusion of employees' families is based on the deep-rooted value of humanism and recognition of Indian familial culture. There are many organizations in India which follow this philosophy in varying degrees. Some anecdotal evidence is provided for this range of organizational responsiveness:

A worker's wife sustained severe burns in a kitchen accident. The worker approached the welfare officer for the company's ambulance, but was informed that the ambulance could be given only after the departmental head's permission had been obtained. The departmental head was not available. Finally, some worker after considerable effort arranged an autorickshaw and took the woman to the hospital where she succumbed to her injuries' (Chaturvedi, 1987: 57).

In this example, the organization had a welfarist policy but lacked responsiveness. This contrasts with the following examples:

One of the employees met with a serious accident while on tour. On receiving the news, two persons of the company immediately went to his house and gently broke the news to his wife. They told her that her presence was needed more by her husband and that the company itself would arrange for someone to look after her children and the house. Thereafter the company's aircraft was put at her disposal and all the necessary arrangements for the children were made at this end (Chaturvedi, 1987: 57–88).

Another example:

After a prolonged sickness a worker died around 6 p.m. On receiving the news the labour welfare officer immediately arranged for the money which is usually given by the company for the last rites. However, after talking to the widow, he realised that the amount was insufficient and extra funds would be needed in this case. The officer went to the residence of the Vice-President (Personnel) and explained the situation. The Vice-President was visibly annoyed. 'For how long have you been working with this company?' he asked. 'For 8 years', was the reply. 'After working for eight years in this company how could you not take an immediate decision on such a matter? What made you think, that we would say 'no' in such a case?' Since that incident, the labour welfare officer has always decided on the spot on all such issues and, in his own words, 'the company has never said "no" to anything which is humane' (Chaturvedi, 1987: 58).

These two examples highlight a high level of organizational responsiveness. Since these may also be interpreted as chance events due to particular individuals involved, a more comprehensive picture is required.

The Tata Iron and Steel Co. (TISCO) and the Tata Engineering and Locomotive Company (TELCO), both of which are among the best in their respective industries, provide illustrations for this model. A word of caution is necessary. It would be unrealistic to presume that none of the negative aspects of the Indian familial *jati* psyche exists in these organizations. Rather, these organizations suggest a managerial approach which attempts to minimize the negative aspects while mobilizing the positive potential of this psyche.

There are a number of studies available on TISCO. Mamkoottam (1982) and Bahl (1995) have studied the company from the vantage point of industrial relations and trade unions. While both acknowledge the welfare activities of the company, they tend to interpret these as part of the managerial strategy to suppress class consciousness while using various strategies to manipulate or buy off trade unions. The scholarship behind these studies leaves no scope for doubting the facts, but the interpretation of the intent behind the welfarism is a matter of ideological frame of reference. Without denying the possibility of manipulation on the industrial relations front, we are concerned here with the visible efforts of the organization to reach out to employees' families. Two books by S.N. Pandey (1989; 1991) provide useful information based on internal documents and research-oriented surveys. Chaturvedi's (1987) study of 'achieving harmonious industrial relations' provides a comparative picture of six successful organizations in India, in which both TISCO and TELCO were included on the basis of the judgement of a panel of management consultants, trade union leaders, management researchers and a retired senior labour commissioner. Chaturvedi uses a multi-method approach including documents, interviews and observations. The following details are drawn from these studies.

Though the philosophical utterances of leaders are difficult to rely upon in an increasingly demagogic world, the letters of J.N. Tata, founder of TISCO, to those close to him provide a rare and reliable glimpse of his philosophy at the time of establishing the first and most prominent heavy industry in India. He wrote:

> We do not claim to be more unselfish, more generous or more philanthropic than other people. But we think we started on sound and generous business principles considering the interests of the shareholders as our own, and the health and welfare of the employees, the sure foundation of our prosperity.

Further, in a letter written in 1902 to his son he wrote about his vision of the town where the steel mill was to be established:

> Be sure to lay wide streets planted with shady trees, every other of a quick growing variety. Be sure that there is plenty of space for lawns and gardens. Reserve large areas for football, hockey and parks. Earmark areas for

Hindu temples, Mohammadan mosques and Christian churches' (quoted by Pandey, 1989: 12–13).

Pandey also provides evidence of many welfare benefits introduced by TISCO decades ahead of their being enforced by law (ibid.: 16).

Another philosophical statement by J.R.D. Tata, the later architect of the present Tata Culture, was:

> Every company has a special continuing responsibility towards the people of the area in which it is located and in which its employees and their families live. I suggest that the most significant contribution organized industry can make is by identifying itself with the life and the problems of the people of the community to which it belongs and by applying its resources, skills and talents, to the extent that it can reasonably spare to serve and help them (quoted by Chaturvedi, 1987: 53).

In the case of TISCO, such philosophical statements find direct expression in a number of formal policies and practices. The company provides free education to the children of its employees up to matriculation, and also provides facilities for training in crafts and trades. It provides some help for higher education as well; the educational facilities continue even after retirement or disablement. The company has built more than 16,000 flats and provides very low interest loans to employees with lower salaries. It provides extensive medical facilities to all employees, their families, dependent relations, and to retired employees and their wives. It has a hearse service for all. It has provision for the employment of employees' dependents, but that cannot be sufficient in the Indian context. Therefore, it has a number of training schemes for gainful employment through its community development service centres for the families of its employees. Loans are available for various family needs, including for getting out of the clutches of loan sharks. A unique feature upholding familial values is the existence of community committees at the level of localities. Comprising prominent elders, these committees review the progress of various schemes and suggest new directions. As Chaturvedi (1987: 168–69) points out:

> These committees which today number over 45 are also involved in settling petty disputes in their respective areas and the company cooperates whenever necessary. For instance, if the relations of an employee's widow did not look after her or if an employee of the company does not take care of the basic needs of his parents on the recommendation of the committee, company deducts a certain amount from the son's salary and pays to the

widow/parents. The union does not object and does not bring in the law in such cases, because they also accept that it is a moral duty of the children to look after their parents especially since it is only in the light of this obligation that the policy of jobs to relations/dependents has legitimacy.

In many ways, TISCO is a unique organization which believes in 'caring' intensively and extensively. Almost every need of an individual is attended to and their concern extends not only to the employees, 'but includes their families, pets and also entire communities located coterminus with the company's geographical boundaries' (ibid.: 52–53). 'The name of the company spontaneously arouses the image of an organization that cares and is socially alive' (ibid.: 52).

In some ways TISCO is an incomparable organization because its management also manages the city of Jamshedpur where it is located. However, the business house of Tatas, whose flagship TISCO is, has adapted its philosophy to a more common situation in Pune where TELCO is just one of the many large industrial organizations. According to Chaturvedi (1987), TELCO, Pune, is a case of 'an innovation in welfare' through worker cooperatives. She quotes from a brochure of the company's voluntary schemes:

> We believe that our employees are adult members of the family and a paternalistic approach to their needs would stifle their own growth. Our employees also understand that they are members of a large social community and that many of their own needs can more lastingly be met with by slowly changing and improving the fabric of society around them. It is not their, or our ambition to change the world. Only to make humble contributions to each other's lives within the time, strength and comprehension given to us (ibid.: 153).

Starting with the untimely death of an employee the management encouraged and persisted with the formation of a cooperative of employees' wives. Today there are five 'cooperatives owned and run autonomously by 1020 women all of whom are wives or dependents of the company employees. . . .' There are twenty-three centres at different locations (in Pune) offering members the facility of bringing work to their doorsteps. Women work only for four flexible hours so that their families and households are not neglected. Then there are industrial cooperative societies which provide full-time employment to the male dependents of company employees.

Apart from these economic activities, a trust has been formed to facilitate the admission of employees in schools. There are hobby training centres for children, where training is imparted by skilled company employees. Further, twenty-five community centres have been established in localities where the company's employees reside as places 'to get together and relax'. A cultural forum with a membership of over 1,500 conducts activities in literature, music, theatre and fine arts. In addition there are four creative clubs. For other needs there are housing cooperatives, employees' mutual benefit funds, medical and mobile hospital societies and so on.

Summing up, Chaturvedi concludes:

> TISCO people mostly felt that the company had been taking genuine interest in their personal problems and was concerned with their well-being. TELCO, Pune orientation cannot be categorised with any degree of definiteness because two opposed perceptions existed. While managers usually tended to view these schemes as enlightened strategies for conflict management, the few workers who were interviewed, took them as expression of concern and commitment to the philosophy of 'self-reliance'. Many managers and observers. . .did not view these welfare schemes as expressions of company's concern for the workers' well being. The workers themselves, however, appreciated these schemes and admitted that these are some of the major attractions of the company. In fact, the commitment of the company to these welfare schemes and its flexibility and interest in evolving the schemes in the light of the present and future needs of the people, the perception of the workers does seem to have a justification (Chaturvedi, 1987: 152).

These examples from TISCO and TELCO illustrate the extent to which some organizations have gone in establishing tangible linkages with employees' families. Employees' testimony indicates that such an approach increases the attractiveness of the organization for its existing and prospective employees. An overall goal orientation is, of course, essential to harness this attractiveness for organizational efficiencies and effectiveness in a competitive marketplace. In the absence of concern for result, the outcome is likely to be otherwise, as evidenced by the innumerable financially sick public sector organization in India which provide bountifully for employees and their families (J.B.P Sinha, 1990). There is some, though not systematic, evidence that in a result-oriented organization such truly familial orientation not only arouses spontaneous commitment but also works as a deterrent to delinquent tendencies. For example:

> contact with the family is maintained by the Labour Welfare Officer who every day visits few houses of the workers and meets with their families. Interestingly, while generally workers are appreciative of the close

contact which the companies are trying to build, sometimes they resent it because it 'curtails' their 'freedom'. 'You cannot take casual leave by giving a wrong excuse because through the community centre the company will come to know of the facts'—as a worker from Telco, Pune, observed (Chaturvedi, 1987: 245).

There are many examples, though not documented, in which the organization uses its positive linkages with the family to discipline truant workers. For instance, an organization may resort to involving relatives in public reprimand of indisciplined employees if private counselling and reprimand do not show positive effect. In another organization, employees' resistance to learning about and using computers was overcome when their children were given computer lessons by the organization, which led to pressure on them from their children to acquire knowledge of computers. In still another example, truant workers were brought back to honest work by showing them how their negative attitudes to work were perceived by their own children.

In conclusion, there is ample evidence that genuine multidimensional linkages with employees' families stimulate their sense of belonging, generate a result-oriented atmosphere, and evoke superior performance. Since the focus is not on the micro interpersonal behaviour at work between supervisor and subordinate, the evidence related to the established concept of Nurturant Task Leadership (J.B.P. Sinha, 1980) has not been presented. However, it is to be presumed that such leadership at the micro level is an integral part of the familial orientation of the organization with respect to employees' families. It is also emphasized that in the Indian context 'organization as a family' is not an optimal metaphor unless the emotional boundary of the organization is extended to include the actual families of the employees. Familial orientation within the organization coupled with an effective extension of the organizational boundary to include employees' families as much as possible is what constitutes a truly familial organization.

VI

The foregoing discussion indicates that organizations and management in India need to see employees' families in a different light from that in America or Japan to evoke the maximum possible commitment to and involvement of employees in the organization. Doubts may be raised as to whether companies that have so far been successful in this direction can afford to continue to pay such attention in an increasingly competitive marketplace. Only time will testify their strength. Both TISCO and TELCO, however, are confidently adapting themselves to the new realities without giving up their philosophy (*Business India,* 19 June–2 July 1995: 54–62). Actually, many other companies are beginning to find sound business logic in 'networking into a family and winning over employee loyalties by creating a sense of belonging' (*India Today,* 15 June 1995: 90–91). This popular article in a leading Indian magazine takes its examples from NIIT (a leading information technology educational and software company), HCL (a leading computer hardware company), Kirloskar Cummins and Thermax (both large engineering companies).

The initial discussion of the attitudes of American and Japanese employees and organizations illustrated that the exceptional business successes of their organizations implicitly took into account their respective cultural assumptions about the family. Thus, at a more general level it can be proposed that the optimal business organization in a society or culture needs to achieve a fit with cultural assumptions about family and work life. As a corollary it also follows that business organizations need to recognize that they are not dealing with atomistic individuals but individuals who received their initial socialization in a family and continue to be an important member of another family. While pursuing the ever-demanding goals of cut-throat capitalism on a global scale, the role of the family—the most fundamental cultural institution—cannot be brushed aside.

7

JAPANESE AND INDIAN WORK PATTERNS: A STUDY OF CONTRASTS

Anshuman Khare

BACKGROUND OF INDIAN AND JAPANESE BUSINESS CUSTOMS

The Japanese have always stressed the needs of the company over the needs of individuals, and they have been successful in this. It is very interesting to analyze how such commitment can be drawn from individuals in Japan, while this effort fails in India. Perhaps this acceptance of the authority of the company comes from Japan's centuries-old feudal tradition of obligation between companies and employees (and also between big companies and their smaller suppliers and distributors). Further, government policy also focuses on production rather than on individual consumption. The enormous benefit of this Japanese tradition has been the ability of big companies to focus on the needs of the entire value stream unimpeded by functional fiefdoms, career paths within functions, and the constant struggles between members of the value stream to gain advantage over each other.

Another aspect of the Japanese system lies in preserving these feudal relationships, rather than responding to shifts in the market or international working environment. A case in point is the fact that Japanese companies with massive export surpluses are encouraged to redeploy production so that their output in a given region corresponds more closely to sales in the region. This implies that they work under constraints like the inability to reassign employees to new enterprises and to abandon the traditional second- and third-tier suppliers. This causes many big companies to invest in additional domestic capacity for making the same families of products. The *relationship preservation act* works both ways—company to employee and employee to company; company to supplier and supplier to company. In spite of the associated constraints, the system gives good results as one of the precious links between the organization and the individual is *commitment*. In Japanese companies there is special effort to inculcate and preserve this element. In fact, they do not have to work very hard for this as a new entrant (from the university) normally comes with an already adopted set of socially correct norms of behaviour. Thus, it does not take long to understand what is missing in the Indian context. The most essential missing link between actions and results is *commitment*.

Let us take a closer look at the evolution of today's Indian business and work environment. It can be said to have evolved through two different routes—one can be traced to the origins of Indian civilization and the other to the Western influence originating from the Industrial Revolution of the 18th century (D.P. Sinha, 1996). India's relationship with the British prior to independence reduced the cultural aspect of Indian business, making it much less prominent compared with Japanese business. The Indian feudal system was systematically destroyed by the British to further their goal of colonization of the Indian subcontinent. After independence, India was left with a hybrid system: Asian culture with European social structures. The heart and the mind of such systems do not often work together. This conflict is apparent in the lack of results today. Little or no effort was made to develop an *Indian system*; the systems in vogue were strong enough to repel efforts to change.

SOCIALIZATION PROCESSES: SOCIAL NORMS AND EDUCATION

Change can be initiated in the system not from the time of entry in the organization, but much before that—through the education system. However, this too has proved to be a futile exercise in India as the education system is very American and/or European in content and methodology. Let us try to appreciate the sharp difference between the Japanese and the Indian management education system. In Japan, students use

basically Japanese books which help them understand their own management styles and their own work environment; secondary to this is
information about other management styles, e.g., that of America. The
situation is just the reverse in India, where the basic books are about
American or European management styles. Very few education centres
make available information about anything Indian. In short, in the Indian
context, a truly Indian system never got the opportunity to emerge and
grow.

Let us take a closer look at the average Japanese and her/his beliefs.
From early childhood, the Japanese are taught to be socially correct. Other
important, visible factors are their sense of discipline and honesty. There
is also an emphasis on building and maintaining relationships over long
periods of time. The emphasis on peaceful maintenance of relationships
is distinctively Japanese. The stress laid on being socially correct leads to
respect for the elderly and for seniors. The relationship of *sempai* (senior)
and *cohai* (junior) is further strengthened in the school and the university.
The club organization structures at the university level are based on strict
adherence to senior–junior relationships. In every activity, the senior
leads the junior or helps the latter in achieving her/his goals, and /or shares
the responsibility. Most of the activities at this stage are group activities.
Sometimes the seniors, after graduating from the university, assist their
juniors during the most demanding of times in a Japanese student's life—
job hunting. This makes a Japanese understand the power and benefit
of being group-oriented very early in life. The ideal is individual self-
sacrifice and conformity with the group.

The fact that human beings have to coexist is not appreciated in many
parts of the world. Perhaps the Japanese understand best the meaning of
the well-known phrase, *man is a social animal.* An individual's growth
at the expense of another may be the norm of today's social climbing,
but this is still alien to Japanese society. Living for oneself is perhaps
the easiest way, but living for others and suppressing one's own desires
for their benefit reflects greater social consciousness and understanding.
Concern for others finds a prominent place in Japanese society.

What makes an Indian's situation different from that of the Japanese? In
India also there is an immense emphasis on the sanctity of social relationships. However, lessons of social correctness are received only at home
from parents and family members. Outside the home, an individual fails
to appreciate the advantages of social correctness because, for example,
there are no constructive, meaningful and prominent senior–junior relationships visible in the student's life. There are very few group activities

where a student would be exposed to working in a group. Also, due to the huge population and the ever-increasing competition in every field of life, the average Indian cannot but become individualistic, although not as much as the average American, but certainly more than the average Japanese. However, the strong ties binding Indians to their social structure and work groups do not altogether disappear. They do think about those who will be affected by their decisions, but their ambitions are not restrained as in the case of the Japanese. When it comes to making a decision, an Indian normally takes an individualistic decision rather than conform to the wishes of the group (Sinha and Tripathi, 1994).

The lack of senior–junior relationships also means that there is no reason why an individual should not eye a senior's position once he/she is capable enough (or thinks that he/she is capable enough). There are no sentiments attached to the senior as in the case of the Japanese. In Indian organizations, therefore, there is an atmosphere of high competitiveness. Further, there is a high possibility of the status quo being disturbed for the least reason. Insensitivity or lack of concern toward others often leads to tensions avoidable in a group-oriented system like that of the Japanese. Thus, situations in Indian organizations are more volatile. This is further aggravated by the arrival of the new generation of educated, competitive, career-conscious managers proficient in using the new technological tools. They are also aware of their *rights* as industrial workers. Being individualistic in approach, they are not shy in demanding what they think is due to them. Under similar circumstances, the Japanese would not demand their rights as it would be socially incorrect behaviour. For an Indian, however, there is no way out. As most companies are not sensitive enough, individuals are forced to protect their interests and fight for their rights. Job security in organizations also becomes a right which, once ensured, acts as a *demotivator*. In short, the new generation is influenced by Western individualism and style of working.

Management of human resources is another area where the concerns of the Japanese are very different from those of the Indians. Their workforce is smarter than anywhere else in the world (*Business Week*, 1994). They have been masters of innovation (even though the West tends to call them 'imitators') and still continue to be the leaders. This is because of their investment in technicians and engineers. While organizations in India seek out management graduates and place them above engineers, this does not happen in Japan. An engineer is the most respected person in organization and society. Managers as such are an invisible class. Everyone is a manager whose job is to assist fellow workers. In India, engineers are 'second-class citizens' in an organization, comparatively poorly paid and neglected. In such an environment most engineers turn to management schools for ensuring better living standards and higher status in the organization and in society. The Indian system produces managers who only believe in 'managing people' and not in 'assisting' them. Organizations in India have so far failed to give engineers the place due to them in the hierarchy and treating them on par with the managers. This has resulted in the deterioration and degradation of the technical base as engineers have either migrated or turned into managers. The success of Japan has been due to heavy investment in technical and vocational education and in courses in engineering (Watanabe, 1991). Only selected universities offer MBA courses, and investment in 'making' a manager is low.

BEHAVIOUR AT THE WORKPLACE

The very facts that Japanese culture and work environments are *typically Japanese* and that Indian culture and work environments are *Indian with Western influence*, makes the comparative study of behaviour of Japanese and Indian employees at the workplace absorbing. This paper discusses Japanese and Indian work patterns with respect to some specific issues which stand out among many others. The argument does not favour either system, because two situations cannot be identical. Even though the two countries are Asian, their historical backgrounds, cultures and people are very different. The idea is to identify and appreciate these differences and to work towards achieving organizational goals keeping them in mind.

In Japanese society, when a new entrant starts working in an organization, the last thing on her/his mind is to compete with seniors. Their gratefulness stops them from pursuing narrow individualistic goals. For them social acceptance is of greater significance than individual achievement. Group recognition is the only reward they seek. They are fully committed to the group and to their organization. Cooperativeness and devotion to the goals of the company count more in the Japanese context than ambitious drive and decisiveness. Status in society is due to the company for which one works rather than the profession one is in. This is reflected in the way Japanese individuals normally introduce themselves. They first mention the name of the company they work for, and then their names. In other cultures the opposite is the case. At the workplace, being group-oriented leads to cooperation and suppression of individual competitiveness and ambition. Competitiveness in Japanese organizations is *controlled* and senior–junior relations are not easily disturbed. Some may view this as a drawback as it hinders, for example, the growth of talent. However, this system has provided Japanese organizations with discipline and stability resulting in unbounded success in many areas of business. In contrast, not all senior–junior relationships in Indian organizations remain positive and conducive to work. More often than not, this relationship degenerates into manipulation (Tripathi, 1981) and ingratiation (J. Pandey, 1981).

In most Japanese offices, superiors and subordinates sit together. The communication channels between them are not formal. As there are no job descriptions, there is freedom to rotate work amongst employees. This makes everyone capable of handling almost all types of jobs handled by a given section. After work, office colleagues and their superiors often socialize and go out to drink and shed their tiredness from work in each other's company. During such meetings there is freedom to discuss anything. There is hardly any status consciousness visible. This keeps the organizational social relations intact and, in fact, makes them stronger. The superior is normally aware about subordinates' desires and expectations because they interact regularly.

Many companies take care of their employees by ensuring what is popularly known as *lifetime employment*, in expectation of an individual's lifelong commitment. An average Japanese does not demand it as a matter of right, but accepts it gracefully as a gift from the company. To express gratefulness they pledge their commitment to the company.

The seating arrangements in Indian offices are more like those in Western countries. There are formal communication channels between the superior and the subordinate. There is also a tight compartmentalization of work due to job descriptions and well-established responsibilities for each individual. As regards informal interactions, they are very few. People mix normally with people of their own level and status. Drinking and going out for dinner with juniors or subordinates is not very common. People do not express their inner feelings. A subordinate does not speak much in the presence of seniors, but the superior is expected to understand the problems and wishes of subordinates.

Sharing of responsibility is another aspect in which there is a difference. In Japanese companies most people work late hours. That includes both the staff and the executives. This is not a common practice in Indian organizations where only executives work late. The staff leaves early. It is believed that if there is work pending, it is the responsibility of the person who is in charge of the section. There is no feeling of collective responsibility.

This aspect is further reflected in the way people work in offices in India. Let us look at some of the performance attributes: the working is bureaucratic (in its negative sense); the approach is cautious (very non-committal); people avoid taking decisions till they are very sure of a favourable outcome or depend on their senior to take the decision; they are not very concerned about the correctness of the task being done nor too concerned if the work remains incomplete; delaying work is normal (especially in government organizations), leaving it for the next day is also normal; job security tends to discourage good performance; quality consciousness is still very low. Company goals and objectives are not very well understood by workers and group decision-making is not very common. Many factors can be said to underlie the caution and insensitivity to organizational needs. One is the fierce competition inside the organization. There is always somebody ready or willing to take your place and one has always to be cautious to maintain one's position. Second, the responsibility of poor performance or incorrect decision-making is not shared. It is focused on the individual because of the rigid and specific requirements of job description and the Western system of evaluation. As such, in adverse circumstances, an individual stands alone and exposed. Third, there is no social support and protection accorded by colleagues and social alienation is easy to encounter. Fourth, an individual is never properly educated about company goals and mission; one is only made aware of the job one is expected to perform. Thus, in general, a person dose not identify with the company goals and objectives. As employees cannot anticipate the ultimate goal, their vision is restricted to their own narrow sphere of activities. Also, they are incapable of realizing the consequences of their actions—good or bad. Fifth, as identification with the company and its objectives is minimal, there is a lack of commitment. All these factors (and many more not discussed here) underlie the cautious and insensitive behaviour generally witnessed at the workplace.

As a matter of fact, companies in India do little to change the situation. Because of the availability of the human resource in abundance, they do not feel the need to spend time and energy in gaining the commitment of their workforce. From the very first day, an individual feels the coldness of an Indian office. It takes some time before a person settles down largely because of her/his own efforts. There are instances where new employees have to do everything—right from planning their own induction and training programme. In India, companies normally start contacting students after they graduate or obtain the requisite qualifications. Sometimes, a guarantor has to vouch for the candidate. The companies make little effort to introduce themselves to the students. Some companies make this effort when they recruit directly from the campus. Students are tested rigorously in their areas of specialization (written tests, interviews and group discussions are common) and also on their knowledge about the company. This process of selection may take over a year to complete.The reason is the large number of candidates for any kind of selection. There are no active college senior–junior relationships visible in students' getting jobs. The Japanese case is very different. Most companies arrange seminars for students in their final year at school. Here, the prospective candidates are provided with information about the company. After the selection process is over (about six to eight months before the student graduates and joins the company), companies keep in touch with the new employees giving them information about the company. The feeling of belongingness to a certain company soon develops; the presence of seniors in the company further reduces the feeling of entering a strange place. In short, one finds a constant effort on part of the Japanese companies to be concerned about their employees right from the day they first meet them as job-seekers.

Training is one vital area which receives a lot of attention in all types of organizations. However, the approach to training is different in different countries and cultures. In the Japanese system, individuals receive training and information about the entire working of the company. Apart from the training in specific work or skills, they get a general view of the organization they have opted to work for. An effort is made to make them understand the philosophy of the organization and its goals and objectives and to know about its customers. They are thrown again and again into the company of those they are going to work with, resulting in the building up of social bonds so sacred in the Japanese system of working. In sharp contrast, most Indian companies give their employees on-the-job training for the work for which they have been hired. Sometimes they are familiarized with the work of the other sections or departments of the company or with the customers with whom they will be expected to interact. During training one has to work as a responsible executive of the company. It is a very formal and rigid approach and it is at this stage that new employees in Indian organizations start becoming individualistic. From the very first day they are expected to defend their position and to seek their rights as employees of the organization. This is reflected in their behaviour at work. Lack of comradeship in the early stages in the organization accentuates individualistic orientation. It is at this stage that they begin assimilating all the attributes of Western managers.

The next important factor in an employee's association with a company is the issue of promotion. As mentioned earlier, in the Japanese system, senior–junior relationships are not easily disturbed. The employees show no desire to *jump* because that would disturb their social bonds. Seniority is the most important factor deciding who is promoted and who is not (Watanabe, 1991). The Indian system is different because of the presence of two things—job descriptions and, as a consequence, job evaluation. The concept of merit emerges from this. Promotions in Indian companies are based on merit and seniority, and both aspects are supposed to be equally important. It is, therefore, obvious that inside the organization there is 'cut-throat' competition (and politics) and rivalries. Every employee tries to out-pace or out-perform colleagues and appear more meritorious. This form of unrestrained competition often results in discontent and has a negative impact on organizational performance. Being self-centred in India and to protect one's own interests makes more sense under such circumstances.

Since information is power in every form of organization, information hoarding is more common than information-sharing in the Indian setting. This is the reason why group decision-making is not yet very popular in Indian companies. This power is invariably used (or misused) for promotion of self-interest. In sharp contrast, in the Japanese organization information-sharing is part and parcel of the business culture (JETRO, 1982).

At the workplace, Indian employees are not completely free of social compulsions. In this respect, they are typically Asian in character. They are tied to informal groups based on religious beliefs, languages, profession (for example, a steel worker may be a member of the union of steel workers), political affiliations (most trade unions in India are sponsored by or affiliated to political parties), or even the state or the region they belong to. Therefore, while a Japanese employee feels social compulsions *inside the company*, for Indian employees, the influences ordinarily emanate from *outside the workplace*. In general, it is not surprising to find an Indian having pressing commitments outside the workplace or organization. Commitment to the organization, at times, is found wanting since priorities exist outside the organization. Indian public sector chief executives have often lamented the lack of a committed industrial workforce. It has been pointed out that Indian workers' priorities are linked to their family, friends, neighbours, caste, religion, political ideology and so on. The organization probably occupies the last place. An industrial workforce entirely committed to the organization is yet to emerge.

Another issue that stands out relates to group formation and its role. The problem in India starts from the stage of formation of groups (specially the ones at the shopfloor level). In an industrial setting, first, it would be difficult to voluntarily get together a group of workers for a common cause. If this is achieved, the group soon starts setting up its own objectives (for example, related to unfulfilled demands) which are unrelated to the real objectives for which the group was formed. The main objective is soon lost and the new ones become the preconditions set by the employees for considering the real objectives. As a result, while searching for solutions to issues related to the organization, the management often finds itself beset with problems not directly related to the main objectives of the organization.

Looking at the same issue from another angle, we find that in the earlier days of the Indian industrial revolution there was hardly any encouragement for group activities, and formation of groups was viewed with concern. 'Groups of workers' were synonymous with 'unions'. Also, India adopted the Western system of evaluation of performance in which only individual assessment and achievement of goals were emphasized. Slowly, the system as well as its administrators (managers) developed an attitude that can be called 'anti-group'. In the 1980s, with the advent and success of Japanese business philosophies in almost all corners of the world, the administrators of the system tried to adopt group-oriented activities without however changing the system or their business thinking. This strategy therefore started to backfire, because the employees, used to the restraints of the earlier period, now saw it as an opportunity to get organized and raise their voice against the system. The formation of groups, therefore, often diverted attention from real organizational problems to merely grievance handling on a larger scale. The organizational ethos and its orientation are not conducive to working as groups, but to working as individuals. This needs to be changed if Indian organizations are to experiment and succeed with group-oriented business methods.

The point to be noted here is that if we cannot form, or work in, groups, we cannot achieve success with issues like productivity and quality. These cannot be achieved by individual excellence alone. They require group excellence. To the Japanese, working in groups comes naturally and as such they have excelled in these areas (Watanabe, 1991). Their commitment to the organizational cause is also remarkable and adds to their success.

The performance evaluation systems in the two countries are remarkably different. A successful employee in the Japanese setting is not necessarily the most talented one. Emphasis is on individuals who can understand and work with others. In other words, employees who can work in groups are sought after. The case is just the reverse in India. A sought-after employee is one who stands out amongst fellow workers.

The concept of time in Japan is well known all over the world. Being group-oriented and while working with others, people develop an understanding of the value of another person's time. Not much needs to be said on this issue. In India, wasting time is a rampant problem. Every public service organization, every government body is plagued with it. Things just do not move, be it banks, hospitals, post offices, the electricity department or telephone department. Coupled with dishonesty and bureaucracy, this issue poses a formidable challenge to anyone attempting to do business in India.

There are other aspects that make for a lot of difference between the situations of the two countries. One is the homogeneity of the Japanese population. Here is a case of one language, one culture and one expectation. In the case of India, the heterogeneity is remarkably unmanageable. There are many languages, many religions, many cultures and many expectations. The environment in the organization is therefore sometimes difficult to understand, and at times chaotic. A second aspect is the profile of the Indian workforce. In general, one can identify three groups of people: executives (people with specialized professional qualifications and education), clerical staff (persons with average education, e.g., graduates with vocational certificates), and workers (poorly educated without any meaningful formal qualifications). Managerial jobs like planning, controlling, organizing, executing and client visits are handled by the executives, while the desk jobs are handled by clerical staff. Daily menial jobs are handled by the third category of people. A third aspect is the use of English as the language for work. India is a country of many languages and many cultures; Hindi is the national language, but mostly English is used for official/organizational communications. A fourth aspect is the lack of compulsory education for a large section of the population. And a fifth is poverty. How do these factors play a part in the Indian situation? Use of English acts as a barrier to communication between the third and upper two levels of the organization. The lowest-level worker is normally a local resident, maybe with poor education and with little or no understanding of the English language. Lack of education also means lack of the capability of understanding one's own position in the organization and of understanding the significance of the work one is doing. Poverty means a very different set of priorities—personal needs are more pressing than the big invisible goals of the organization. The case of Japan is different, because of a common language which is used and understood throughout the organization and the country, limited division of labour and stratification, availability of compulsory education to everyone, and near absence of poverty.

JAPANESE APPROACHES THAT INDIAN COMPANIES WISH TO EMULATE

So far, we have discussed the differences in the Indian and the Japanese situations. Given this scenario, let us try to focus on problems that many Indian managers face when attempting to emulate Japanese approaches like just-in-time, quality circles, continuous improvement and total quality management. Some Indian factories have been successful in emulating these systems, but have found it difficult to sustain the changes. The question that needs to be addressed is: are they really the right approaches for the Indian environment? Can these be transplanted wholesale to a different cultural setting?

QUALITY CONTROL CIRCLES

The phrases *quality circle* or *quality control circle* mean different things to different people. They suggest that quality control (QC: the improvement of quality within an organization) and quality circles (participative decision-making groups) are one and the same. Although quality circles generally do focus on quality control, the two concepts are not synonymous.

In Japan, quality control circles are organized within a department or work area for the purpose of studying and eliminating production-related problems. They are problem-solving teams which use simple statistical methods to research and decide on solutions to workshop problems. Similar types of activities are known by many names, such as *Ai* (chemical industry: all members' ideas) movements, big brother or big sister groups, *Jishu Kanri* (or JK) in the steel industry, level-up movements, no-error movements, management by objectives, mini–think-tanks, new-life movements, productivity committees, safety groups, suggestion groups, workshop involvement groups, workshop talk groups, and zero defect movements (Imai, 1982).

Presently in Japan, quality circles and other small group activities have expanded beyond the manufacturing sector, especially into the sales and marketing fields. They focus on much more than quality and productivity improvement. Employee development and the improvement of communication and morale among co-workers are also important.

My experience of initiating the application of QC in an Indian organization is relevant here. I attempted to initiate QC for a business associate of a well-known Indo-Japanese collaboration in car manufacturing. I could make hardly any headway. It was difficult to explain the reasons for initiating such an exercise to the employees. Every time I tried to go a step further, I found myself dragged two steps back. I could understand the reasons for my inability to convince the shopfloor-level workers. The initial response was good, as I was interacting with executives. The company and its environment had taken good care of their needs and they were able to associate themselves with the goals of the organization. When it came to making the workers understand the concept and its utility, there were many obstacles in the way. Some of them came immediately to my notice—lack of education (and therefore inability to understand the documents that were handed out to them by the company), poverty (therefore inability to relate to the needs of the company, as their own needs were hardly satisfied), lack of awareness about the company and its goals (they only understood what they were expected to do; the company had never made an effort to make them understand the goals of the organization), and so on. I could not blame them for asking me questions like 'Why should I change my approach to work?', 'Why should I think about the company?', 'I must think first about earning my living, rather than thinking about how the company earns its revenue.' What was missing was *commitment*—of both parties (company and the workers) to each other. Commitment is a rare commodity in Indian organizations. This was precisely a case of the absence of *commitment between elements inside the organization*. This explains the employee's lack of identification with company goals and objectives, as well as the company's lack of understanding of its employees' perceptions and needs.

This made me realize the futility of the exercise of trying to adopt Japanese approaches in India, without preparing the ground for the same. This preparation will not be quick and easy due to the differences that exist between the two cultures (in spite of the fact that they are both Asian and resemble each other in many ways). One has to go back a long way to extract the kind of commitment, honesty and discipline required for an exercise as complicated as quality circles. If an organization forces quality circles on its employees using its power to do so, it would find it difficult to sustain, as quality circles are a voluntary employee exercise.

JUST-IN-TIME

The Just-In-Time (JIT) concept of making nothing until it is needed and producing it at the highest level of quality sounds simple. The application of this concept becomes essential as economies move from an era of undersupply to an era of oversupply. In a situation of oversupply, old beliefs no longer hold good as the needs of the consumer undergo a dramatic change (as many options are made available). One encounters a high rate of obsolescence and feels (in terms of falling sales and rising costs) the rigidity in countering price cuts from competitors.

This philosophy seeks to establish a production technology that uses a minimum amount of equipment and labour to produce defect-free goods in the shortest possible time with the least amount of unfinished goods left over.

This is another concept that revolves around commitment. The difference is that there is a need for commitment from external parties like suppliers and other business associates. Without commitment and sincerity it is impossible to achieve the results obtained by the Japanese companies. Again, in Japan, one sees the nurturing of suppliers and other downstream and upstream partners by the biggest or the core organization (even in the most adverse circumstances). The case of Nissan's British subsidiary provides a striking example of what has to happen and the extent of commitment required (Cusumano, 1985). When Nissan launched its first car, *Primera*, designed for the European market, several suppliers failed to deliver workable parts on time. The normal reaction would have been to replace the miscreants. Instead, Nissan's British purchasing department teamed up with the Nissan R&D centre to place supplier development teams of Nissan engineers inside each supplier for extended periods to improve their key processes. Nissan's theory was that setting high standards and giving the suppliers advice on how to meet them would produce better and desired results. A few years later, when Nissan introduced *Mica*, a new small car, this approach had transformed Nissan's worst suppliers into its best.

It is not only a case of expecting commitment from others, but also of showing deep commitment towards those who assist the company in doing business. Such commitment is not easy to extract and express in a fiercely competitive situation characterized by narrow individualistic behaviour of firms. Further, application of the JIT approach depends on the efficiency of various infrastructural facilities like telecommunication, transportation, and so on. This probably explains the reasons behind the difficulties in practising these Japanese concepts in India, or in many other parts of the world.

The absence of something like the Japanese *keiretsu* (cartel) system in other parts of the world also has its bearing on the reasons for the failure of JIT outside Japan. In India, too, such an agreement between a group of companies would be viewed with concern rather than as an agreement that makes good business sense. However, a near *keiretsu* system developed carefully over the last fifteen years by Maruti Udyog Limited (MUL) has borne results (Khare, 1997). The emphasis of MUL was on being a *partner* in the progress of its suppliers (and not a dominant buyer) and it *assisted* (not dictated) suppliers in meeting its requirements. This joint venture with Suzuki Motors Limited in India has a lot to teach about how to work with Japanese concepts and draw the same benefits as in Japan.

CONTINUOUS IMPROVEMENT

Embeddedness of such a concept in an organization's culture is possible only if the employees identify with the company and understand their responsibilities. It requires sincerity, commitment, knowledge about the company and understanding the significance of one's own job. Many of these things are possible with an educated workforce (like the Japanese workforce) with a strong urge for achievement. Further, this urge is possible only if the employee's basic needs (physiological, security and social needs) are satisfied. Given the diverse heterogenous situation in the Indian context (different languages, religions, expectations, etc.), it is a difficult task for any manager to motivate subordinates to such high levels of performance.

CONCLUDING REMARKS

Many authors have pointed out the *simplicity factor* in Japanese systems and approaches. This is easy to understand. Any society (or organization) that is characterized by commitment, honesty and respect for social structure can do things easily and simply. Societies (or organizations) that do not incorporate these attributes have to set up checks and controls to derive the necessary requirements from the system. This complicates the system.

The Indian situation is very different from Japan's in the sense that the systems encountered in India are control/restrictive systems, while those in Japan are facilitating (or helping) systems. As such, the individual's inner feelings are different when he encounters either of these systems. In the Indian situation they feel impatience, anxiety and/or expectation of failure to achieve; while in the Japanese system the feeling is that of being relaxed and safe. The former is the legacy of the British, and such systems still continue to exist after over fifty years of independence.

It is not the change in management style that can make an organization (or a nation) competitive and successful, but the basic change in thinking, understanding of its background, its social and business environment, evolution (emergence) of its own systems and a sense of commitment and identification with one's work that would make all the difference. It would take a long time to get all this in place. Merely copying will not bring results. There has to be a concerted effort toward modifying and adapting foreign approaches to work in new settings. There is hope, as many Indian firms have begun to understand such compulsions. However, it requires a collective effort from all sections of society. Changes in an individual, a company or a system are not enough. It is a dilemma one must face because the solution lies outside the purview of the company.

The foregoing discussion conclusively indicates that unless Indian management practices are soaked in the Indian cultural ethos adequately, corporate India may not be able to cope with the managerial challenges in the globalized milieu (D.P. Sinha, 1996). Lessons from Japan are not only instructive, but also illuminating. They have demonstrated that the successful management practices are those which blend the indigenous cultural ethos of a nation with the requirements of techno-economic systems.

III

VALUES AND ORGANIZATIONS

8

THE EVOLUTION OF WORK ETHIC AND MANAGEMENT THOUGHT: AN ISLAMIC VIEW

Abbas J. Ali

The issues of work and organization and their relation to religious beliefs have captured the attention of scholars since the 1930s. Most discussions of these topics, however, have been concerned with Judeo-Christian contributions. Despite the fact that many other religious and ethnic groups have achieved tremendous economic prosperity during parts of their history, their contributions have been almost totally ignored in management literature. Islamic contributions to organization and management thought are either misunderstood or not widely known in the field of organization studies. This paper provides insights into the various Islamic schools of thought and their relevance to management thinking. In addition, the paper reviews the meaning of work in Islam. While acknowledging that there is no single voice in Islam regarding daily or worldly affairs, the paper investigates the meaning of work and organization in early Islamic teaching.

The author wishes to thank Prof. Steve Osborne for his comments on an early version of this paper.

ISLAM AND WORK

It is fair to suggest that many management practices in the Islamic world have their roots in the Islamic and pre-Islamic empires. The birth of Islam in Arabia in approximately A.D. 610 should not be seen as a sudden and isolated event. Rather, it was a creative evolution of existing religions (e.g., Judaism, Christianity, Zoroastrianism), beliefs and practices that prevailed in Arabia and the surrounding empires (Persian and Roman).

Today, Islam is one of the most influential forces in the Islamic world that moulds and regulates individual and group behaviour and outlooks. Religion is an influential force as reflected in a number of practices: (*a*) most Islamic societies are still traditional in the sense that the commitments to honour, honesty, respect for parents and older persons, loyalty to the primary group, hospitality and generosity remain the deeply held beliefs of a majority of the population; (*b*) the family and other social institutions still command the respect of almost all individuals regardless of their social backgrounds. These institutions utilize Islam to sustain their endurance and influence; (*c*) most people recite/listen to Quranic verses more than once a day; and (*d*) Islam is a comprehensive religion that regulates not only asceticism but also worldliness. Almost all social, political and military precepts are covered in the Quran along with the piety of the soul and moral aspects of individual behaviour.

Quranic principles and the Prophet's prescriptions serve as a guide for Muslims in conducting both their business and their family affairs. The Quran persistently instructs Muslims to pursue whatever work is available whenever it is available. 'He [God] has also made subservient to you all that is in the heavens and the earth' (Holy Quran, 1981: 45 : 13). Prophet Mohammed preached that hard work caused sins to be absolved and that 'no one eats better food than that which he eats out of his work' (M. Ali, 1977). Similarly, Imam Ali (A.D. 598–661), the fourth successor of Prophet Mohammed stated: 'Persist in your action with a noble end in mind. ... Failure to perfect your work while you are sure of the reward is injustice to yourself,' and that 'poverty almost amounts to impiety' (Imam Ali, 1989).

During the first six centuries of Islam's Golden Age (beginning in the 6th century), knowledge, trade, industry, agriculture and the construction of complex organizations flourished. Work and creativity were honoured in all their forms. Quranic principles and Prophetic prescriptions served as guides for Muslims in conducting their business and family affairs. Izzeddin (1953) examined the contributions of Arab/Muslim people during the Golden Age to organized work, noting that:

> The industries and trades were organized in corporations or guilds. These corporations were of great social importance. They maintained the standard of craftsmanship and prevented underhand competition, thereby insuring a friendly society. Based on religious and moral foundations, they impressed upon their members a sense of duty toward one's craft and toward one another. Honesty and sobriety were characteristic qualities of Moslem artisans. A tradition of mutual aid prevailed (ibid.: 30–31).

It was during this Golden Age that highly esteemed organizations emerged. The status of merchants and trade in Arab-Islamic thinking is reflected in Prophet Mohammed's saying: 'He who brings supplies to our market is like a warrior in the war for God;' and 'the truthful, honest merchant is with the prophets and the truthful ones and the martyrs' (quoted in M. Ali, 1977). Likewise, Imam Ali, in his letter to the governor of Egypt, held merchants in a respected social position. He stated:

> Take good care of the merchants and artisans, and ensure their well-being whether they are settled or traveling, or working on their own. Those are the providers of benefits and goods which they bring from far away by sea or by land through mountains and valleys, securing them for people who are unable to reach them. Those are the people who will assure you of durable peace and respected allegiance. Give them due care in your vicinity and in other areas of your land (Imam Ali, 1989: 329–30).

This view is in contrast to the belief that prevailed among other civilizations that prospered before or after the Islamic empire. For example, Dessler (1986: 15) pointed out that in ancient Greece, 'Business in general, and money-lending in particular, were...carried out by slaves and less-than-respected citizens; manual workers and merchants, in fact, were not permitted citizenship in the Greek democracy.' Likewise, the European peoples regarded business as a degrading occupation. In *The Wealth of Nations* (first published in 1776), Adam Smith indicated that businessmen are 'an order of men, whose interest is never the same with that of the public, who have generally an interest to deceive and even to oppress the public and who accordingly have, upon many occasions, both deceived and oppressed it' (quoted in Koontz et al., 1980: 31).

Islam emerged in Arabia when the community in Mecca was thriving commercially and intellectually and when the Arab elite of the city of Mecca was accumulating wealth by controlling trade and trade centres. Naturally, members of the commercial class assumed political positions and leadership. It is this class of 'merchant warriors' which was able to integrate the Arab world and who transformed it into a centre for international trade between Asia, Europe and Africa. This provided the basis for knowledge, trade, agriculture and the construction of a sophisticated system of government to develop. Work and creativity were honoured in all their forms. A case in point is the Arab capitalist sector. It was the most extensive and highly developed sector in history before the establishment of the world market by European businessmen (M. Robinson, 1974). The 'merchant rulers' supported and encouraged trade. It is worth noting at this point that the Ommeyyade dynasty (A.D. 661–750) had held power and wealth before Islam. Initially, the dynasty led the opposition to Islam. After the establishment of Islam, however, members of the Ommeyyade dynasty managed to position themselves strategically. Leading members of the dynasty had accumulated wealth that had to be invested. Since the environment in Arabia was not conducive to industrialization and agriculture, the Ommeyyade dynasty had to rely on commerce to expand and invest the available capital. Thus, they lured Arabs into the army and extended their tribal loyalty to national loyalty in an attempt to capture new regions (e.g., Africa, Spain, South Asia). They used material rewards and ideological bases (Arab solidarity) in service of their economic and military expansionist goals (Abdel-Rahman, 1989). Gradually, a form of partnership evolved between the state and the merchants. This partnership continued until the late years of the Abbasid empire.

Certainly, in the Arab world, any approach to organizational change is assumed to be influenced by existing work ethics and norms. The Islamic Work Ethic (IWE) is an orientation that has tremendous influence on people and organizations. It stands not for life-denial but for life-fulfilment and holds business motives in the highest regard (Ahmed, 1976). The concept has its origin in the Quran, and in the sayings and practice of Prophet Mohammed.

The IWE flourished during the Golden Age of Islam. The defeat of the Arab Caliphate and the ascendancy of the non-Arab Ottoman empire (1412–1918) however helped to institutionalize autocracy and further the demise of trade associations and freely organized business activities in Arab/Islamic lands (A. Ali, 1990). Turner (1981) argues that Islamic stagnation and the servile imitation of traditions were the inevitable consequences of Turkish military absolutism. Further, in order to maximize their control over the Islamic *umma* (nation), the Turks encouraged a conservative theology of strict obedience to authority. Knowledge and formal schooling were prohibited and *Jabria* principles were advanced (see the section on Islamic schools of thought later in this paper). The absence of written communication and the isolation of Muslims in different parts of the world induced many Muslim people to treat various foreign rituals and legends as original. With no knowledge of general Islamic principles, each generation came to treat foreign habits and customs as its own. The supremacy of Western colonial powers over the Arab/Islamic lands, especially after the breakdown of the Ottoman empire, further reinforced cultural discontinuity and alienation. For example, even though the Western powers allowed schools to open in various Arab states in the first decades of the 20th century, they established authoritarian regimes and attempted to replace Arabic with French or English. In fact, in Morocco, Tunisia and Algeria, the French colonial power forced its language on the indigenous people. After independence, the new governments did not make serious attempts to transform the colonial legacy, and the French language is still used for instruction at the university level and in the workplace as well.

It is important to note that the dominant features of the IWE are contained in all Islamic schools of thought except in the *Jabria* school. In its spirit and meaning, the IWE stands in contrast to the teaching of the *Jabria* school, which is currently sanctioned by existing Arab/Islamic governments. Since the Iranian revolution, however, a cultural awakening has spread through the Islamic countries, and many groups and associations have been established to advocate cultural revivalism. The IWE thus appears to attract many segments of the population, not only for cultural reasons, but because it encourages individuals to better themselves and to strive for economic prosperity. In a survey regarding the IWE in Arabia and in the United Arab Emirates (UAE), A. Ali (1992) and Ali and Azim (1994) found that Arab managers scored high on IWE. The overall mean of IWE is 4.16 (5-point scale) in Arabia and 4.26 in the UAE; both are relatively high. Previously, A. Ali (1988) found that Arab students scored high (M = 4.26) on the IWE scale.

The strong commitment to the IWE is manifested in a number of workplace practices. First, there is an emphasis on hard work, meeting deadlines and persistence. This means that in introducing change, the establishment of a timetable and clarification of goals and responsibilities are essential for carrying out a successful intervention. Second, work is viewed not as end in itself but as a means to foster personal growth and social relations. In this context group interactions and team activities, if designed appropriately, could result in optimal facilitation of intended changes. Third, dedication to work and work creativity are seen as virtuous. Managers and consultants should focus their process design on the new method of change and on producing results that reinforce existing commitment and enthusiasm. Fourth, justice and generosity in the workplace are necessary conditions for the society's welfare. This has three implications: (*a*) managers/consultants must show that they are attentive to and concerned about human needs; when considering firing employees, for example, managers may consider factors other than performance before a decision is made; (*b*) social skills and mastering public relations are essential for effecting change through a successful intervention. In a highly personalized society, once a commitment is obtained there will be smooth implementation; (*c*) goals for change are directed toward serving the community or society as a whole; that is, managers should emphasize the fruits of the results for the organization and society. Finally, unlike the Judeo-Christian ethic, the IWE places greater emphasis on intentions than on results. Prophet Mohammed stated, 'Actions are recorded according to intention, and man will be rewarded or punished accordingly.' That is, unlawful work that results in accumulation of wealth (e.g., gambling, prostitution, drug trafficking, deceiving, extortion, hoarding and monopoly) is condemned and those who engage in it are looked upon with contempt. Thus, the process of managing in an organization should be assessed carefully.

ISLAM AND MANAGEMENT

Contemporary management as a concept and as a process differs from the management of human affairs in pre-industrial societies, including the Islamic empire during its Golden Age. Nevertheless, there are some similarities with respect to desired behaviour and conduct. Despite the fact that major and leading merchant enterprises existed during the Islamic empire, their organization and actions may not resemble today's complex organizations. True, they had representatives (before the emergence of Islam, Mohammed worked as the representative of a merchant woman whom he later married) and offices across the empire, but they relied on moral commitment and trust, a bond between employer and employee, to perform their activities. In managing the state and the society, two major aspects can be identified which may shed light on management issues in the Islamic world and differentiate Islam's management experience from that of other civilizations. First, the Islamic concept of management places an unusually strong emphasis on the humanistic aspect of managing people's affairs. Second, there is the changing aspect of management that evolved as a result of the dynamic nature of the relations between the state and religion. The humanistic aspect is found in the tradition of the Prophet and his successors. The Prophet's sayings are often quoted as evidence: 'The blessing is with the group;' 'The best of you are those who have the most excellent morals;' and 'Every one of you is a leader and every one of you shall be questioned about those under his responsibility; the Imam is a leader and shall be questioned about his subjects; . . .the woman is a leader in the house of her husband and shall be questioned about those under her care; and the servant is a leader so far as the property of his employer and shall be questioned about [that] which is entrusted to him' (quoted in M. Ali, 1977).

Imam Ali was more explicit in his humanistic thinking. In his letter to the governor at Mecca, he stated:

Sit with them [the people] every day from dusk to sunset to answer their queries, to educate the ignorant, and to discuss matters with the learned. Let your tongue be the only ambassador to your people and your face be the only barrier between you and them. . . . Disburse what God has placed at your disposal for the welfare of the needy and (especially) those with dependents, in order to eradicate poverty and misery (Imam Ali, 1989: 350)

Similarly, in his instruction to the governor of Egypt, he stated:

Never regret any forgiveness you extend, nor rejoice for any punishment you impose. Do not react on the urge of anger as long as you can help it. Do not say, 'I am in charge and I shall be obeyed.' That is a sign of weakness in the heart and of a shaken faith, and an invitation to trouble. . . . Observe. . . people's right in your own behaviour and in that of your close relatives, your employees and those who have access to you. Otherwise you will not be fair. . .Put in charge of each service a person who is not afraid to shoulder big responsibilities or hesitate because of diversity [complexity]. Any fault in your employees which you overlook is your own responsibility (ibid.: 305)

Fear God in all matters relating to the less advantaged members of society: the poor, the needy, and the disabled. Among those are people whose need is obvious and those who are too proud to show their poverty. By God! They have rights that you will be accountable for before God. (ibid.: 331)

While these instructions set out the collective and moral foundations for administering state and market affairs, they did not specify certain peculiarities that evolved over the life cycle of the Islamic empire, especially during the Islamic Golden Age, the break-up of the Islamic empire, and its collapse around the year A.D. 1220.

ISLAMIC SCHOOLS OF THOUGHT

Several schools of thought flourished during the first six centuries of Islam. These schools ranged from an extreme adherence to rules and procedures to a more rational school that advocates self-discipline, self-control and the power of mind. Since there is no separation between state and religion in Islam, these schools have had profound influence on various political and economic structures in Islamic and Arab states. S. Ali (1964), in an effort to bring order to this vast body of experience, divides Islamic thought into six schools. The first, *Jabria*, which had its roots in pre-Islamic Arab thought, emphasizes compulsion or predestination. This school asserts that man is not responsible for his actions, and that tradition must take precedence over the power of choice. It relies on clearly defined rules and complete obedience to authority. For this school, a man does not need to use rational arguments but only to follow and accept the leader's instructions. An extreme version of this school, called *Sifatias* (attributes), asserts that man has no power, knowledge or free will. It adheres strictly to the doctrine of predestination in all its gloominess and intensity. The absolute leader who has answers to everything and dispenses reward or punishment is glorified. The organization and organizational work group roles are subordinate to the role of the figure of authority.

The second school is the *Tafwiz*. This school emphasizes free will and unqualified discretion in the choice of right and wrong because rules and regulations constrain human and organizational life. In the organizational context, there should be no clear sets of responsibilities and duties. Employees assume different tasks and duties, and collective responsibility is preferred. Organizational change is seen as a normal course in serving people's interests.

The third is the *Ikhtiar* school, which shares the *Tafwiz's* emphasis on free choice, but differs in its beliefs about man's capacity to turn evil into good. Unlike the *Tafwiz* school, it holds that man is at liberty to commit a good or bad deed, experience pain or joy, and that he is solely responsible for his actions. Man is believed to be a responsible social actor striving to work with the group and to achieve the group's goals in a harmonious and cooperative environment. Members of an organization should follow the authority that represents the consensus of the community and that was selected on the basis of its qualifications. A harmonious and cooperative group environment is sought.

The *Mutazilas*, or the rationalistic school, believe that all knowledge must be attained through reason. This school holds that nothing is known to be right or wrong until reason has enlightened us on the distinction and, further, that everything is liable to change or annihilation. As in the *Ikhtiar* school, the *Mutazilas* believe that performance is the criterion for reward and punishment. Man is capable of distinguishing between right and wrong. It maintains that free will and democracy are prerequisites for action and for the prosperity of society. Denial of ability and free will stifles creativity and destroys the soul. Commitment to logic and reason is a necessary quality for a leader. Self-reliance is viewed as a virtue. Organizational change is not only a possibility but a necessity for growth and development.

The fifth school of thought, advocated by *Ibn-Rushd* (or Averroes, *c.* A.D. 1126), holds that actions depend partly on free will and partly on external environmental forces which serve to restrain and/or determine individual and collective actions. The participative democratic process is thought to be the ideal organizational form, and autocracy is believed to open the door to human misery. Furthermore, this school believes that perfection can only be attained by study and speculation, not by mere sterile meditation. In addition, women are considered equal in every capacity to men. This school of thought views change as a collective responsibility. Furthermore, conflicting ideas are seen as the source of positive change.

The sixth school, the *Ikhwan-us-safa* (Brothers of Purity), arose in the 10th century in response to the oppressive practices of the *Jabria* school. During the 10th century, liberal-minded thinkers and philosophers were tortured and prosecuted. Nevertheless, a small body of thinkers formed themselves into a brotherhood to hinder the downward course of Muslims toward ignorance and narrow-mindedness. They established secret organizations across the Islamic nation and used letters as a way of disseminating thought. The school advocated rationalism, self-discipline and self-control. *Ikhwan-us-safa* believed that faith without work and knowing without practice were futile. They displayed a strong faith in man's ability to make progress and control the environment. Although this school contributed to setting high moral standards in commerce and politics, its main contribution was the belief that liberty of intellect is an essential precondition for a creative and healthy society. They believed that corruption and disorder are symptomatic of tyranny.

These schools had tremendous influence on the way in which states were organized and on the way business and personal transactions were conducted in various parts of the Muslim world. For example, the Ommeyyade empire (661–750) subscribed to the *Jabria* school where centralization of government affairs and strict adherence to specified rules were the norm. The position of the elite was glorified and submission of the public to the elite was considered a virtue.

It is important to note that the rest of the schools flourished during the era (especially during the period 685–866) when the Arabs intimately interacted with other civilizations (e.g., the Greek and the Persian) and energetically translated their intellectual and philosophical contributions. Nevertheless, these schools, to some degree, relied on the teachings of Islam and Prophet Mohammed. The Quran states that 'Whoever gets to himself a sin, gets it solely on his own responsibility' (4 : 111). The Prophet dismissed many pre-Islamic Arabic traditions, including concepts and behaviour condoned by the *Jabria* school. Prophet Mohammed asserted the free agency of man and the liberty of intellect (S. Ali, 1964). For example, he stated that 'Obedience is due only in that which is good,' and 'The seeking of knowledge is obligatory upon every Muslim' (quoted in M. Ali, 1977). Furthermore, these schools seemed to be affected by the philosophy of Imam Ali who valued the virtue of knowledge and hard work, appeared to promote idealistic principles and displayed distrust of the tribal elite. He set an example for his deputies and instructed them to have an open door or participative policy and to observe justice at any cost. He stated:

> Let your choice in all matters be the most righteous and the most in terms of justice, those that command the acceptance of the majority of the people. The satisfaction of the people may often be at variance with the interests of the elite whose dissatisfaction may be condoned if the people at large are content (Imam Ali, 1989: 307)

The rationalistic view and the *Ikhtiar* or *Mutazilas* forms prevailed during the enlightened reigns of the Abbasid caliphs Mamun and Mutasim and in the Fatimide state. During the Fatimide era (969–1171), the power of the mind, the concept of liberty, and the role of knowledge were promulgated. The increasing influence of non-Arab elements in the Muslim world contributed to the gradual disappearance of this participative approach and to the solidification of traditional or authoritarian forms of government. The defeat of the Arab Caliph in the last years of the Abbasid empire and the ascendancy of the non-Arab Ottoman empire (1412–1918) helped to institutionalize autocracy and furthered the demise of trade associations and freely organized business activities in Islamic lands.

All these schools of thought, except the *Jabria*, have come to play an insignificant role in the contemporary Muslim world. Following the *Jabria* school, the newly established nation states subordinated the role of religion to that of the ruler. Single-minded thought is advanced to serve the goals of each regime. Religious figures (e.g., sheikhs or mullahs) have been recruited and appointed as mosque functionaries, teachers and judges. They are given titles and lucrative salaries, and many have become paid employees of the state bureaucracy. Their roles vary slightly from one state to another, but their function remains the same. In Saudi Arabia, they play very vital roles and have been integrated in daily functions of government (e.g., approving new laws, advising, and participating in official ceremonies). Their principal duty, however, focuses on providing religious validation to actions taken by the ruling family. In Egypt and Iraq, on the other hand, their roles are highly regulated and the government makes sure they do not exceed their prescribed limits.

APPEARANCE OF AMBIGUITY

Islamic teaching and tradition often specify desired business conduct and dealing. Nevertheless, like other religions, it opens the door to exploitation by the rulers. The Quran (Holy Quran, 1981) contains many references to the conduct of business. For example, 'Do not exchange your property in wrongful ways unless it is in trade by mutual agreement' (4 : 30), and 'It is he who has made the earth subservient to you. You walk through its vast valleys and eat of its sustenance' (67 : 15). Islam also has specific prescriptions regarding investments and the undesirability of preventing commodities from circulating, depriving the owner as well as the community of their benefits. For example the Quran advises:

> Those who hoard gold and silver and do not spend for the causes of God, should know that their recompense will be a painful torment on the day of Judgment and that their treasures will be treated by the fire of Hell and pressed against their foreheads, sides and back with this remark, 'These are your own treasures which you hoarded for yourselves. See for yourselves what they feel like.'

There is a contradiction between the ideal, as specified in the Quran and Prophet Mohammed's sayings, and reality in the Islamic/Arab world. For example, interest charges on loans and bribes (money and gifts given or promised to a person in a position of influence to facilitate deals or change his or her conduct) are publicly acknowledged in most Muslim states. On many occasions, in fact, business cannot be conducted without bribes being given. Islam, however, considers interest and bribes sinful. The majority of financial institutions in the region adopt the predetermined rate of interest on loans. Muslim thinkers believe this is not Islamic. They suggest establishing an interest-free banking system. The principle of this system is that profits and risk should be shared by both partners (lenders and borrowers) in the loan transaction (Boase, 1985). Likewise, bribery is a customary practice in the region even though it was condemned by Prophet Mohammed, who said: 'Those who offer and those who accept bribes are in hell.'

Another contradiction is related to the process of consultation. In conducting business and political affairs, true adherents of Islam hold consultation among peers to be religiously positive, as this statement from the Quran attests: 'Reward will be for those who conduct their affairs with consultation among themselves.' Furthermore, the Quran denounces kings: 'When kings enter a town they destroy it and disrespect its honorable people' (27 : 34). Likewise, Prophet Mohammed says: 'I am not a king or a Jabar [oppressor]' (quoted in Amarah, 1988). Rulers and religious leaders, however, have chosen to emphasize other passages of the Quran which instruct believers to obey God, the Prophet and those in positions of leadership. For example, 'God grants His authority to whom he wishes (2 : 247)' and 'Obey God, and obey the apostle, and those charged with authority among you (4 : 59).' Thus, there is a high degree of tension between participatory or consultative approaches on the one hand, and authoritative approaches to management on the other.

The case of employee recruitment and appointment in Arab/Islamic societies provides a further example of the contradiction between theory and practice, the ideal and reality. Prophet Mohammed says: 'When a person assumes an authority over people and promotes one of them because of personal preferences, God will curse him for ever (quoted in Al-Fingary, 1996)' and

If a man in authority left the better and the fitter person in favor of another because of relationship between them, . . .or of being from the same locality, nationality—Arab, Persian, Turk or Greek, or because of a bribe received in kind or service or for any other cause, . . .he who does this is a cheater of God, of his Messenger and of the Faithful.

Similarly, Imam Ali stated in his letter to the governor of Egypt:

Monitor the behaviour of your assistants and use [tenure] them only after probation. Do not nominate them on account of favoritism or egoism [nepotism]. Those two attributes reflect injustice and treachery. Select from among them those who have experience and decency (Imam Ali, 1989: 321).

Despite the clear instructions regarding recruitment of personnel, the typical practice in the Islamic world has been often based on nepotism and friendships. This is especially true of middle- and upper-level positions. In contemporary Islamic states the most important jobs are generally saved for relatives and clan members regardless of their qualifications.

In conclusion, the Islamic civilization has treated trade and work as necessary acts for enriching self and society; they are religious and worldly duties. Hard work, quality and discipline have in principle been considered virtues. Most of the Islamic schools of thought valued flexibility and creativity. Therefore, commerce and trade were pursued by Muslims as worthy activities that enhance one's own self and others and contributes to the prosperity of society as a whole. As allegiance to ethnicity rather than to Islam took precedence, and as the Arab/Islamic world discounted the power of the mind and the importance of knowledge and hard work in life, the decline of these values became inevitable.

9

THE CONCEPT OF *BAO* AND ITS SIGNIFICANCE IN ORGANIZATIONAL RESEARCH

Chaoming Liu

Bao is a traditional Chinese concept, as well as an important basis of Chinese social relations (L.S. Yang, 1957; 1987). However, there has so far been very little research or discussion conducted on *bao*. Scholars have earlier pointed out that unless the concept of *bao* is clarified, it will be difficult to subject it to study and research (K.K. Hwang, 1990a). In the West, there are concepts that resemble *bao*, such as 'reciprocity', which are considered universal norms in all human societies (Gouldner, 1960). The Social Exchange Theory, which has deeply influenced Western social sciences, is basically compatible with the Chinese concept of *bao* (Wen, 1982; L.S. Yang, 1957). For this reason, before I further analyze the concept of *bao*, let me first clearly define it.

THE TRADITIONAL CHINESE CONCEPT OF *BAO*

THE MEANING OF *BAO*

In the Chinese language, *bao* has wide connotations. In ordinary usage, it basically means repayment (such as returning a favour or gratitude or

Table 9.1
The Six Subconcepts of *Bao*

Characteristic	Positive Direction	Negative Direction
Instrumentality	Repayment of favour	Retaliation
Affectivity	Repayment of gratitude	Revenge
Causality	Good retribution	Evil retribution

acting in revenge), causality (as in retribution) and the act of informing (such as making a report). In the literature related to the social and behavioural sciences, L.S. Yang (1957) takes *bao* as the basis of Chinese social relations. He believes that the central idea behind *bao* is reaction or repayment, or a type of causality between persons or between man and the supranatural. Wen (1982) views both repayment of gratitude and revenge as exchange behaviours. Wei (1987), however, points out five different types of concepts related to *bao*, namely, repayment of gratitude, revenge, returning a favour, retribution and *karma*.

In the past, *bao* was viewed as a single concept, or at most classi-fied from one angle, both of which perspectives easily led to a confusion of the concepts. Here, a two-pronged approach to defining *bao* by ana-lyzing Chinese classical works and writings, folk sayings and academic discussions has been adopted. The first approach is concerned with the nature of *bao*, which can be divided into instrumentality, affectivity and causality. The other approach is related to the direction of *bao*, which can be either positive or negative. These two approaches cover six different concepts which correspond to six terms in the vocabulary: repayment of favour, retaliation, repayment of gratitude, revenge, good retribution and evil retribution (Table 9.1).

Regarding its instrumentality, *bao* is an instrument by which people maintain equilibrium in their mutual relationships, or reach certain goals. For the Chinese, a person who has received a favour is bound to repay it. A person who has suffered wrongdoing must retaliate. Treating each other with respect and decorum has been a Chinese concept of repayment since ancient times. This idea can be traced to the Confucian classic 'Book of Rites' (*Li-chi*) and has inspired a popular folk saying to the effect that mutual exchange and dealings are in conformity with rites and decorum. Such a relationship of mutual dealing is itself a way of repaying each other. This well-disposed way of repayment is necessary for the maintenance of good relationships among persons.

In the real world, interpersonal exchange is not always a well-disposed observance of decorum. Often, these relationships involve one party being a victim of misdoing or ill-treatment, which gives rise to grudges and finding ways to get even. Confucius proposed the 'repayment of a grievance with rectitude and returning virtue with virtue'. Chu Hsi identified 'rectitude' with 'forgiveness', an idea often stressed in Confucian teachings. The proposal made by Confucius, therefore, means that 'evil intention must be repaid with pardon.' This way of forgiveness has always been proposed in Confucianism as the paragon of human behaviour. However, forgiveness has its limits, usually referred to as a person's 'self-cultivation' (*xiuyang*). Whenever a misdoing exceeds limits, acts of reprisal readily result. Mencius proposed 'the repulsion of evil words'. This describes in vivid terms the meaning of retaliation.

Repayment and revenge are basically manifestations of mutual dealing. Most of the methods of showing *bao* and their frequency are governed by social norms (such as equity). *Bao* can also serve as an instrument for a person to achieve certain goals (such as good conscience, interpersonal harmony and social stability). However, the Chinese concept of *bao* includes a very strong affective component. For this reason, it cannot be totally explained in terms of its characteristics as an instrument. For instance, the attitude of finding ways to repay gratitude is one example of repayment for affective reasons. The Chinese often figuratively compare the immensity of their gratitude with the mountain or the sea specifically to emphasize that their feelings of gratitude cannot be easily repaid by material means. In the *Book of Songs*, a passage reads: 'My parents gave birth to me and reared me...my gratitude is as lofty as the heavens.' This illustrates how, on the affective level, *bao* is perceived as limitless and its repayment similarly so. A person who has received a favour is filled with a sense of gratitude. The behavioural manifestation of this gratitude (such as doing anything to repay it) usually surpasses the tit-for-tat level of the concept's instrumental character. Tang (1980) further points out that in the Chinese humanities, repaying gratitude lies in returning all the favours received by an existing 'ego' to their origins in the past. Thus, it can be seen that repaying gratitude is not limited to returning a favour to its original giver; it can also mean repaying other people at other times. For instance, a person may rear and educate his children to repay his own parents, or a teacher may repay his own teachers by also practising the profession well.

Grudges are the opposite of gratitude. In comparison with retaliation as earlier mentioned, grudges, although also arising from ill-treatment, are much more serious than 'grievances'. In the Chinese language, sayings that decry the intensity of interpersonal grudges illustrate how grudges, as negative feelings, deeply affect a person. Typical examples of these sayings include: 'The grudge resulting from the killing of one's father will not allow sharing the same sky with the enemy' and 'A man who fails to avenge himself is not a gentleman.' Revenge is substantially a means of releasing this negative feeling and is not an instrument for reaching certain goals (for example, deterring the belligerent behaviour of the aggressor).

Causality constitutes another important factor in the concept of *bao*. The Chinese believe in retribution. Evil acts deserve evil retribution while good deeds are rewarded with good retribution. For this reason, the concept of retribution developed early in Chinese civilization. The folk saying 'the family that gains merits will not be deprived of joy' and the Chinese people's ethical emphasis on 'accumulating merits' both reflect the concept of retribution. Retribution is further classified into evil or good retribution. When this concept is combined with religious ideas on reincarnation, it leads to the concept of *karma*. The latter refers to the concept that if someone commits evil acts in this life, there will be retribution in the future life. In serious cases, that person will not be able to leave the reincarnative cycle for several generations. This causality of retribution has a strong influence on the behaviours and attitudes of the Chinese people (Wei, 1987; L.S. Yang, 1987).

Diverse meanings of *bao* have been discussed, and I have used six different terms to explain six corresponding subconcepts. It is worth noting that these terms may not totally overlap with their usage in daily life. To cite an example, there is no clear demarcation between the terms 'repayment of favour' (*baoda*) and 'repayment of gratitude' (*baoen*) in Chinese. Furthermore, the meaning of the terms may slightly differ from the way they are used in the literature.

OTHER TRADITIONAL CONCEPTS RELATED TO *BAO*

Since *bao* forms the basis of Chinese social relations, it is related to many traditional concepts in social relations. For instance, L.S. Yang (1957) observes a difference between *bao* and righteousness (*yi*) by explaining that the latter is a moral act wherein a person refuses to accept repayment for doing a certain favour. Yang also believes that filial piety is the principle of mutual repayment within a family or clan. In recent years, researchers who have been promoting research on indigenization have often brought up concepts related to *bao* in their study of the traditional ideas on social relations. Two of these concepts that share the closest connection with *bao* are *renqing* (favour) and *mianzi* (reputation or face). These two are worthy of discussion and analysis.

King (1980), in his discussion of the Chinese concept of *renqing*, said that 'forgiveness' forms the basis of social ethics among the Chinese and that *bao* forms part of 'forgiveness', and is even included in the concept of *renqing*. I strongly agree with this opinion, since forgiveness is a noble virtue interpreted in different ways by different schools.

In his discussion of *renqing*, K.K. Hwang (1987) points out that the regulations governing *bao* fall within and form the basis of the laws of *renqing*. He writes: 'Upon receiving *renqing*, the recipient must, on the first appearance of an opportunity, try to repay the favour. The giver, while bestowing the favour, can also expect the recipient to finally repay the favour in the future.' This description of the 'regulations governing *bao*' overlaps with the concept of repaying a favour from the perspective of its instrumentality as discussed earlier.

In the same work, Hwang proposes a theoretical model for *renqing* (favour) and *mianzi* (face) in Chinese societies. He classifies interpersonal relations into instrumental ties, expressive ties and mixed ties. *Renqing* and *mianzi* both belong to the mixed type of interpersonal relations. According to Hwang, in the mixed type of relationship, the recipient and the giver usually know each other and share a certain level of expressive relationship. This expressive relationship, however, is one which has not developed to such a depth wherein both sides can openly show sincere behaviour. For this reason, the mixed relationship easily leads to the so-called dilemma of *renqing*, which relies on 'face work' for reinforcing mutual relationship.

In conclusion, therefore, I believe that from the perspective of interpersonal relations (that is, excepting *karma* relationship between man and the supranatural), *bao* can be categorized under *renqing*. *Renqing* is a mixed relationship resulting from the fusion of the instrumental relationship with the affective relationship. In turn, *mianzi* is a concept that belongs to the mixed relationship type. It shares a certain degree of overlapping with *bao*. As discussed earlier, that part of the relationship between *bao* and *mianzi* in which these two come closest corresponds to 'repaying a favour' or 'revenge', and they fall under the instrumental type. Figure 9.1 is a schematic representation of the relationships among *renqing*, *mianzi* and *bao*.

Figure 9.1
Conceptual Relationships among *Renqing*, *Mianzi* and *Bao*

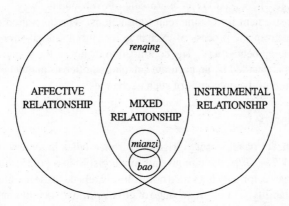

WESTERN CONCEPTS RELATED TO *BAO*

For researchers of Western social sciences, the interpersonal exchange of repayment has always been taken as the foundation of social behaviour. The most representative concepts include the Social Exchange Theory, reciprocity and indebtedness. These concepts do not totally overlap with the Chinese concept of *bao* although they share certain similarities with it.

THE SOCIAL EXCHANGE THEORY

The Social Exchange Theory, influenced by 19th century Western utilitarianist ideas, stresses a person's rational choice in terms of individual benefit. It proposes that interactions between persons are nothing but the maintenance of equilibrium between giving and receiving (or in other words, exchange). Homans (1958) presents six major propositions on the exchange theory. He proposes that a person repeats actions that merit a reward (the success proposition), repeats his reactions to stimuli that lead to reward (the stimulus proposition), decides whether or not to continue action based on the value of its results (the value proposition), that repetition of reward will lessen its value (the deprivation–satiation proposition), that the proportionality between reward and expectation leads to acts of personal aggression or approval (the aggression–approval proposition), and that when a person makes a choice, he chooses actions that can lead to results with the greatest value (the rationality proposition).

Homans' six propositions are basically centred on reward, and are thus close to the viewpoint of behaviourism. From the perspective of the Social Exchange Theory, *bao* is an instrument of exchange the way money acts as an instrument for commercial transactions. The derivation of things of value from the process of exchange leads to a mutual strengthening of exchange behaviours. The continuation or not of these exchanges of rewards is decided by an accurate calculation of costs and benefits or an evaluation of the outcomes of such exchanges.

RECIPROCITY

The concept of reciprocity originated from studies in anthropology. In his work *The Gifts*, the famous anthropologist Mauss (1925) stresses his belief that reciprocity is a social norm closely related to the maintenance of social stability. Through exchange of gifts, primitive societies maintained internal cohesion and also averted wars. Gouldner (1960) proposes the universal norm of reciprocity in human societies. Without this norm, there would be social division.

In the literature on anthropology, reciprocity is classified into three different types (Sahlins, 1965). The first is balanced reciprocity. This refers to that situation wherein a person who received a gift or service from another must make an equivalent repayment within a certain period of time. This is the most typical mode of reciprocity. However, reciprocity is not totally balanced in human societies. For instance, among close relatives, although there is a duty to give, the duty of returning the favour is not always clear, neither is it necessary to repay immediately. In this case, it is called generalized reciprocity. A mode of exchange between strangers or enemies is the exact reverse of the spirit of reciprocity and is known as negative reciprocity. This refers to a situation wherein, after receiving something or an act of service, the recipient uses means such as bargaining and argument to make a repayment whose value is lower than that of the favour received. In this case, it leads to an unbalanced transaction.

The concept of reciprocity serves as the basis of the Social Exchange Theory (Gergen et al., 1979). However, Homans' exchange theory, bearing the strong influence of behaviourism, involves concepts and research methods that are criticized for psychological reductionism (Gergen et al., 1980). Anthropological studies in recent years (Pryor and Graburn, 1980) also point out that certain societies have the capability to develop different social mechanisms to handle unbalanced reciprocity. This viewpoint suggests that *bao* and reciprocity can have different meanings in different cultural settings and may not be explained fully in terms of instrumental exchange behaviours.

INDEBTEDNESS

Indebtedness is a small-scale exchange theory developed by the psychologist Greenberg (1980) within the framework of the Social Exchange Theory. Indebtedness has been defined as 'a duty to repay others'. It refers to a condition of emotional discomfort when a person has not yet returned a received favour. Only after the recipient has repaid the donor can this emotional discomfort be lessened.

Based on the assumptions of Greenberg, the degree of indebtedness varies according to four factors, namely, donor's motive, recipient's benefits and donor's cost, attribution of donor's behaviour, and social comparison. When the donor's motive is concern for the recipient's benefits, or when the recipient's benefit and donor's cost add up to a higher value, the recipient's degree of indebtedness is higher. The same is true when the donor's actions come from his own free will (and not by chance or part of his duty) and when there is higher social expectation. The higher the degree of indebtedness, the stronger is the motive for repayment. The fundamental content of this theory lies in the calculation of costs and benefits and the restoration of emotional balance through repayment. In substance, this exchange still bears a strong instrumental character.

CHINESE AND WESTERN CONCEPTS: A COMPARISON

A comparison between Western concepts of social exchange and the Chinese concept of *bao* can be made in six areas: nature, direction, social character, time of repayment, quantity of repayment and source of motive (Table 9.2).

In terms of the nature of the concepts, the Social Exchange Theory (including reciprocity, indebtedness and other extended concepts) has an instrumental nature. The goal of exchange lies in maintaining balance in mutual benefits or in attaining interpersonal harmony. The exchange theory seldom deals with 'gratitude', 'feeling' or other affective concepts. In contrast, the concept of *bao*, as noted earlier, involves not only this type of instrumental exchange, but encompasses a great deal of affective content. In fact, it includes supranatural concepts as in the cases of causality and retribution.

Table 9.2
Comparison between the Social Exchange Theory and the Concept of *Bao*

	Social Exchange Theory (Western Concept)	Bao (Chinese Concept)
Nature	Instrumentality	Instrumentality + affectivity + causality
Direction	Positive	Positive and negative
Social character	Weak (takes the individual as target of study)	Strong 1. Hierarchical status in social relations affects the practice of *bao* 2. The target of *bao* extends from the individual to the clan
Time of repayment	Immediate or within a short period of time	Immediate + lifetime + next life
Quantity of repayment	1. Equivalent repayment 2. Allows clear calculation of costs and benefits	1. Additional repayment 2. May not need clear calculation of costs and benefits but emphasizes the actual significance of *bao*
Origin of motive	Reward (reinforcement)	Reward + ethical principle

It is worth noting that the lack of affective content in Western exchange does not reflect in any way the absence of emotional relationship among individuals in the West. Instead, it can be explained by the fact that in the individualistic societies of the West, the satisfaction of personal feelings is not normally used as an instrument for social exchange. For this reason, emotional relationships are rarely dealt with in the Social Exchange Theory. F.L.K. Hsu (1971) compares the Western concept of love with the concept of *bao*. He points out that in an individualist Western society, an individual may freely choose things he/she likes to do. This leads to such 'emotional' expressions as 'I love to...'. In the collectivist cultures of the East, the individual is tied down to the complex web of interpersonal relationship. For this reason, the emotional side always tends toward feelings of being indebted to others (I owe to...). The West has such romantic mythology as the one centred on Eros, the god of love, while the Chinese let the concept of *bao* regulate human feelings. Tang (1980) compares 'loving-devotion' between the Chinese husband and wife with the Western concept of love. He believes that in the

West, only love binds husband and wife together. Among the Chinese, the relationship involves loving-devotion, loving-duty and loving-kindness. Thus, the spirit of repaying gratitude so common in Chinese societies is also manifest in the mutual accommodation between husband and wife which transforms love and passion into 'loving-devotion'.

The Social Exchange Theory is basically positive in direction. It mainly deals with the attainment and exchange of benefits. In contrast, the Chinese concept of *bao* may take either direction. For instance, gratitude and revenge are opposites. Retribution can also be good or evil. K.K. Hwang (1990a) observes that after the rule of law was instituted in Western societies, acts of revenge committed by victims gradually declined in number. The lack of a fair judicial system in traditional Chinese societies probably led victims to seek revenge on their own and even consider reprisals against malefactors as being in conformity with the will of Heaven. This helped form the concept of causality and retribution, notably the idea that evil acts beget evil retribution.

On the concepts' social character, the Western Social Exchange Theory basically deals with the exchange of benefits between individuals. Most cases take the individual as the object of their study. The Chinese concept of *bao* is not limited to exchange behaviour between individuals. In the literature on *bao* (cf. K.K. Hwang, 1990b; Wen, 1982; L.S. Yang, 1957), most authors point out the connection between the concept of *bao* and the family. L.S. Yang (1957) even cites Weber's ethical universalism and particularism to discuss the features of *bao*. He observes that in terms of its nature, *bao* can be identified with universalism (i.e., the Chinese universally accept the principle of cross repayment). However, L.S. Yang believes that the practice of this principle tends towards ethical particularism. He cites the fact that in any Chinese society, the practice of *bao* varies according to existing relationships between individuals or clans (i.e., the so-called 'hierarchical status in social relations' of Fei Hsiao-tung). It is extremely rare that *bao* is practised as a simple exchange behaviour between individuals. For this reason, acts normally considered as favouritism in the Western mode of thinking are considered normal acts of *bao* in Chinese societies.

Chinese and Western concepts also differ in terms of timing. In the Social Exchange Theory, the practice of repayment is mainly carried out immediately, or is completed within a short span of time or within a certain period of time. In contrast, the concept of *bao* does not necessarily imply immediacy. L.S. Yang (1957) points out that with the exception of the exchange of gifts during the lunar new year festivities, the giving of gifts on other occasions, such as birthdays, weddings and funerals, is repaid whenever these occasions arise among counterparts. He believes that this can be explained by the fact that the family is the foundation of social relations among the Chinese. Family ties may be maintained over a long span of time, and a speedy repayment is not called for. In fact, the Chinese extend the duration of repaying to the whole lifetime. This is attested to by the saying: 'Once a teacher, father for a lifetime.' When gratitude is so great that it cannot be repaid during one's lifetime, there is another concept that applies: repayment in the next life.

The core factor in the Social Exchange Theory is balance. Thus, all exchanges seek a balance between costs and benefits, both of which can be calculated accurately and clearly. The Chinese concept of *bao* does not require quantitative equivalence in repayment. In fact, most of the time, the repayment is greater than what is received. Wen (1987) observes that *bao*, after combination with such factors as *renqing* and *guanxi* (inter-relatedness), makes an otherwise simple exchange behaviour undergo a delicate transformation. Gifts exchanged increase in both value and quantity. In his analysis of behaviours of repayment and revenge in Chinese history, Wen (1982) also cites substantial and not quantitative equivalence as the major concept in *bao*. For this reason, the Chinese do not necessarily calculate the actual costs and benefits in practising *bao*. Instead, they stress its actual significance.

In terms of the source of motive, the exchange theory explains continuous exchange behaviour using the concept of 'reward'. In the process of exchange, material or spiritual satisfaction, or even social recognition, plays a reinforcing function on both sides, such that in making subsequent acts of repayment, they usually anticipate a return from their counterparts. The recipient will also make efforts to repay and thus, the exchange behaviour is extended. In contrast, Wen (1982) points out that *bao* follows certain ethical concepts. For instance, it is considered a manifestation of filial piety for offspring to take revenge for their parents. Similarly, gratitude is taken as an observance of 'decorum' (*li*). This exchange behaviour is in fact a practice of ethical values and is closely linked to the traditional Chinese social structure and Chinese ethical norms.

It can be seen that the Chinese concept of *bao* is more comprehensive than the Social Exchange Theory of the West. It would be proper to say that the latter is included in the concept of *bao*. Therefore, studying the concept and practice of *bao* from the viewpoint of the Social Exchange Theory is likely to lead to erroneous conclusions.

THE SIGNIFICANCE OF *BAO* IN ORGANIZATIONAL RESEARCH

The Social Exchange Theory reflects the system of values that evolved in the West after the Industrial Revolution. Any discussion of social relations or interpersonal relations is always influenced by this theory. The same is true with organizational research. Contributions of the Social Exchange Theory to organizational studies in the West are discussed before analyzing the issues of *bao* that can be subjected to study in organizational research.

THE SOCIAL EXCHANGE THEORY: ITS ROLE IN ORGANIZATIONAL RESEARCH

Organizational research is usually classified into three levels: individual, group and organization. The Social Exchange Theory exerts a strong influence on all these three.

The most direct influence of the exchange theory at the level of the individual is in the study of work motivation. Adams (1965) proposes his equity theory from the viewpoint of the Social Exchange Theory. He believes that in the workplace, an employee is constantly making comparisons between the work input he/she contributes and its outcomes, and those of others. Whenever a person finds that the ratio of his inputs to outcomes is different (greater or lesser) from those of others, he experiences a feeling of inequity. The employee will then adopt various measures to relieve this feeling. For instance, when an individual feels he is underpaid, a possible reaction will be to reduce input, or even sabotage others' achievements. On the other hand, when someone feels he is overpaid, the reaction may be to lessen his outcome. If the payment calculated is based on the amount of work done, he may reduce the quantity and improve the quality. Another reaction may be to increase input. If remuneration is based on the amount of time, he may increase his working hours. Under circumstances of inequity and when the individual cannot alter his or others' input and outcome, the individual may distort his own view of the matter or even resign from his job. Adams proved these assumptions with a series of experiments and has received much recognition.

The equity theory adopts the viewpoint of the Social Exchange Theory. Although there are no clear indications of the influence of the exchange theory on other important theories on work motivation, their concepts show strong similarities with those of the exchange theory. For instance, in the expectancy theory (Vroom, 1964), the concept of instrumentality is explained as viewing efforts in work as a type of instrument in exchange for personal goals such as promotion, salary increase and so on.

On the group level, the Social Exchange Theory has been used to explain and predict interactive relationship between leaders and their subordinates. A case in point is the transactional approach which proposes that the rise of a leader is the result of a series of exchanges of benefits between a person who wants to be a leader and other members of the group. A person who wants to lead a group will initially show careful observance of the group's regulations to gain other members' trust. Then this individual will make all types of special contributions to the group (idiosyncrasy credit) that will bring benefits to group members. Once these contributions reach a certain level, members of the group will start to accept the potential leader's innovatory ideas and suggestions for change. These ideas and suggestions will further clarify his role as a leader. If the reforms prove advantageous to the group, the leadership role will be strengthened. On the other hand, if the leader brings failure, his influence will gradually weaken. Proponents of the transactional leadership theory view leadership effects as a type of equitable exchange wherein the leader obtains power and sway to reach goals set by the group or organization. In turn, subordinates feel that their input to the group or organization gets an equivalent reward. To be successful, the leader must take care to prevent subordinates from feeling that their inputs are not worthwhile and from feeling any inequity (Hollander, 1980).

The transactional leadership theory views the relationship between leader and subordinates as a universal exchange relationship. In contrast, the vertical dyad linkage theory proposes that the leader and the subordinates will develop relationships of varied degrees of closeness and distance. The leader will form a tight circle with a small minority of the group who are capable and worthy of his trust. Members of the in-group mutually share a close relationship while keeping a certain distance from members of the out-group. The formation of these small circles depends on the exchange of mutual benefits. The leader gets one or two trustworthy assistants who can shoulder part of his burden. Subordinates who form part of the in-group increase their influence, take more interest in their jobs and as a result get better chances for promotion (Graen and Cashman, 1975).

At the organizational level, the Social Exchange Theory was used to explain collectivistic exchange within an organization, power and dependence, as well as exchanges between the organization and the environment and between organizations. Ekeh (1974) observes that social exchange is not necessarily a reciprocity between two persons; it can be through a third person, and can gradually turn into an intra-organizational collectivistic exchange. For example, A gives a benefit to B, and B gives a similar benefit to C who, in turn, repays A. If this network of exchange cycles is expanded, members of the organization will, because of benefit-sharing, engage in exchanges with other members (not with only one person). In terms of power and dependency, Emerson (1962) points out that the power of an individual over others is established based on whether or not they depend on things of value provided by that individual. Blau (1964) further points out how power imbalance occurs in the exchange process. Walder (1983) cites the example of mainland Chinese workers treating their superiors with courteous respect and a high degree of obedience in attempts to build up private relationships they need for greater job stability or for promotion. This example is more or less identical with the viewpoint of the exchange theory. Furthermore, the resource exchange theory was likewise adopted in explaining how resources controlled by the organization can influence individual behaviour and how the capability of an organization to obtain resources from the environment or other organizations affects the structure and behaviour of the organization (Nord, 1980).

The concept of *bao* can prove useful in obtaining a deeper understanding of the interactive relationship between the individual and local organizations. In this context, the significance of *bao* in organizational research is analyzed in terms of five issues: work motivation, leadership, *renqing shigu*, organizational type and social vicissitudes.

ORGANIZATIONAL ISSUES IN THE ANALYSIS OF *BAO*

Bao and Work Motivation

The core question in the study of work motivation is: 'Why do people work hard?' (C.M. Liu, 1992). Western theories on motivation cite such reasons as satisfaction of personal needs, sense of value and goals (Locke and Henne, 1986). In studying the work motives of Chinese workers, however, the social significance of hard work requires analysis. A term in the Chinese language—*gufu* (let down, disappoint)—has significance in studying the relationship between *bao* and work motivation. In writing classes, elementary and junior high school Chinese students often write sentences such as 'I will study hard so as not to let down my parents.' In the interview data I have collected on work motivation (C.M. Liu, 1993a), some respondents claimed that they work hard so as not to disappoint the company or their superiors. Some workers work hard because of concern from their superiors. In the Chinese classics and biographies, there have been writings on 'dying for a friend' (*Sima Olan*) or 'repaying the favour of a supportive and appreciative superior'. All these suggest that motivation for hard work among the Chinese may not be limited to the instrumental level (satisfaction or exchange); it may also involve the affective level (gratitude).

Western literature refers to withdrawal behaviours and includes such topics as tardiness, absenteeism, theft and even turnover. Adams (1965) points out that 'inequity' may lead to these withdrawal behaviours. The Chinese concept of revenge (classified earlier in this paper as a negative, affective practice of *bao*) is perhaps linked with these behaviours.

Bao and Leadership

Leadership is a top–down interpersonal relationship. Among the Chinese, this top–down relationship is influenced by *bao*. L.S. Yang (1957) points out how examiners in traditional Chinese civil service examinations engaged in social investment through their positions. Tang (1980) also cites the fact that gratitude among the Chinese is shown to teachers, friends, sovereigns and officials whom they personally know. In discussing the influence of the Social Exchange Theory on Western leadership theories, I have mentioned that leaders in the West also form in-groups with their subordinates. However, this formation of in-groups is based on ability and mutual trust. In contrast, in-groups among leaders and their subordinates in Chinese societies are determined more by 'hierarchical status in social relations' and *bao*. Among family corporations or in the civil service sector, both of which are 'ruled by man', the promotion or training of a subordinate is one way through which leaders strengthen their power base.

Of course, the Chinese model of leadership is not totally built on narrow, instrumental repay-relationships. It is based on 'gratitude' and 'righteousness' when a leader bestows a favour without expecting something in return. When a leader and a subordinate come to know each other, they feel a sense of gratitude. If they repay each other's gratitude, a union of gratitude and righteousness results. In contrast, if the superior fails to be supportive, the subordinate may turn his back on the superior. Tang (1980) cites the moral lesson of the classic novel '*Romance of the*

Three Kingdoms' as being centred on this gratitude–righteousness concept. The issue whether or not the concepts of gratitude and righteousness still influence Chinese attitudes and behaviour on leadership is worthy of investigation.

Bao and Renqing Shigu

Renqing shigu is a term commonly used in Chinese societies. *Renqing* means interpersonal relations. Based on the foregoing analysis, *renqing* is a mixed type of relationship that combines both affective and instrumental relationships. The term *shigu* connotes 'methods adopted to maintain personal relationships'. The Chinese concept of *renqing shigu* is complex and, by using the concept of *bao*, it is easier to understand the exact connotation of, interpersonal relations.

Bao and Organizational Type

Family business is the traditional organizational type of Chinese companies. K.K. Hwang (1995) uses Weber's comparison of formal and substantive rationality to explain the formation of family businesses. The so-called formal rationality refers to the calculability of means and procedures while substantive rationality refers to the values of ends and goals which are difficult to calculate. The concept of *bao* extends to the affective level and is thus closer to substantive rationality. By using the concept of *bao*, it would perhaps be easier to understand the organizational structure and management style of family businesses. Furthermore, differences in the cognition of *bao* between family members and non-members can explain the internal conflicts often seen within family businesses. This may be the key to helping family businesses achieve a breakthrough in their process of modernization.

Bao and Social Vicissitudes

Since the 1960s, Taiwan has witnessed a transformation from an agricultural society to an industrial one. The same period has also witnessed a decline in people's social orientation and a corresponding rise in individual orientation (K.S. Yang, 1981). Whether or not the concept of *bao* has followed the same trends is an issue worthy of further study.

In my comparison of the Social Exchange Theory with the Chinese concept of *bao*, it has been pointed out that the former is instrumental in nature and emphasizes the exchange of benefits between individuals. In contrast, *bao* possesses a considerable degree of affective content over and above its instrumental character and is influenced by social factors. In the process of modernization, will the rise of individual orientation lead to a gradual weakening of the affective level of *bao*? Will it instead turn into something more akin to the instrumental concept of the West? These are basic questions involved in analyzing the behaviours of modern Chinese people.

The significance of *bao* in the field of organizational research according to five related issues has been analyzed. From the perspective of the six subconcepts of *bao*, organizational research appears to share only three, namely, repayment of favour, retaliation and repayment of gratitude. Revenge and retribution (good or evil) will offer some possibilities for study in other fields in psychology, including criminal psychology, judicial psychology and folk psychotherapy.

RESEARCH STRATEGY ON INDIGENIZATION

In summary, one can see that *bao* is a complex concept. Current studies related to *bao* mostly deal with its manifestations in Chinese classical works and discussions in the literature of Western social sciences. These discussions are of assistance in the analysis of the concepts, but are not sufficient to help in understanding the ideas and behaviour of contemporary Chinese vis-à-vis *bao*. What is required is not narrow assumptions based entirely on Chinese literature and classics, but a well-designed empirical survey to determine the current state of the concept among the Chinese people, and then developing appropriate theoretical frameworks. In view of the complexity of the concept of *bao*, it would not be fruitful to put it under one all-embracing theory. Instead, middle-range theories are likely to be more useful, not only in providing insights into Chinese organizational behaviour, but also highlighting its complementarity with similar concepts in the West. In any case, the concept of *bao* constitutes a fertile area for indigenous theories of managerial and organizational research in Chinese societies.

10

EMPLOYEES' PERCEPTION
OF DISTRIBUTIVE FAIRNESS
IN THE PEOPLE'S REPUBLIC OF CHINA

Yu Kai-cheng and He Wei

Fairness or justice, as a kind of social ethics and value, has long been pursued as a lofty ideal. People everywhere have been interested in the fair distribution of societal and organizational resources and wealth—the products of collective effort. Fairness, in essence, relates to the issue of entitlement, i.e., who ought to be allocated how much. In general, justice is a core value holding together societies and organizations. It has attracted much scholarly attention in fields of political economics, ethics, law, religion, sociology and psychology. Organizational behaviour focuses on the rules that govern the generation, formation and functioning of employees' perceptions of fair distribution of rewards in business administration.

The negative impact of perceiving unfairness on employees' motivation has been widely recognized. But the pursuit of fairness has not usually been considered a very powerful motive in the West. That may

The authors are grateful to the STEC program of the Land & Sky Foundation International for their support of this research. Correspondence concerning this article should be addressed to Yu Kai-cheng, School of Management, Dalian University of Technology, Dalian, Liaoning 116024, P. R. China; E-mail: kcyu@dlut.edu.cn.

be the reason why the equity theory has been less influential in Western social and behavioural science than need theories or even expectancy theories. In China, however, it is different. Fairness is one of the most influential and sensitive socio-political issues that relates not only to employees' morale in industries but also to the stability of the society. Perceptions of unfairness have, in the past, triggered a number of peasant uprisings and the matter remains significant today. It is attributed to two kinds of factors. First, objectively, there are many inequities in present-day China, especially those concerning the corruption of officials. Second, subjectively, Chinese people are said to have high sensitivity and low tolerance towards interpersonal income gaps. The characteristic has been referred to as 'Red Eye Disease' or 'Oriental Jealousy'. Hence, fairness has been a major focus of people's attention in China. Many Chinese scholars have tried to specify the traditional, cultural, ideological, and situational factors that have affected the formation of a distinctive Chinese concept of fairness and its social and psychological implications.

The task is, however, complicated. First, the formation of one's perception of fairness is a subjective process that includes judgements against certain norms. Unfortunately, there have never been any objective criteria or norms that are universally recognized and accepted. A person may apply different norms to judge fairness when different types of rewards are distributed (Foa and Foa, 1974; 1980). Even when the same type of reward is allocated, an individual may apply multiple norms simultaneously, but assign different weights to each of them to form an intricate matrix of fairness norms (Yu, Bunker and Wilderom, 1989; Yu, Wilderom and Hunt, 1989).

The second reason lies in the relativity of people's fairness judgement. People often make judgement via social comparison. Hence, one's perception of fairness relies heavily on which targeted individual or group one selects as the reference in the comparison (Adams, 1965). In addition, it also relies on one's feeling about the referent target. For example, Chinese people, who are supposed to be more collectivism-oriented than people in the West, are more tolerant to in-groups when reward allocation deviates from accepted fairness norms (Chiu, 1988; Young and Hui, 1986). Bles and Moag (1986) have pointed out that one's perception of fairness is affected by the nature of the interactional relation between the reward distributor and the recipient. They have suggested the term 'interactional justice' to distinguish it from the conventional concept of fairness that mainly focuses on resource distribution.

The third factor concerning the complexity of the study of fairness is the asymmetry of fairness perception—a derivative of its subjectivity. People tend to be more sensitive to unfair distribution when they feel that they are underpaid than when they are overpaid. W. Yu (1991) found, when identifying people's unfairness-sensitivity thresholds, that the sensitivity threshold for the underpaid situation was much lower than that for the overpaid situation. Borrowing the term from Herzberg's (1966) Motivation–Hygiene Theory, Wu (1991) refers to these characteristics as 'hygienical'. Although some people form their perception of fairness on the basis of a certain ideal or moral value, the fairness perceptions of many others are based on protecting or securing their self-interests. Since their judgement is purely subjective, it is easy to readjust their perception to reduce the sense of being guilty whey they feel overpaid.

Despite its complexity, we can still approach the issue by narrowing the scope of enquiry to a specific aspect of this broad topic. In this paper, the focus is on the basic norms that Chinese people use in judging the fairness of reward allocation and the cultural and ideological sources of those norms.

BASIC NORMS OF DISTRIBUTIVE FAIRNESS

Deutsch (1975) identifies a series of internal values or norms concerning distributive fairness:

1. Outcome gained proportional to each one's input
2. Equal treatment for all
3. To each according to one's need
4. To each according to one's ability
5. To each according to one's effort
6. To each according to one's achievements
7. To give each one equal opportunities for competition, free of any bias or discrimination
8. Based on market supply and demand
9. Based on common interests
10. Based on the principle of mutual interests
11. To make no one's gain lower than a preset bottom line

Deutsch believes that there has never been an absolutely objective ranking of these norms in terms of their significance that inherently fits human nature. This is understandable given the subjectivity and complexity of the formation of fairness perception. However, he further pointed out that

172 Yu Kai-cheng and He Wei

only the top three norms in the list are fundamental and universal. Each of these has certain specific functions and would be perceived as being fair in a specific situation. These norms are:

1. The *equity norm*: This says that one's gain (outcome) is proportional to one's contribution (input), so it may be variously labelled the norm of contribution, performance, merit or proportion. One's perception of fairness (or equity) is not determined by a comparison of the absolute amount of gain with that of a referent target, but rather by a comparison of outcomes to inputs.
2. The *equality norm*: This says that everyone should be allocated equal resources without considering any other factor.
3. The *need norm*: This says that the share of resources one gains should be based on one's need.

As far as the specific function of each basic norm is concerned, the equity norm is supposed to produce high average group productivity. Distribution based on this norm is most beneficial to high performers who are motivated to perform better resulting in the maximization of the productivity of the whole group. The equality norm is expected to lead to group harmony and stability. It is the poor performers who are most benefited and happiest, though they are the minority; the average performers who tend to constitute the majority would live with the norm with few complaints because they receive equal rewards; the better performers, though angry and dissatisfied, have little voice in the distribution decisions since they constitute the minority. The need norm is humanistic and most helpful to individual well-being and development. On the other hand, each basic norm tends to have certain negative effects. The equity norm generates conflicts, especially when the income gap is big and people's equality orientation is strong, while the equality norm tends to turn out low group productivity. As for the need norm, it seems ideal but too unrealistic to be actualized in present circumstances.

THE MARXIAN PERSPECTIVE ON SOCIAL FAIRNESS

A full appreciation of the unprecedented changes in the perception of distributive fairness of contemporary Chinese employees requires an understanding of the Marxian perspective on social fairness. There is a popular bias in the West that the Communist Party of China (CPC) always claims to be striving on behalf of the working class for the goal of social equality. This bias implies that the norm of equality conforms with socialism while equity is capitalistic because it encourages a gap between the rich and the poor. Many people in socialist countries, having little exposure to the classical works of Marxism, also share this misunderstanding. As a matter of fact, classical Marxism has never advocated egalitarianism; instead, its extreme form—absolute egalitarianism—is generally criticized in socialist politics as being reactionary, because it does not promote but instead hinders the growth of productivity in society.

It is true that in Marxism, the need norm is regarded as an ideal. Being humanistic in nature, it should be pursued as the ultimate goal for distributive fairness. But it is unrealistic, because it requires a number of preconditions including an abundance of material wealth in the society that is almost impossible to attain. In fact, the key tenet of Marxism, the principle of distribution appropriate to the 'primary phase of communism' i.e., socialism (since China is a developing country, the CPC claims that China is still in the primary phase of socialism), is: from each according to his ability, to each according to his work. The latter part is virtually a statement of the equity norm. The implementation of the equity norm seems the only way to promote the growth of China's productivity, a basic objective of the socialist revolution.

As for the need norm, Marx (1970), in his *Critique of the Gotha Program*, remarks:

> In a higher phase of communist society, after the enslaving subordination of an individual to the division of labor, and therewith also the antithesis between mental and physical labor, has vanished; after labor has become not only a means of life but life's prime want; after the productive forces have also increased with the all-round development of the individual, and all the springs of cooperative wealth flow more abundantly—only then can the narrow horizon of bourgeois right be crossed in its entirety and society inscribe on its banner: From each according to his ability; to each according to his need!

Two points in the quotation need analysis: first, 'from each according to his ability' which forms a vital part of the principle of distribution; second, the preconditions set for the implementation and the expression of the 'narrow horizon of bourgeois right'. When an individual has contributed the best of his or her ability to society, but his or her performance (given similar working conditions and training) is still poorer than that of some others due to poorer ability, then why should he/she, as an individual of equal status with all the others, be distributed less 'cooperative wealth'? In actuality, he/she really needs more, because he/she should not be held responsible for poorer ability and physical or mental defects. The equal right of distribution according to one's work, as Marx argued, is really only equal when one acquiesces to the fact that unequal talent and hence unequal abilities are a natural right. Therefore, equal right in terms of its substance is inherently unequal. Marx called it a bourgeois right. In this sense, only the need norm is authentic.

However, Marx was a historical materialist who knew that the development of society is not independent of the constraints of historical conditions. As an underdeveloped socialist country, China inevitably retained traces of the old society from which it had emerged. Its wealth being far from abundant, the equity norm was the only real choice.

EGALITARIANISM ORIENTATION AND ITS CULTURAL SOURCES IN CHINA

Since Deng Xiaoping initiated reform in the late 1970s, Chinese leaders have begun to call for the elimination of egalitarianism and the re-establishment of the socialist principle of distribution, i.e., from each according to his ability, to each according to his work. They also claim the necessity of breaking down the 'Three Iron System', i.e., the 'Iron Rice Bowl', the 'Iron Chair', and the 'Iron Salary' (standing respectively for lifelong employment, stable position, and rigid compensation) and to enlarge reasonably the income gap between people by allowing some people to become wealthier first. Some Western observers believe that the CPC is going to give up its socialist revolutionary principles and implement certain capitalist ones—a misunderstanding based on the wrong assumption that the equity norm is appropriate only to capitalism.

As a matter of fact, Chinese leaders have never advocated or supported equalitarian distribution. Instead, they have consistently and clearly held the opposite position. Mao (1963) criticized it, as early as 1929 when he was leading his Red Army in a life-and-death military struggle with Chiang Kai-shek, by pointing out that absolute equalitarianism beyond reason must be opposed because it is not required by the struggle; on the contrary, it hinders the struggle.

However, no one can deny that the most noteworthy characteristic of the Chinese perspective on distributive fairness is that of equalitarianism. Chinese people are said to be sensitive and intolerant of income gaps that are regarded as potentially disruptive in a collective society that places group harmony and social integration as a top priority. The equalitarian orientation is variously labelled by Chinese people as 'Red Eye Disease', 'Comparison Disease', or 'Oriental Jealousy'. It is the combined outcome of a series of historical, cultural, ideological and situational factors, two of which constitute its major causes.

The first is the traditional feudalistic culture, especially the peasant mentality. Mao (1964b) has pointedly observed that equalitarianism is 'the product of a handicraft and small peasant economy and is a mere illusion of peasants and small proprietors'.

The danger of unequal distribution has long been the focus of attention of scholars and politicians. As early as 2,500 years ago, Confucius in his well-known saying claimed, 'no worry about scarcity but unevenness; no worry about poverty but instability.' In the past, perceptions of unfairness have triggered hundreds of peasant uprisings. As early as the 10th century, Li Shun and Wang Xiaobo, the peasant leaders of a well-known uprising during the North Song dynasty, wrote the slogan, 'to equalize the poor and rich; to even the noble and humble on their banners'. The major characters in the great Chinese classical novel *Shui Hu* were Robin Hood–style heroes who allocated equally what they gained among themselves. When the wealth and resources available to society are so scarce, equal distribution seems to be the only feasible or even desirable option.

Unfortunately, leaders of all the previous peasant uprisings, having overthrown the old and corrupt feudal dynasty, soon established their own dynasty on the same basis as the old one. They themselves became new emperors enjoying enormous prerogatives and riches. That is why, when Mao (1964b) pointed out that equalitarianism is but 'a mere illusion of peasants and small proprietors', he also asserted that even under socialism there can be no absolute equality, for material things will then be distributed on the principle of 'from each according to his ability, to each according to his work as well as on that of meeting needs of the workers'.

The second major cause of equalitarianism lies in the distribution practices implemented in the military and administrative systems led by the CPC for decades during the revolutionary war, right from the time of the formation of the Red Army in 1927 until the beginning of the People's Republic in the early 1950s. The distribution system practised was called the Supply System, a system of payment in kind providing working personnel and their dependents with equal amounts of the primary necessities of life. Mao (1964a) has given a specific description of the practice:

so far the Red Army has no system of regular pay, but issues grain, money for cooking oil, salt, firewood and vegetable, and a little pocket money. . . .
In addition to grain, each man receives only five cents a day for cooking

oil, salt, firewood and vegetables, and even this is hard to keep up.... Fortunately we are inured to hardships. What is more, all of us share the same hardships, from the commander of the army to the cook, everyone lives on the daily allowance of five cents, apart from grain. As for pocket money, everybody gets the same amount, either it is twenty cents or forty cents. Consequently, the soldiers have no complaints against anyone.

Mao was aware that the system was not an ideal one but rather a temporary measure about which he had little choice, because it was determined by the extreme scarcity of materials as well as by what was required by the circumstances of the struggle they were facing. It is this policy of unity and equality between cadres and soldiers that made the Red Army able to endure extreme hardship bravely.

At first glance, the Supply System seems to be based on the equality norm. In essence, however, it is based on the need norm, because at a very low supply level it is only an equal distribution of resources that can maintain people's survival. This is understandable, because it fits the basic assumption of historical materialism that there is no innate value of fairness that is natural and universal to any society at any time. Instead, the prevailing value of fairness in a society is always determined by the physical living conditions of the society which consistently change in terms of both their content and form with change in the society's economic relationships (Li, 1984). In a society with such a low level of productivity and scarcity of material, one cannot imagine any deviation from the distribution practice based on the need norm at survival level in the form of equal distribution. In the final analysis, the value of fairness, like all other values, as a part of societal superstructure, is determined by its economic basis—the production capability of the labour force.

With the continuous improvement in the country's economy after 1949, the Supply System began to be given up and substituted gradually for a regular pay system, first in the government and state enterprises in 1952 and then in the military in 1955. Various incentives, including the piece rate, were also introduced in the mid-1950s. The socialist principle of distribution was advocated and officially recognized.

The party, however, does not exist in a vacuum. Instead, it inherits a heavy load of tradition and a huge population of which peasants constituted 80 per cent. The revolution took peasants as its principal force and they formed a majority of the party's cadre, whose belief that the major objective was to equalize all members of society in terms of both their status and wealth was strengthened by the equalitarian distribution practised for decades in the revolutionary team. It became the basis of the ultra-left ideology. Zhang Chunqiao, then just a careerist of the middle rank cadre but later the chief theorist among the Gang of Four, began to whip up the ultra-left ideology by publishing a notorious article with the title 'Do away with the Bourgeois Right Ideology' (Zhang, 1958). He attacked the then prevailing compensation system by asserting that the system had corroded the mind of cadres and workers, making them think of nothing but their personal interests, and caused them to be preoccupied with their personal gains and losses. He insisted that the abandonment of the Supply System was a serious retrogression. During the Cultural Revolution, the ultra-left ideology dilated malignantly. This time, the ultra-leftists attacked even more fiercely, insisting that any kind of material incentives were poison for all working people (Zhang, 1975). They deliberately depreciated the value of 'mental' labour and sent hundreds of thousands of intellectuals to do physical labour. They took the average of the total fund for bonuses as a fixed additional component of compensation and labelled it 'additional salary'. Everyone was then given a fixed pay unrelated to performance, and material incentive was eliminated. The fixed pay system, without any adjustment for thirteen years, plus lifelong employment, were called by the masses satirically the 'Iron Rice Bowl' system and eating meals from the shared 'Big Pot'. These perverse acts led the country to the verge of economic collapse.

Deng Xiaoping brought order out of chaos when he took over the control of the country again in the late 1970s. He soon rehabilitated the socialist principle of distribution and called for the abolition of the 'Iron Rice Bowl' and the 'Big Pot'. With increasing interaction with the outside world, the values of Chinese people changed. The norm of contribution had struck root in the hearts of people, including managers, to such an extent that in a comparative study, Chinese managers' preference for highly differentiated distributive patterns consistent with an equity-based logic was found to be even stronger than that of their US counterparts (Meindl et al., 1987).

A document issued by the Central Committee of the CPC (1993) with the title 'A Resolution of the Central Committee of CPC about a Number of Issues in Establishing the Socialist Market Economy' proclaimed that it was necessary 'to insist on the system of taking "to each according to his work" in individual income distribution as the main body, coexisting with multiple distribution patterns to reflect the principle of giving priority to efficiency and at the same time giving consideration to justice'. The statement does not provide a clear-cut definition of the term 'justice'. However, it implies that justice, is the opposite of efficiency and equality is the synonym of justice, without being aware that efficiency, or its basis, equity, is also another kind of justice.

As for the distribution practice in contemporary China, the Structural Pay System has become popular both in administrative and public institutions as well as in business organizations. One's pay is composed of three major components. First, the *basic pay* is the same for every working person for maintaining one's basic level of living and is similar to the Supply System. Second, the *position pay* is the reward for one's performance in fulfilling the major responsibilities of one's job as required by the job description. This component is relatively stable, and a distinction is made between it and the bonus that is contingent upon one's current performance during a period, e.g., a month, six months or a year. Third, the *seniority pay* increases by a definite amount for every working person after every year. This component, at first glance, seems to be based on the equality norm, because everyone enjoys the same amount of increase for the same period of work, no matter what job one holds. But that is not the case because, contrary to the equality norm, those who have greater seniority receive more than junior colleagues. In essence, the seniority component is the pay for additional work experience accumulated in the past. It is still based on the equity norm, because work experience, like one's education, reflects one's potential for greater contribution, and thus should be rewarded. However, with more and more joint ventures and subsidiaries of international corporations established in China, the Structural Pay System has been fading out, and the concept of Contemporary Compensation System has been introduced to act as a reference for designing China's new pay system.

EMPLOYEES' SPECIAL CONCERNS IN PERCEPTION OF FAIRNESS

Although the equity norm of distribution is prevalent and dominates in China, the impact of traditional culture and practices on the minds of Chinese employees cannot be ignored. Chinese social scientists began to study the unique perception of distributive fairness in the mid-1980s (Han, 1987; Jin, 1986; Lan, 1987; Xu and Sun, 1987; Zhou and Lu, 1985). But few of these studies are empirical. In collaboration with a few western colleagues (Yu, Bunker and Wilderom, 1989; Yu, Wilderom and Hunt, 1989), the senior author conducted some field studies, the findings from which are useful in understanding Chinese employees' perception of fairness.

According to Adams (1965), since one's perception of distributive fairness is a purely subjective judgement, different people have different understandings about the variables concerned, which may lead to quite different conclusions and consequences. Since Adams' theory is based on the concept of social exchange, the outcome or reward one gains is defined as resources allocated to employees by the organization in exchange for certain contributions made by them. Traditionally, people focus on merely economic rewards, i.e., Herzberg's (1966), 'hygiene factors' which satisfy mainly lower-order needs and are mediated externally. Scholars of the humanistic school of thought have emphasized rewards that satisfy higher-order needs by providing non-financial rewards (Likert, 1967b; McGregor, 1960) or by mediating these rewards through the employees themselves (Deci, 1972). With this enlarged view of rewards, a variety of resources have been identified and added to the inventory, ranging all the way from economic and tangible ones like pay, bonus and fringe benefits to intangible and symbolic ones such as praise, recognition, titles, trust and respect, as well as enriched job characteristics such as skill, variety, task significance and identity, access to feedback, participation in decision-making and opportunities to get trained and to self-actualize oneself. The definition of resources as 'anything that can be transmitted from one person to another', is also broad enough to include things as different as a smile, a cheque, a haircut, a newspaper, a reproachful glance, or a loaf of bread (Foa and Foa, 1980).

It is increasingly recognized that distributive norms vary in accordance with the types of resources to be distributed (Deutsch, 1985). Therefore, people are interested in a reasonable, meaningful and systematic classification of resource and reward types. As a result, a variety of ways for differentiating rewards have been found. One basis for classification is the material versus socio-emotional dimension. The lower-order need satisfiers mentioned earlier are material in nature, and provide for the physiological well-being of employees, whereas the higher-order need satisfiers are socio-emotional resources that mainly enhance the psychological well-being of employees. The two, however, overlap to a certain extent and there is no clear-cut distinction between them. For example, a promotion that enhances one's status and prestige, and that should be regarded as a socio-emotional and non-financial reward, also simultaneously brings a rise in pay.

According to Maslow's (1943) Need Hierarchy Theory, a higher-order need begins to function only when its adjacent lower need is satisfied. So, material rewards are very effective in motivating employees in China, a country that is still underdeveloped. It is worth noting that, in China, housing is an important reward and is a basic necessity for survival. But in the West, whether an employee would buy or rent a house and what kind of housing he prefers are his personal business. In China, however, housing has always been a significant benefit provided at a nominal rent by one's organization, a policy that can be traced to the Supply System. Second, with very low wages, employees simply cannot afford their own houses. Therefore, providing adequate housing is a primary concern in the reward package of organizations and is crucial to employees' morale and commitment.

Another interesting aspect of housing as a reward is that the average area occupied by members of an employee's household is generally taken into account in house allocation. The crowdedness of one's house is taken into consideration. This implies that the need norm is recognized as the most important consideration for housing distribution, which is not the case with the distribution of other types of resources (Yu, Wilderom and Hunt, 1989). Thus, a resource that is scarce and concerns basic living conditions is distributed on the basis of the need norm irrespective of seniority.

Non-economic rewards are also important in China, of which respect, trust, opportunities to be trained abroad and conditions for self-actualization are of particular significance, especially for white-collar workers and managers.

In the West, the quantity and quality of employees' contribution to an organization are the bases for expecting or demanding a reward as requital. The contribution one has made to the organization has multiple components, roughly categorized into two groups viz., those that are *personal* in nature, such as one's job performance and the merit one wins and those that are *environmental* in nature, including poor work conditions, responsibilities, risks, high levels of work requirement and so on. To a considerable extent, these involve subjective judgement. As such, the perception of reward depends on the significance an employee attaches to various factors. However, in spite of this relativity, Chinese employees brought up in the same cultural setting share some common features. First, there is a popular Chinese saying, that 'if I have no merits, I do have hardships; or at least I have exhaustion.' This implies that Chinese employees assign a big weight to one's work attitude and the effort one has put in no matter what results one has produced. This can be labelled the 'effort norm', and may be attributed to the impact of the equalitarian orientation and the traditional attitude of being content with ordinary status and not being concerned with rewards. This attitude is usually labelled the 'Spirit of an Old Yellow Ox', and is traditionally regarded as a virtue and encouraged.

Second, a distinctive feature of Chinese society is the weight attached to morality. Morality has many components, including one's political integrity (like patriotism and loyalty to socialist ideals and the reform policy), honesty, accountability, justice, and diligence in one's work and in social life. In China, morality not only plays a key role in the decision about promotion, but is also significant in the distribution of other kinds of rewards like pay, prestige, housing and even opportunities for training. The CPC has traditionally accorded the highest importance to morality. This implies that, irrespective of how good one is at one's job, one can be placed at the bottom of the waiting list for the distribution of any kind of reward if one is perceived as guilty of certain misdeeds in terms of morality.

Third, seniority is another input which is of significance in determining reward distribution. In China, morality, ability, and seniority have been traditionally juxtaposed as key determinants for promotion. This policy reflects not only the recognition of work experience accumulated over the years, but also the influence of the equalitarian tradition.

Some unique factors in present-day China concerning reward alloca-tion are situational in nature. For example, the CPC began to reform its cadre system in the mid-1980s through a Four '-ize' Policy, i.e., to make the cadre force revolutionized (in political harmony with the party), intel-lectualized (better educated), professionalized (qualified to act as leaders and managers in the new economic system), and youngerized (i.e., if candidates for promotion are almost equal in other aspects, the younger ones are preferred). On the surface, the 'youth norm' may appear contra-dictory to the seniority norm, but in fact each of them governs different aspects of the promotion decision.

China is in a period of transition. It has not abandoned the rigidity of its central planning system completely. Its newborn market econ-omy, especially in the field of labour, is far from mature and perfect. The so-called system of organizational ownership of employees has just begun to unfreeze. Workers' mobility is limited, causing special problems concerning fairness, i.e., the problem of equal outcomes versus equal opportunities. Some scholars have questioned the validity of Adams' theory in contemporary China by arguing that it is unfair to emphasize equal ratios of employees' outcome to their input till equal opportunities are not available to all of them (Bi, 1988).

There is a basic conflict between the traditionally equalitarian values and the value of performance-contingent rewards that is due to differences between classical Marxism and the practices recently introduced in China from abroad. Obviously, the basic issues of fairness are closely related to the struggle of those who would like to preserve the status quo with those who seek to change it. Even under the most stable social conditions, flaws in the basic values of fairness are revealed, and some of the traditional values that have served in the past require revision and reinterpretation to be readjusted to new needs and newly aroused consciousness. The issue of fairness has been further complicated by the process of radical reform currently happening in China. It appears that the major changes concerning distributive fairness are moving towards the acceptance of international values.

A SURVEY ON THE UNDERSTANDING OF FAIRNESS

The basic norms that the Chinese utilize in judging the fairness of reward allocation, and their cultural roots and ideological sources in Marxism that have operated since the revolution have been discussed. Against this background, a field survey was conducted to analyze the opinions of the average Chinese and to determine empirically the specific content of the concept of fairness prevailing today. The sample on which the study was conducted consisted of 220 university undergraduate freshmen and juniors, ranging in age from 17 to 21 years, who had taken the course on Organizational Behaviour (OB).

Taking the cue from Herzberg's (1966) two-factor Motivation–Hygiene Theory which posits satisfaction and dissatisfaction not as bipolar ends of the same dimension but as two separate and independent constructs, it was hypothesized that the concepts of fairness and unfairness similarly constitute independent dimensions with separate sets of determinants.

Utilizing the method of critical incidence, two questions were raised in the OB class just before the topic on motivation (including the equity theory) was discussed. They were:

Question 1: In your opinion, what is fairness? (Please give example[s] to support your idea.)

Question 2: In your opinion, what is unfairness? (Please give example[s] to support your idea.)

Responses elicited to the two questions were content-analyzed, and coded and categorized separately under four broad groups as follows:

1. *Content fairness:* This relates to the content in the resource distributions or exchange relations, mainly focusing on the sequential relations between conditions and results, such as input–outcome,

performance–reward, effort–reward, competence–reward, virtue–reward, equal distribution and trade-off.

2. *Procedural fairness:* This relates to the perception of the fairness of the procedure followed in the realization of the sequential relations just mentioned, such as the availability of equal opportunities and conditions, the guarantee of applying strictly identical criteria for judgement, uniform criteria in implementation and so on.

3. *Environmental fairness:* This pertains in a broad sense to the social norms and rights of people such as social equality, social norms and natural equality, and forms the basis for the realization of content and procedural fairness.

4. *Subjective fairness:* The foregoing three types of fairness can be regarded as objective fairness. But subjective fairness relates to people's perception of the fairness involved in reward allocation with respect to content, procedure and environment. It is this perception that determines the behaviour of people.

Table 10.1
Contents of Fairness and Unfairness

Categories	Fairness Frequency	(%)	Unfairness Frequency	(%)
Content	80	43.5	53	28.8
input–outcome	5	2.7	8	4.3
performance–reward	23	12.5	16	8.7
effort–reward	13	7.1	6	3.3
competence–reward	14	7.6	5	2.7
virtue–reward	2	1.1	5	2.7
equal distribution	8	4.3	3	1.7
trade–off	15	8.2	10	5.4
Procedural	60	32.6	88	47.8
equal opportunities/conditions	32	17.4	26	14.1
identical criteria	17	9.2	12	6.5
criteria implementation	11	6.0	50	7.2
Environmental	31	16.8	32	17.4
social equality	10	5.4	8	4.3
social norms	19	10.3	14	7.6
born equality	2	1.1	5	2.7
accidental	0	0.0	5	2.7
Subjective	13	7.1	11	6.0
personal preference	6	3.3	4	2.2
neither fairness nor unfairness	7	3.8	7	3.8
Total	184	100.0	184	100.0

The categorization of responses to the two questions are given in Table 10.1. It is not necessary to discuss the table in detail. It would suffice here to indicate that the perception of *fairness* was more content-oriented, i.e., related to the constituents of the output or reward allocated. But the perception of *unfairness* was more procedure-oriented. That is, it was related to the appropriateness of the procedure followed in ensuring the reinforcement of the condition of equal opportunity and the like. On the other hand, unlike the content and procedure categorizations, differences in responses relating to fairness and unfairness were not significant for the environment and subjective categories. It appears that in the perception of fairness and unfairness, a similar framework operates, but there are differences in emphasis.

11

VALUE CLARIFICATION FOR A SYNERGETIC WORK CULTURE IN ORGANIZATIONS

Mala Sinha

In recent years there has been an upsurge in organizational development (OD) interventions in business organizations in India to cope with the challenges thrown up by globalization. The overall aims of these efforts have been to raise the performance level of the workforce so that the customer-driven and international norms of quality are reached. At the same time, breakthroughs achieved in the area of information technology and communication have forced corporations to restructure organizational forms and re-engineer work flows. Mergers, alliances and diversifications have become frequent and necessary tactics, not only for survival but for gaining competitive advantage. Human resource in developing countries is already underutilized, and organizational change is adding to the pressures faced by them. Numerous interventions are regularly imported from the West by management consultants and used in India. Job enrichment, management by objectives, transactional analysis, team-building and quality cycles are some OD techniques frequently used in India. Often there is lack of fit with the societal culture, suggesting that change agents may have intervened at a depth that was inappropriate, leading to short-term or piecemeal results (Srinivas, 1994). Vision-sharing through value clarification is an intervention technique that is becoming increasingly popular in India but which emanated from the West. Broadly, the technique strives to understand the mental models of the workforce and then align the organization's systems and structures to it, striving to achieve a fit between culturally determined attitudes, values and beliefs of people and organizational form. The end result is synergy, the identification with corporate vision leading to profitability and well-being (Senege et al., 1994). This paper is based on a series of 'vision-sharing through value clarification' workshops conducted by the author in a number of business organizations.

THEORETICAL UNDERPINNINGS OF VISION-SHARING THROUGH VALUE CLARIFICATION

Constant and frequent changes in the environment have led to a paradigm shift in the way work is done in organizations. Organizational goals are no longer defined quantitatively; the end is always qualitative, like 'consumer satisfaction' or to be 'leaders in one's business area'. Facts and figures are subservient to a superordinate goal which is intangible (Jacobs and MacFarlane, 1990). Employees never know the limits of performance expected from them. They are expected to remain in a perpetual state of readiness to change working styles, adjust to new work forms and learn new skills, without diluting their overall performance. All this requires high levels of motivation, identification with corporate goals, commitment and total involvement in work.

Work in the West and in most Indian organizations today is based on contractual obligations, which ensures explicit definition of duties, obligations, rules and regulations, and compensation and outcomes in lieu of performance. This system worked in the West (Udy, 1970), but in India it led to a soft work culture due to a lack of fit with Indian social values, habits and extraneous considerations (J.B.P. Sinha, 1990). Western nations are beginning to question the efficacy of the work values promoted by Taylor, Weber, McGregor and Mayo, and are looking for alternatives to arrest the decline in economy. Quick to respond to the changing definition of work, they know today that the employer–employee relationship needs to be based on sharing of vision and goals, loyalty, emotional bonding, trust and faith. The contract basis of work is against this spirit. The past economic success stories from East Asia have led to the belief that leverage to Asian countries have been their traditional values in this era of environmental uncertainties and globalization (Kao et al., 1994).

The West also carries deeply ingrained values of the rational and scientific approach. Vision-sharing is a rational strategy to generate and inculcate values amenable to organizational effectiveness through the experiential mode in the workforce. Frequently used in Western countries, it has led to the creation of organizations of excellence (Senege et al., 1994). Brought to India by management consultants, this organizational development technique has the potential for achieving the end result of designing organizations which have a cultural fit with the local needs and circumstances. If successfully executed, it can create a synergetic work culture which, in the words of R.C. Tripathi (1994), is a hybrid of East–West mix adapted to local situations, fashioned by specific cultural and historical legacies, and set against the background of a global extension of world markets, competition, economic restructuring as well as enhanced mobility of capital and labour across national boundaries.

CONCEPT OF VISION-SHARING THROUGH VALUE CLARIFICATION

Visions are pictures of the future that people or organizations create, representing the best in themselves. They are like future dreams or goals that give meaning to the present, shaping activities and behaviours today. Visions release an extraordinary energy in all those who share them, locate creative abilities and bind people into a critical mass geared to make the vision a reality. Gandhi's vision of a free India, which he consciously shared with both masses and elite through grass-roots interactions and the setting of personal examples, made an enormous contribution to the independence movement. This vision found instant recognition and shared meaning in the personal dreams of many Indians. It was translated into smaller elements called missions that defined the small steps needed to fulfil the larger vision. For example, the Swadeshi movement was launched to teach people respect and love for all things Indian. The Dandi Yatra, culminating in the making of salt, was undertaken to assert that a basic necessity like salt did not require to be taxed by the British. Indians would make their own salt, and this endeavour would teach them the meaning of *swavalambh* (self-sufficiency). Gandhi also defined certain core values, which told people how they should behave to fulfil this vision. These values were derived from what people had already imbibed through their cultural, religious and historical heritage. Values like selfless service (*niskama karma*) and non-violence (*ahimsa*) are examples. Thus, Gandhi's vision, mission and core values evoked recognition and empathy in the masses, and they were collectively motivated, energized, involved and committed to the vision of free India.

Organizations articulate visions based on the founder's aspirations, certain standards of excellence, or demands of the market. They may be qualitative visions, such as, 'to be leaders in telecommunications' or quantitative: 'to achieve $5 billion by the year 2000'. Top management, a cross-section, of employees and even management consultants get together and frame this vision, which is then translated into strategic purposes or mission statements which let people know what it takes to fulfil that vision. For example, to be a leader in telecommunications one needs to (a) ensure complete customer satisfaction; (b) empowerment; or (c) constantly innovate. Finally, guidelines or core values are stated which indicate how people must operate or behave on a day-to-day basis. Some examples of core values are (a) treat everyone with respect; (b) share knowledge and resources; (c) recognize and support initiative. Formal articulation of vision, mission and core values tells people where they are heading, how they will reach there and how they must act. It also makes top management accountable in creating an organizational climate for practising what has been articulated.

It is often found that some members of organizations do not identify with the documented and articulated vision, mission and core values. They do not see a consonance between these and their personal visions and values. While there are operating values resulting from interactions among members, systems and structures which are historical and consistent, there are also personal values, as ideals to be upheld and practised given the opportunity. *Vision-sharing through value clarification* tends to reduce gaps between organizational core values and those of members. Studies have shown that congruence between the two sets of values leads to greater member integration and organizational effectiveness (R.C. Tripathi, 1994).

The present author was approached by some organizations to facilitate vision-sharing through value clarification. Each organization had a document stating its corporate vision, mission statements and core values. As an OD consultant and trainer the author had to induce vision-sharing by getting organizational members to align themselves with corporate values. This paper relates to findings obtained through value clarification which formed a subpart of the overall vision-sharing intervention. Two main objectives were to be achieved through value clarification:

1. To facilitate alignment with *corporate core values* by exploring *personal desired values* of members and their relationship with corporate core values.
2. To identify gaps between members' personal desired values, *practised organizational values* and stated corporate core values, these gaps being starting points for future OD interventions.

METHODS AND PROCEDURES

Vision-sharing through value clarification workshops were conducted in two Indian organizations and one multinational organization in India during 1994–1995. The organizations were in the power sector, telecommunications and air traffic control. Ten workshops, each of 8 hours' duration, were conducted with ten to fifteen participants in each. Participants were from the junior-to-middle management level, between 30 and 40 years of age and holding postgraduate professional degrees. Two experiential exercises were used interchangeably for the sake of cross-validation to derive desired values.

EXERCISE 1

Through various iterations, participants chose one or two most desired values from a list of values. Whenever there was a doubt while choosing a value, situations showing two values in conflict were presented by the facilitator. The participant analyzed the situation and gave up one value which led to value clarification. Subsequently, groups of five to six members were formed, each representing a hypothetical corporation with the emergent desired values being the company's core values. Members had to formulate various policies to cope with competition within the framework of core values. Some values had to be given up as they impeded progress. At the end, the group was left with a set of values they would never give up and these also represented the best interest of the company and its people. These were the desired values needed to create a synergetic work culture in the organization.

EXERCISE 2

Participants were made to recount real-life experiences where they had been part of a winning team which had achieved outstanding results. With the help of questions and probes, the values that led to a synergetic work spirit and finally the success of the team were articulated. These values represented desired values that could lead to synergetic work culture even in organizations.

Corporate stories and folklore discussed during the proceedings and that had consensual validation formed the basis for practised values in the organization. Corporate core values were given to the author and participants by the organizations as a written document.

The findings in this paper focusing on the emergent desired values, practised and corporate core values will be referred to for comparisons and discussions only.

RESULTS AND DISCUSSIONS

Some trends were observed during value clarification exercises across different groups:

1. All groups showed a great deal of congruence between corporate core values and desired values.
2. Practised values were perceived to be a result of inappropriate organizational systems and structure, lack of skills and abilities, and poor work habits acquired over years.
3. There was expressed need and sense of ownership towards desired values. Replacing the prevailing practised values by these was considered extremely important. Results and discussion pertain to only those values which were common to all three organizations and across groups.

CONCERN FOR FAMILY

This was the central desired value for all groups. Performance in organizations was for the purpose of achieving the end results of caring for and improving the quality of family (D. Sinha and M. Sinha, 1990). Family was considered a major support for members, and relying on it for any contingency was normal. There were regrets that, despite the family being the most important factor in life, there was a tendency to ignore its emotional and social needs and to take it for granted. None of the three organizations referred to the well-being of the family even remotely in their corporate core values. On asking the senior management about this, the common reply was that if care for family is formally stated, it is opening up a Pandora's box and there would be no end to demands. The attitude reflected a lack of willingness to understand what members meant by family salience. The main concern was not economic but emotional and social neglect of family because members were putting in long hours of work and were too tired to respond to family needs on reaching home. Familism as a desired value has stood the test of time in all South Asian countries (R.C. Tripathi, 1994). However, there was a strong belief that the value needed to be revitalized and supported by organizations.

LEADERSHIP VALUE (HIERARCHY)

Participants clearly emphasized the need for effective leaders in all working groups. The analogy given was that, just like work groups need a common goal as an objective necessity, people in a group also need a leader as a subjective necessity. Numerous authors have repeatedly stated that family socialization patterns predispose Indians favourably towards hierarchy (Kakar, 1978; J.B.P. Sinha and D. Sinha, 1994). In these studies, hierarchy is ascriptive and related to seniority, roles, position or status. A distinct change was observed in the definition of leaders symbolizing hierarchy. An acceptable leader needed to possess and display (a) integrity in all dealings and the ability to set personal examples; (b) competence and abilities for the tasks to be performed; resourcefulness or expertise; (c) charismatic qualities and mentorship. There was to be no permanent hierarchy but new leaders could emerge depending upon situational needs. Such a leader would be natural and accepted by all. But once acknowledged as a leader he would be looked up to. Historically, also, the traditional model of authentic Indian leadership has always been that of *rajarshi* (*raja-rishi* or king-sage). It symbolizes the keynote of the Vedantic ethos: 'management of secular in the light of sacred' (Chakraborty, 1995b).

Most participants agreed that practised leadership in organizations was imposed by senior management. Leaders lacked integrity, skills and abilities and were misfits and unacceptable. This diluted organizational effectiveness in large measures. None of the corporate core values talked about providing effective leaders. Since most organizations are undergoing restructuring and acquiring flat structures which would need empowerment at all levels, the concept of hierarchy and leaders is losing salience in the rational sense. The corporate core value which came closest to the leadership concept was developing personal leadership in all.

SERVICE

Quality and customer satisfaction were treated as synonymous values. The desired value of *service* was the only way these corporate values could be achieved. Service was understood roughly as the English equivalent of the concept of *dharma* (to do one's duty acquired by knowing one's true nature and role played in life). Work has always been understood by Indians as discharging one's duty. Excellence in work is generally seen to occur in a family or personal context (J.B.P. Sinha, 1990). Participants were willing to bring this concept to the organizational setting due to the environmentally imposed imperatives for excellence and quality. Further customer satisfaction was seen as synonymous with excellence in work and the epithet 'customer is king' meshed well with the traditional Indian value of *athiti satkar* and *athiti deva bhav* (hospitality and respect should be given to a guest as he is an image of God). The customer is like a guest to be pleased in organizations.

The concept of 'service' also has its roots in the Vedantic tradition of the five-fold debt system or *rin*. It means that individuals must pay back *dev rin* (debt to gods), *rishi rin* (debt to seers and sages), *pitr rin* (debt to parents and ancestors), *nri rin* (debt to humanity at large) and *bhuta rin* (debt to plants and animals) for making possible bounties given to them (Chakraborty, 1995b). The customer must also be served for making it possible for individuals to excel in work and pay something back to the system. Therefore, quality was not seen as an alien modern value but an extension of indigenous value already in practice as *dharma* in the personal context.

At various points the discussion centred around another important Vedanta concept—that of *niskama karma*, which means doing one's duty without attachment to results. Participants were clear that in organizational settings it was not possible to delink rewards from efforts. If one was delivering selfless service and excellence in work, the expectation of reward was high. This finding is endorsed by Chakraborty (1993) in various OD interventions in different companies. It is possible that in a developing country, where paucity of resources is juxtaposed with growing consumerism, not expecting rewards is unrealistic. Cultural values are therefore sometimes limited in terms of applicability to present societies which are already transformed due to Western and modernization influences. Participants also said that the practice of such orientations as service to customers was not possible due to poor support systems and inadequate empowerment of organizational members.

Table 11.1
Desired Values, Corporate Core Values and Practised Values in Organizations

Desired Values	Corporate Core Values	Practised Values
Family (improved emotional and social life)	–	–
Effective leaders (competent and with integrity, and situationally determined)	Personal leadership (empowerment)	Ineffective leaders (poor competence)
Achievement (challenge and meaning)	Nurturing innovation	Systems and attitudes which do not support achievement
Service is equivalent to excellence and quality	Quality and customer satisfaction	Skills, systems and work flows not aligned to service

Note: Values common to all work groups and organizations are reported.

ACHIEVEMENT VALUE

The desire to accomplish interesting and challenging work and be recognized for it was another desired value that could contribute to a synergetic work culture. The corporate core value which came closest to this value was 'encourage and recognize innovation, creativity and achievement'. Indian studies have shown that urban people and those at higher organizational levels value ability utilization, achievement and personal development (Padaki, 1988; J.B.P. Sinha and D. Sinha, 1994). The achievement value had individualistic and collectivistic orientations. Participants said achievement should be nurtured without diluting group harmony. Individual accomplishments are possible only with the help of group members, because all work is an outcome of interdependence between group members. In fact, the relevant work group should recognize and recommend the high performer for reward from the organization. The juxtaposition of individualistic and collective orientations in the achievement value is quite different from McClelland's (1961) need for achievement which was purely individualistic. Mehta (1994) has talked about social achievement which is quite similar to the achievement value obtained in this study. According to him, developing societies are ridden with insecurities and lack of resources, and people generally have a history of failures. Due to extraneous conditions people find it difficult to obtain admission to good schools, professional courses and even finding and holding good jobs. Fear of failure instils the need to excel, achieve and improve the quality of life, but it also makes people concerned about the collective good, and value cooperation and collaboration.

Table 11.1 gives in summary form the values according to their salience for the members.

IMPLICATIONS AND CONCLUSIONS

Vision-sharing through value clarification is an effective OD technique for bringing about organizational change. It leads to an understanding of the mental models of members, and of whether or not they are aligned with organizational goals, systems and structures. The process approach used for vision-sharing gives members an opportunity to review their own values, habits and beliefs and to become open to change. It therefore fufils the criteria of openness and embeddedness for system development as suggested by R.C. Tripathi (1988). Value clarification starts the process of supplanting and modifying dysfunctional practised values with the functional desired values and corporate core values, making the organizational system open, since members are activity-involved in the process. It does not overly disturb the system, and contributes to making members and systems more embedded.

The desired values obtained in the study for creating a synergetic work culture in organization had a cultural core and elements representing change. Some corporate core values matched well with desired values while others did not. Practised values in organization were dysfunctional for organizational effectiveness, resulting from poor systems and structure, inadequate skills and abilities and poor work habits. The family value was the central value for all members, but organizations did not consider this a corporate core value. Perks and welfare schemes for the family are present in organizations but they do not relate to the actual concerns of members vis-à-vis the family. These schemes do not contribute to improving the quality of interactions with the family, which suffers due to long and exacting work hours and an antagonistic attitude of family towards the organization. A participant mentioned that while a trader's or farmer's wife talks of 'our fields', an employee's wife always says 'his work, his job, his office'. Organizations must strive for greater identification of the family with the organization. Small steps are needed to increase the interaction of organization with family in a direct-approach manner. This would increase bonding of organizations and family and reduce stress and alienation within the family leading to overall gains. In the face of constant environmental change, uncertainty and instability, families play a critical role in acting as stability and comfort zones (Toffler, 1981).

Organizations must strive to convert this value into a strength for organizational effectiveness.

Widespread dissemination of knowledge due to media and the breakthroughs in information technology have led to empowerment at all levels. Traditional, ascriptive hierarchy is unacceptable today. Competence, abilities, and integrity and charisma are qualities valued in leaders. The need to look up to such leaders is still strong and alive. Corporate core values do not talk of providing effective leadership, but refer to developing personal leadership in members. Practised leadership in organizations is regarded as ineffective. It is possible that older employees have traditional values and have never learned to delegate and encourage participation. Younger people demand delegation and scope for exercising autonomy and do challenging work as reflected in the desired value of achievement. Thus, the changing value of leadership is linked with the value of achievement. In an environment where young people desire challenges not possible without the sanction of seniors, true empowerment will never occur and people will always have a subjective need for leaders. This is very similar to what Khandwalla (1994) has said in reference to nurturing the pioneering innovating (PI) motive in Indian organizations. According to him, professionals in developing countries face the dilemma of balancing innovative and challenging work while conforming to the status quo and security, in a scarcity-ridden ascriptive society. Organizations and social environment do not provide an environment conducive to reducing the socio-psychological costs of achievement, and innovation-oriented behaviour, in terms of rewards, accepting mistakes, training and development and effective leadership, is just not present. The implications of these for organizational development are that greater efforts are required to develop senior management which can change managerial styles, upgrade skills and abilities and become creators of a synergetic work environment. The traditional value of treating work as duty or *dharma*, or the service rendered to a guest, was seen to be equivalent to the present-day concept of quality and customer satisfaction. Although in reality these values were not being practised, the chief cause was attributed to mismatch between systems, structures and the values practised. To effectively exercise the spirit of service, factors like work flow, interdependence within the work unit and standardization should be adapted to the cultural values of the group (Menon, 1994).

In conclusion, it can be said that modern Indian organizations need to base their OD interventions on values stemming from religio-philosophical origins. Care for the collective, concern with excellence, performing work as service rendered and learning from a leader can lead to organizational change and growth in a controlled way (Verma, 1987). This paper examined the values desired by professionals for creating a synergetic work organization. All the values have a deep and stable core derived from ancient psychological, philosophical and religious traditions of India. Elements of change are not radical but related to immediate environmental factors. Traditional values are alive and vibrant in the minds of professionals. They are perceived as possessing all the ingredients to cope with the challenges presented by change. Of late, there has been considerable evidence that cultural and religious values do inspire people in secular workplaces. Japanese and Chinese success has been attributed to values based on Confucian ethics (Kao et al., 1994). This paper has conclusively suggested that there is no need to substitute values in totality because change is inexorable and takes place in stages. Once new elements are embraced, there is also a strengthening of the core (traditional) values which provide stability. The core of values is unchanging and applicable across cultures and eras.

12

SOCIAL VALUES IN ORGANIZATIONS: THE CASE FOR COUNTERVAILING SOCIALIZATION

S.K. Chakraborty

The first section of this essay argues for the principle of indigenization of values in the human dimension of management in India. The second section offers an overview of some paradoxes and contradictions in the present Indian social milieu, especially those which seem to have surfaced during the post-independence period. The third section describes a few efforts by the author in educating Indian managers (and students) about some basic principles and methods to reconcile performance and product-ivity with the enduring ethos of India. The concluding section contains the suggestion for selective and appropriate re-socialization towards the primary values-structure of Indian society.

THE INDIGENIZATION PRINCIPLE

India has a variety of stringed musical instruments including the *sitar*, *sarod*, and the *veena*. The musical notes played on them will be identical. Yet, each melody or tune will have its own combination of these notes. Let us suppose one common melody has been chosen to be played on all these instruments. The musicians are seated on the same platform, and begin to perform simultaneously. It will then be readily observed that each instrument is being played with a distinctive tool, held in its own unique physical positioning by the respective musician. Interchanging the tool and posture relevant to the *sitar* for that of *sarod*, for example, will simply mar the final result expected of the former. If the process is reversed for the *sarod*, an identical distortion follows.

The metaphor of musical instruments draws attention to the indisputable fact that each culture has a keynote, a genius, a temper which is its very own. Thus, an Indian Stanford MBA, now a leading industrialist in Bombay, once told us about the sheer impossibility of American and Indian cultures being convergent. In the West, he said, as soon as a boy or girl reaches 15 years of age, he or she cuts loose from the parents. But in India, children live with their parents practically throughout their lives. We have observed in Scandinavian countries men greeting women by embracing them, even though the latter could be the wives of others. This social process is unthinkable in India where even a father is not expected to touch his daughter's body once she attains puberty. We recall the puzzled anguish of a German engineer in Calcutta. One day, he had asked a worker on the shopfloor to remove a spare part lying on the bay at a wrong place. Unawares, however, he had done so by using his foot to indicate the particular object and its proper place. This incident provoked strong resentment amongst the worker and his colleagues, and a tools down–stop work situation seemed imminent. Of course, the matter was resolved through timely counselling by the IR officer and the German engineer offering a friendly apology to the worker.

The foundations of social values, especially in enduring civilizations, usually lie buried in their deep-structure. They crystallize and take root through centuries of experiment and experience in a specific geographical–climatic–topographical context. The very fact of endurance speaks for the robustness of such core social values. All this constitutes the basic stuff and material which, with due care and sensitivity, can be adapted to, as well as used to evaluate, the key elements of each epoch of change.

Assumptions of uniformity about social values across the world also constitute a negation of Natural Law. Diversity in social values is a natural correlate of diversity in the flora and fauna spread over the earth. The strident cries of mass media may produce a superficial impression about the whole world going the same way. The advocates of such a bulldozing process might often condemn the inertia and resistance to change amongst the traditionalists. Yet, more often than not, such conservatism draws its strength from the deeply anchored world-views of specific cultures. It is wiser to respect and conserve the essential Will of each culture as enshrined in its world-view. The world as a whole will be a richer and more interesting place for that—though this might well impede the rolling juggernaut of change progress, springing from one particular world-view, that seeks to dominate all peoples in a particular epoch.

In forcing the pace of change in social values at the dictates of a superficially concocted and culturally alien change model, members of the receiving culture tend to engage in mindless wastage of precious energies simply to keep in step with the fleeting external symbols of change. The more important task of pursuing and achieving inner transformation and development is neglected as a result. Fidelity to the core set of indigenous values is a practical need for breeding and sustaining quality human beings in an orderly and predictable social milieu. Swami Vivekananda (1976) reminded us of this principle a century ago:

> ...every nation has a...national idea. This idea is working for the world and is necessary for its preservation. The day when the necessity of an idea as an element for the preservation of the world is over, that very day the receptacle of that idea, whether it be an individual or a nation, will meet destruction.

VALUE PARADOXES IN THE PRESENT INDIAN SOCIAL MILIEU

A 'balance-sheet'[1] of social values and their opposite, social dis-values, might be a useful starting point for this section:

(A) Social Values[2]	(B) Social Dis-values[2]
1. Commitment and trust within the family	1. Growing indiscipline
2. Neighbourhood social insurance	2. Increasing political and economic corruption
3. Respect for hierarchy-by-age	3. Poor work-ethic in the organized sector
4. Simple living	4. Wastefulness
5. Duty-model of existence	5. Regionalism
6. Sacred religiosity	6. Weak nationalism
7. Strong work ethic in the unorganized sector	7. Interpersonal jealousy
8. Ability to bear hardships	8. Urban dependency
9. Ability to sustain democracy in national governance	9. Ostentation amongst the nouveau riche
10. Rural self-reliance	10. Rights-conscious, duty-avoiding educated class
11. Generally home-centred females	11. Rising money ethic and consumerism
	12. Inter-religious disharmony

---

[1] This is a personal view of this author, based on observation and intuitive feeling.

[2] There is no one-to-one correspondence between items in list (A) and list (B).

There seems to be a definite all-round shift from (A) to (B). Managers caught in this process tend to reveal varying degrees of ambivalence between correct beliefs on the one hand, and correct practices on the other. Since approximately the mid-20th century (especially since the outbreak of World War II), the space and weightage for 'social values' at the front-stage of Indian society seem to have been diminishing. Correspondingly, the space and weightage for 'social dis-values' seem to have been increasing. This process appears to have accelerated after India gained independence from the British in 1947. While the democratic format of running the polity is worthy of acclaim, this very format has bred many of the social dis-values mentioned in the 'balance-sheet'. Shift of emphasis from 'character-oriented education' to 'skills-oriented training' has compounded the problem.

It will be useful now to present some selective data about the ambivalence of Indian managers in the realm of values. They are culled from a recent on-going questionnaire survey amongst Indian managers across the country. As of date, 922 responses have undergone preliminary processing for average scores on two seven-point scales: (a) Never Agree to Always Agree and (b) Never Acceptable to Always Acceptable. Scale (a) is related to 'beliefs', scale (b) to 'practices'.

The response patterns to 'belief' statements 1, 6, 8 and 10 in Table 12.1 seem to indicate a stance of pragmatism-cum-relativism in the discharge of managerial responsibilities. The response to item 3 would appear to contradict the recent advocacy of flatter organization structures—a tall structure is apparently a more 'exciting' setting than a 'flat' structure! Responses to items 2, 4, 5, 7 and 9 produce, on the other hand, a fairly coherent picture of the values-sensitive, culturally congruent mindset. For example, belief 9 captures a fundamental principle of work ethic in Indian psycho-philosophy called *nishkam karma* or *karmayoga* (disinterested/selfless work, or work as a process of union with the Divine). The crux of this value is reduction of self-centred egotism for inner elevation and outward effectiveness (Sri Aurobindo, 1977). Such a spirit blends well with the duty-oriented attitude towards work-life. And both ego-less and duty-oriented work attitudes are essential supports of ethics and morals in the workplace.

Yet, the dichotomy between these two sets of 'belief' responses merits attention. For instance, what can managerial education and training do to prevent the possibility of the pragmatism–relativism tide sweeping away the deeper instinct of ego-less, duty-centred work ethic? The purpose is to achieve long-term, holistic effectiveness in organizations through

Table 12.1
Scale (a) Responses (%): BELIEFS

	Never Agree	Undecided	Always Agree
1. Business decisions, being situation-specific, ought to be value-neutral	31	22	47
2. Ethically wrong actions must produce harmful effects, sooner or later, for the source of such actions	8	8	84
3. A hierarchically tall structure, affording many career growth levels, is preferable to a flatter organization	26	17	57
4. Management philosophy and practice is of such universal character that it hardly needs any inputs from one's own cultural heritage	54	18	28
5. It is adequate to emphasize individual rights, instead of duties, for improving organizational effectiveness	72	14	14
6. An aggressive competitive spirit is the best answer to the challenges of quality and productivity in a liberalized regime	19	14	67
7. Excellent professional management need not concern itself with moral issues	70	9	21
8. The major traditional family values have lost their relevance for modern corporate culture	42	18	40
9. To the extent one works selflessly, one adopts an enriching and healthy psychological approach to work-life	10	9	81
10. Human/ethical values are as much liable to change in time and place as are social customs or rituals	37	12	51

Note: There were 20 statements in all.

cultural congruence. After all, organizations are only a kind of means for achieving a wholesome society and human enlightenment.

We now turn to a selected set of responses to the scale (b)—'practices' items. Except for the responses to items 7, 9 and 10—which are culturally congruent—the other responses seem to be contradictory to both universal as well as culture-specific values. Thus, the 'belief' proclaimed in item 9 of Table 12.1 is negated by the responses to 'practice' items 4, 5 and 6 in Table 12.2. The selfless work or *nishkam karma* principle, which is so strongly agreed upon as a belief, apparently breaks down in the practical

Table 12.2
Scale (b) Responses (%): PRACTICES

	Never Acceptable	Undecided	Always Acceptable
1. Promoting internal competition to get the best out of individuals	11	14	75
2. Recruiting high-powered experts (say in R&D or Marketing) from a competitor to increase business or profits	27	24	49
3. High pressure advertising for consumer goods	19	28	53
4. Attracting and retaining high calibre manpower on the principle 'every head has a price'	18	19	63
5. Progressively increasing and diversifying the number and value of perquisites to employees	17	25	58
6. Motivating youngsters by holding out fast career growth prospects	13	14	73
7. Including respect for age and experience as an organizational value	7	13	80
8. Advance buying up of the entire shelf-space of selling outlets at a premium price for first-time market penetration	40	27	33
9. Paying regular monetary/material gratification to key government officials in various places for smooth clearance of files, etc.	72	14	14
10. The senior (by age and position) should forget that he/she is the senior, while the junior should not forget that he/she is the junior	17	19	64

situation. Similarly, the near-unanimous avowal of belief in the *karma* theory, i.e., you reap as you sow (Table 12.1, item 2), gets short shrift through the response to item 2 in Table 12.2. The ambivalence in a related Table 12.2 item—number 8—is also a sign of the difficulty to hold on to or translate a belief into practice.

The response to item 1 seems to reflect the harm that superficially understood and culturally incongruent cognitive inputs could do to the managerial mind. In the same vein, the social dis-value of mercenariness receives endorsement through the responses to items 2, 3 and 4 in

Table 12.2. All these responses to 'practice' items seem to suggest a widespread lack of ability to appreciate the holistic interconnectedness between fundamentally correct beliefs and their practical translation in the work context. Most managers may not even feel that there is a contradiction between 84 per cent believing that 'like effects follow like causes' which recoil on the source (Table 12.1, item 2), and 63 per cent endorsing in the recruitment market the practice of 'each head has a price' (Table 12.2, item 4). Or, even if they feel this discrepancy, the top management/owners/board do not send down the right signals, thus inducing managers to altogether avoid facing such tension.

The response to item 9 on bribery in Table 12.2 suggests that its practice is strongly resented. It seems to be a 'receiving end-victim' mindset response reflecting the compulsion to offer bribes to get even legitimate issues sorted out in time. But often it is from amongst the same managers, in the obverse setting, that bribes are forced upon the other side. One need not labour this obvious fact. The response to the social dis-value of corruption, manifested through bribes, as revealed here, may thus conceal the tendency to avoid managerial accountability for initiating such practice too.

To sum up, the outline of the social values picture revealed by the managerial mind, tentative and crude though it may be, is something like this:

1. Contradictions amongst 'beliefs' themselves
2. Contradictions amongst 'practices' themselves
3. Contradictions across 'beliefs' and 'practices'

Observing and working with a wide variety of Indian organizations at close quarters, we infer that such unperceived and/or unresolved contradictions leave them devitalized. Continuous psychological energy leakage occurs because of such debilitating contradictions. A mere intellectual, technique-centred, skills-driven approach to managerial development fails to plug these gaping holes.

To this broadbrush picture of organizational setting we might add a general perception of ours. As the Indian citizen today moves up through the rungs of higher education and takes a berth in the organized sector, he/she begins to undermine or disown the otherwise preponderant 'social values' still prevalent in the wider society, and tends to opt for the 'social dis-values' of the smaller, privileged but rootless sector of society. This transition to pseudo-socialization may not yet be universal; still, it is widespread enough to cause concern.

STEMMING THE SLIDE: 'QUALITY MIND' WORKSHOPS

It is contended that the basic cause behind the aggravation of the paradoxes and problems mentioned here lies in both non-education and mis-education about the deep-structure aspects of Indian ethos. This phenomenon is quite widespread, especially in the institutions of higher learning in the fields of technology, management and so on. As Bhattacharya (1977: 37) had pointed out a few decades prior to independence, the educated Indian works with a 'shadow mind'. This shadow seems to have darkened even more since the 1960s.

Over the years, the following characteristics of the Indian deep-structure have appeared crucial for our work in organizations of removing, to a certain degree at least, such shadows in the managerial mind:

1. The ingrained habit of investing all secular activities with the touch of the sacred or transcendent. Thus, Prakash (1995: 52) informs us how, in his hi-tech electronics firm, any new machine installation goes through a process of consecration through worship of the divine master-artisan, Vishwakarma, before being commissioned.
2. Secular work is not an end in itself. It is basically a process of progressive ego-management. It is intended to act as a grindstone to gradually polish the crude and rough edges of selfish egotism.
3. Through ego-management one reaches out for the built-in spirit-core which is Truth, Light, and Wholeness in itself.
4. All social processes—from birth to death—are organized around this keynote of ego-management. Thus, for example, the primacy of the family over the individual is based on the keynotes of infinite patience and adjustment. They constitute the practical side of ego-management. The large joint family is veritably a gymnasium for ego-management.
5. Similarly, a respectful attitude towards elders on the part of youngsters, and a caring disposition towards youngsters on the part of elders are both socialized extensions of the basic principle of ego-management through humbleness and self-sacrifice respectively.
6. Purity of heart or emotions, achieved over time by sustained focus on ego-management, has to become the ground of equitable, fair and effective human relationships and decision-making within organizations.
7. The overarching historical strategy of managing Indian society has been duty-based. The obligations-oriented, indebtedness-centred

keynote of socialization in India (at least prior to the advent of Western-type university education) was a wiser process in principle. For, once everyone in society is socialized into perceiving one's position in terms of duties, the ancient holistic social lawgiver, the *rishi*, was pretty sure that the rights of others would be secured automatically. They saw that performance of duties at any point naturally translates itself into the honouring of rights at other point(s). Many of the social dis-values mentioned earlier could be traced to the erroneous adoption of a rights–claims centred, law-driven, individualistic ethos of the contemporary West. Several social activists today lament the fact that the ordinary Indian citizen is not rights-conscious enough, does not have recourse to the courts often enough. But this springs from the false lure of a rights-driven social dynamics which seems to be unsustainable in the long term.

8. A continuous self-reminding that all activities in the economic, material, social and related fields are *really* spiritual in their final aim. Social values are meant to support and converge upon the ultimate spiritual value within the person. This big-picture, holistic awareness is a matter of conscious cultivation.

Based on premises such as these, we have been offering in-depth workshops on what we call 'Human Values and Indian Ethos'. The backbone of these workshops is the 'mind-stilling' or 'quality mind' exercise which helps to convert cognitive learning into emotional assimilation. This happens because the exercise enables one to lessen the inflexibilities and rigidities of the rational-intellectual mind, making it more supple and receptive to positive feelings and intuitions. The six-step exercise has been evolved by us over the years by drawing upon multiple sources of Indian psychological practice which have stood the test of time. It has been described elsewhere in detail (Chakraborty, 1989). Managers from top to middle levels have been covered in successive groups over long periods in some of the major and very well-known enterprises, e.g., in the public sector, Indian Petrochemicals Corporation Ltd (IPCL), Indian Oil Corporation Ltd (IOC) and Bharat Electronics Ltd (BEL), and in the private sector, Godrej and Boyce (G&B), TELCO and Shri Ram Fibres (SRF). The Godrej efforts have been presented and analyzed fully (see Chakraborty, 1993).

A national seminar was organized at our institute in December 1992 where these and other organizations were invited to present the results of efforts to educate their managers in human values in the light of the Indian ethos. A collection of these papers has also been recently published under the author's editorship (Chakraborty, 1995a). It will be useful to reproduce below some salient points from these in-house reports.

IPCL (public sector):

(a) Soon after the exposure [to the Human Values Workshops], we faced a major mishap in one of our plants in February 1989.... The plant group suddenly...became the target of ridicule, accusations as well as of several enquiry committees.... Coupled with such a demoralising situation, the unavoidable activity of rebuilding the damaged section by full involvement of the same plant group forced an extensively stressful situation with tensions and pressures on the individuals. However, exposure [to these Workshops] came in handy to keep the team intact and mentally strong to withstand the pressure and to concentrate on the goal of rebuilding and recommissioning the plant (1995a: 23).

(b) I like to mention that constant endeavour to practise 'Values-system' has given me more calmness and strength in decision-making and empathetic feeling for others, particularly for my subordinates. In the process I have been able to establish a pervasive values-system in my own group (1995a: 23).

IOC (public sector):

The overall impact of this type of programme (Values Workshops) has been positive. There are definite improvements in the thinking pattern and behaviour of managers after their exposure to such programmes. The process of consolidation of these improvements may be slow, but with consistent efforts...managers as well as (the) organization can expect to reap dividends (1995: 31).

BEL (public sector):

It will be no exaggeration to say that the values-oriented approach achieved many things for a number of individuals such as:

- subduing of individual egos, and acquiring the ability to look at others as equals;
- accepting that each one of us makes mistakes or commits improprieties;
- overcoming to some extent selfishness, unfairness, partiality, anger (and) jealousy;

- avoiding hurried decisions;
- inculcating (the) spirit of giving rather than taking;
- commitment to customer, community;
- pride as an Indian (and) self-confidence;
- setting good example to peers and subordinates to emulate (1995a: 44).

G&B (private sector):

The percentages of response frequencies of 'Very Good' and 'Good' (from participating managers) for the four core end-result factors—Ethical Sensitivity, Coping with Frustration, Introspection Ability and Work for Work's Sake—were 81, 76, 86 and 87 per cent respectively. These were the results just before the beginning of the second module. Thus, a high percentage had been reached on these core variables and (this) was maintained through to the third module (1995a: 57).

TELCO (private sector):

Despite the problems faced, participant feedback everywhere reveals a significant improvement in quality of worklife as a result of VS–MS [VS: Values System, MS: Mind-Stilling] exercises. Also, their faith in the positive role of the two, and the resolve to transform themselves has strengthened over time regardless of organizational policies. Further, as our own experience with middle managers has shown, this philosophy is not overly intellectual and can be adapted to have widespread implications. The fear of some organizations that the resultant calm of these exercises may make one explain away problems or give in to philosophizing is not borne out by experience. At least not ours (1995a: 75).

SRF (private sector):

A mid-term sample survey on officers conducted in July 1990 showed that the MS exercises had:

- Very Significant Effect On:-   colleague relationships, frustration coping, introspection ability, and working for the sake of work.

- Significant Effect On:-   domestic life, superior and subordinate relationships, ethical sensitivity, and creativity.

- Not Very Significant Effect On:-   encouragement from the superior (1995a: 51).

The foregoing excerpts from the managers' own reports on companies which have/had undertaken a planned exposure process for values learning workshops reinforces the hope that with conscious efforts to reincorporate the basic and culturally congruent human/social values, an organization can substantially combat the downslide from social values to social dis-values. Such an exercise also begins, though unobtrusively, to resolve many of the paradoxes and contradictions mentioned earlier. Of course, as already noted, the values culture process is both cognitive and affective. Unless cognitive understanding seeps into the being as affective feeling, no real elevation of work-life quality seems possible.

CONCLUSION: COUNTERVAILING RE-SOCIALIZATION

Liang Shu-ming, the great Confucian, has recently been commented upon by a scholar in the following words:

> Liang established the fundamental dichotomy.... [Modernity was] the equivalent of mechanistic positivism, intellectualization, purposeful action, selfishness and ethical nihilism. All these conditions were inherent in prag-matism, which he saw as the logical culmination of all [modern] thought. The alternative was...the equivalent of emotion, intuition, non-calculation, ethics, unselfishness, and absolute value (Alilto, 1987: 101).

From the viewpoint of Vedantism, this author feels readily attuned with Liang's insight into these two contrary paradigms. India's Nobel laureate poet, Rabindranath Tagore (whom Liang had met), had approv-ingly quoted Lao Tse in an address in China in 1924: 'Those who have virtue attend to their obligations; those who have no virtue attend to their claims.' After quoting thus, Tagore amplified the point: 'Progress which is not related to an inner ideal, but to an attraction which is external, seeks to satisfy our endless claims. But civilization which is an ideal gives us power and joy to fulfil our obligations' (Tagore, 1988: 56–57).

Thus, duty/obligations-centred re-socialization (see point 7, p. 204) of educated Indians, including managers, would seem to be the hub of a comprehensive strategy for revitalizing the enduring social values to serve and, if needed, also to question the process of change. And this primarily 'secular re-socialization' strategy could be naturally linked to the higher-order 'sacred re-socialization' strategy. This is how Chin-Ning Chu (1995: 212) has expressed this higher-order note: 'Every morning in my affirmation I read the following: "being attuned to the Divine Will is the most important factor in attracting success. To discover through the right meditation how to be in harmony with the Divine Will is man's highest obligation."'

Such reincorporation of the 'sacred', the 'Divine Will', seems capable of reviving appropriate social values that flow from Truth. It will be useful to grasp the principle that, just as the finites are derived from the Infinite, so are social values truly anchored in the universal–transcendental domain. Ancient societies were built on this principle. The ordinary human intellect or reason alone cannot fathom this eternal, Natural Truth. Let us quote the words of Swami Vivekananda (1958) uttered in London a century ago:

> Truth does not pay homage to any society, ancient or modern. Society has to pay homage to Truth or die. ...That society is the greatest, where the highest truths become practical. ...if society is not fit for the highest truths, make it so; and the sooner the better (1958: 84–85).

IV

INDIGENOUS FACTORS IN MANAGERIAL LEADERSHIP

13

CORPORATE STATESMANSHIP: A CURSORY NOTE AND IMPLICATIONS

Ng Sek-Hong and Henry S.R. Kao

The notion of 'corporate statesmanship' is in part instructed by the political analogy of the logic of public administration and governance in such a realm as the running and guidance of a nation-state. The secularized management of political affairs in the 'power' arena of electoral game and haggling is often in the grips of the politicians—professionals who are conversant in the art and craft of political manoeuvres. Yet the mentor who is able to pilot and steer the nation and its people to their higher 'realm of the estate' and to do so with vision and charisma, is often enshrined under the more elevated label of the 'statesman', the custodian entrusted with guarding and advancing the altruistic course of nation-building and reconstruction.

It follows that such a quality of 'statesman'-like leadership is also recognizable in the micro context of corporate administration and governance of the human enterprise. As ordained by classical Confucian teachings, the logic of governing the state is basically the dicta of organizing oneself, the family, the nation or other collectivity 'writ large'. It is suspected that there is a parallel in the quality of leadership and governorship between the nation-state and the enterprise. It is the purpose of this paper to explore some of the distinctive features of such a 'statesman'-like regime which excels in the creation, management and development of business enterprises.

THE BOUNDARIES: ENTREPRENEURS AND MANAGERS

The concept of 'corporate statesmanship' is hardly novel in itself. It addresses some of the gaps left unanswered in the conventional body of established business literature pertaining to 'entrepreneurship'. What Wong (1988) has identified as the incapacity of the 'entrepreneur' is helpful in differentiating 'corporate statesmanship' from 'entrepreneurship'. Discussing the popular image of the Chinese entrepreneur, he laments that 'a striking feature of Chinese private industry is that it is strong in entrepreneurship but weak in management', so that the supply of entrepreneurs tends to outstrip the supply of managers and executives. As an illustration he cites the case of the Shanghai spinners who 'pursue technical expertise, but not managerial professionalism' (Wong, 1988).

Managerial impotency of the (Chinese) entrepreneur is not specific to the Chinese character and context. Rather, these propensities are more or less inherent in the role and functions of the 'entrepreneur' who, in conventional wisdom, is associated with the generic quality and power (both inborn and learned) to create, to explore and to capture opportunities with imagination and innovative spirit. Quite expectedly, their usual zeal and capacity to work with risks often imply concomitantly their feeble sensitivity to the organizational imperative of reconciling, assimilating and disciplining novelties like new ideas, new arrangements and new ventures to the workplace, where these inputs have to be fashioned in order to be sustainable as the continuous and managed aspects of a structured, regulated and governed organization. In this connection, it has been commonly said that the irony is that those who are gifted to invent and create are often ill-equipped to manage whatever human enterprise they help gestate. The appearance of such an 'entrepreneur–manager' paradox has posed a dilemma not only in the case of the traditional Chinese family business, but also in the contemporary era of revived market liberalism in the industrialized Western economies (Kaplan, 1987).

In spite of the widely held view that the career entrepreneur is lukewarm about the rules of management whilst the professional manager is insensitive to the art of entrepreneurship, there is an inexplicable hiatus in that the success of modern business is hedged in many instances to the realization of both imperatives in the workplace. In fact, the mainstream body of contemporary management literature has increasingly shifted its emphasis to the popular theme of 'managing change', which is now a zealous concern with instructing corporate managers to rupture their hitherto held image of a salaried technocracy/meritocracy/bureaucracy in order to become a salaried and corporate-coated entrepreneur, contributing thereby to the rejuvenation of ageing enterprises.

Kanter (1992), in her classic *The Change Masters*, refers to the 'awakening of a dormant spirit of enterprise at all levels of organizations, among all workers'. Such a renewal ethos entails an intellectual agenda of corporate reforms—fundamental, far-reaching and engendering long-term and enduring endeavours such as human resource development, fostering organizational commitment and cradling a solidaristic enterprise culture. In such wholesome endeavours to re-discover the vitality of corporate existence, the pivotal idea highlighted is that of a corporate mission, which is that self-conscious corporate search for a sense of purpose, identity and philosophy in organizing and managing the corporation's affairs and activities.

The thesis of 'corporate statesmanship' advanced in this paper deals with this puzzle by postulating, with reference to empirical case studies conducted in the East Asian context of Chinese culture, that a bona fide non-synthetic form of corporate entrepreneurship is more likely to evolve and consolidate where the owner-founder is sufficiently statesmanlike in steering the enterprise to a new and innovative horizon while at the same time conserving its bounty as a manageable/sustainable entity with an appropriate etiquette of governorship as implied in the notion of 'corporate statesmanship'.

CORPORATE GOVERNANCE AND 'STATESMANSHIP'

An emerging agenda in management literature today is the issue of corporate governance, as business corporations are increasingly beset by the dearth hitherto of an appropriate protocol, or a properly institutionalized mechanism, for governing the administration of corporate business in the face of (*a*) the fragmentation and commercialization of ownership as a sequel to the development of the open 'stock and shares' market; (*b*) the fluidity of its structural configuration and composition forum due to the trendy waves of business mergers, takeovers, acquisition and restructuring (often packaged under the label of moves of 'rationalization' as 'downsizing', 'de-layering' 'streamlining', etc.); and (*c*) the ascendancy of the 'marketplace' ethos which has in a sense emasculated organizational commitment and stability with its characteristic emphasis upon the logic of flexibility, competition and autonomy devolution. The nervous qualm centred on what to do about 'corporate governance' is further aggravated by the growing concern with 'human rights' and global expectations of business ethics.

The classical approach of corporations of the industrialized West to dealing with these 'governance' issues has been anchored in their board as the governing body, which is *ipso facto* the institution guarding the domain of internal governance, analogous to the executive committees of voluntary associations or the ministerial cabinets of parliamentary governments. Conceivably, corporate governance can only excel in a consistent fashion where it is safeguarded constitutionally through 'rules of law', rather than dependent upon the whim of the individuals who happen to head the corporation. However, a cursory glance at the multiplex problems afflicting corporate business everywhere suggests a rather pessimistic prospect of any vigorous appraisal and workable blueprint(s) for meaningfully reforming the board in order to uplift its quality of constitution and efficacy in performance (*Corporate Governance*, 1993; 1994).

Such an institutional hiatus brings us to the second theme of our thesis on 'corporate statesmanship'. The art of governance in corporations does not necessarily rely mechanically upon the provisions of formalized arrangements, as epitomized by a governing body and its functional prescriptions for intervening in the business organization which it is supposed to lead and direct. Rather, it is argued that the key to effective government—especially in achieving a corporate-wide *esprit de corps*, in nurturing a collective commitment to excellence in performance, as well as in sustaining an altruistic sentiment of corporate membership, involvement and commonwealth—has to reside in the governing ability of corporate leaders beyond the ordinary horizon of either 'management' or 'entrepreneurship'. Such an aptitude is suggested in the qualities and vigours of 'corporate statesmen' in their governorship. In other words, the thesis of 'corporate statesmanship' offers an alternative perspective to the 'mainstream' orientation of the Western theoretical prognosis which basically utilizes an institutional mode of treatment in approaching the corporate agenda of internal 'governance'. It is here proposed that the reign of man—with a flair for 'statesmanship'—can be equally, if not more, efficacious in welding together the human enterprise collective and advancing it to a higher realm of responsible 'governance'.

STATESMANSHIP, CULTURE AND SUCCESSION
IN CORPORATIONS

This brings us to the third dimension of our idea of 'corporate statesman-ship'. The agenda of governance is not exhausted simply by its orthodox definition as 'the exercise of power over modern corporations' and stop-ping short at the doorstep of the board of directors and the formalized relationship it has with the top management and other stakeholders in the firm. Often the issue encountered is not just erecting a governing or regulatory system alone, which may either work or else lapse into ritual-istic rhetorics and routines. Even more important is the question of the continuity of an efficacious regime of governance that often gets eroded due to the attrition caused by such traumas as management succession and other organizational crises, which disturbs the 'culture' of corporations.

As an alternative, it is suggested that the ingenuity, insights, imagina-tion and discipline of the top echelon of corporate leaders be consolidated into a body of corporate ethics and code of excellence in practice. Their mode of governance, as well as its underlying *raison d'être*, evolves to constitute the 'core' superstructure of what is named in the relevant liter-ature as 'corporate culture'. It has worked well enough to be considered valuable and is hence enshrined, upheld, applied and cultivated so that it is sustainable through the generations. It is, therefore, 'to be taught to new members as the correct way to perceive, think and feel in relation to those problems' (H.E. Schein, 1984).

It is felt that if corporate leaders are able to govern well, and have the foresight to translate the ingredients of such a governing practice into their 'corporate culture', it is probable that such a normative mechanism is perpetuated through managerial succession. The continuity hence engen-dered represents, among others, the hallmark or insignia of 'corporate statesmanship'—in making possible the perpetuity of effective and ethi-cal governance which does not necessarily rely upon the legalistic effects of the governing board, and of its regulatory pretence. In this respect, corporate statesmanship is noticeable in nurturing a corporate culture of 'normative consensus' as the *raison d'être* of 'corporate governance', which in turn suggests, for both its existent and future membership, a unison of purpose, a bond of mutual trust and identity, as well as a faith in ethical and non-exploitative behaviour and relationship. 'Corporate statesmanship' helps upgrade and reinforce the spirit and practice of cor-porate governance by engendering a series of 'psychological contracts' that transcend both the managed and the manager, the governed and the

governor, espoused and expressed in a corporate culture which persists
through generations.

Often, the hereditary practice of managerial succession is traced
through an 'in-house' lineage of descent, as given by the corresponding
inheritance norm in such cultural traditions as the Chinese. Yet this type
of practice, in nurturing essentially a 'patrimonial dynasty in business', is
often abhorred for its self-perpetuating inclusivity, and its insensitivity to
its propensities for breeding inefficiencies due to the heirs' incompetence.
However, if such patronage could be practised in a technocratic manner
so that the heir groomed for future helmship could be sought, without
discrimination, from either the 'consanguine' posterity or a network of
entrusted and capable associates, it can be argued that 'statesmanship'
may excel where these succession processes are combined with, first, the
inculcation of the sponsored legitimacy of the heirs designate, second,
the technocratic grooming of their leadership and, third, the enhancement of the organization's bureaucratic continuity. In other words, what
have been postulated in the celebrated Weberian typology of governing
mandate as the three types of ruling authority (viz., charismatic, traditional and bureaucratic), can be nurtured in a hybrid fashion to sponsor
the accomplishment of statesmanship in the next generation of corporate
leaders. The 'superstructure' of such statesmanship would then rest upon
a corporate-wide, cherished body of business ideology, vision, assumptions and values, while its infrastructure has its roots in a workable and
efficacious power structure, division of labour and administrative arrangements instituted to ensure the activation, governance and continuity of the
human enterprise.

Corporate leadership, in order to be 'statesman-like', is virtually
always altruistic. Instead of allowing maximum latitude simply for self-
betterment and excellence (typical, for instance, of the aggressive and
self-aggrandizing image of successful career managers in Western corporations), business leaders in the Asian context are in general more oriented
towards the holistic integration and harmony of their enterprises, and
often take a genuine interest in the collective well-being of their staff as a
'commonwealth'. In the Asian context, this is attainable partly because
of the relatively invisible 'we–they' class divide separating the manager
and the managed, capital and labour, the employer and the employed in
the enterprise. Dore (1973), for instance, has reflected vividly upon the
irrelevance of any 'class' distance for the Japanese organizational men,
insofar as both supervisors and workers interact and associate in a solidaristic fashion in group actitivities and collective endeavours, both at
and outside work.

Another dimension is the capacity and readiness of these corporate leaders to endure personal sacrifices for the sake of their staff when business is in the doldrums. Even more significant is their charismatic quality of being able to inspire their subordinates to contribute their sacrifices concertedly. Naturally, such aptitudes for 'putting up' with privations are better noticeable in crisis situations. These are the embodiments of such cherished virtues as thrift, austerity, self-discipline and mutual aid— which, however, may not be readily appreciated for their logic, let alone emulated, in Western cultures. However, there is an apparent logic governing the Asian proneness to the will to suppress and contain oneself in contributing to the 'related others' in a collectivity, like the firm or the family. The thesis advanced in explanation is the notion of the 'minimum self', a mental terrain which helps explain why business leadership in many Asian enterprises is corporate-centred rather than egocentric in its consciousness (Kao and Ng, 1988).

Understandably, corporate leadership is hard to excel in, but it can more easily attain a realm of 'statesmanship' in an altruistic context, where a 'spontaneous' normative 'consensus' is felt and shared throughout the work hierarchy between the top echelon and the shopfloor. Thus, in the governance of Chinese enterprises, there is always an implicit assumption that the subordinates' deferential consent is better elicited by a humble, modest and self-effacing helmsman than a self-seeking, aggrandizing and ambitious leader. In a sense, the imagery of the Chinese mandarin, that of gentry, scholar-official and gentleman, is also cherished in the parallel domain of benevolent business administration.

Attesting to the qualities of statesmanship are, therefore, the noble deeds of the corporate leader in deflating himself and in his readiness to indulge in self-sacrifices for the benefit of his significant and related others. In the Chinese tradition, for instance, such a mental inclination or moral yearning is possibly a mix of both 'grass-roots' religious lore-cum-metaphysics (notably Buddhism and Taoism) and the comparatively regimented ethical code of 'governing' prescribed by Confucianism to regulate the hierarchy of socio-political relationships. Moreover, contributing to such containment of the 'ego' are also the established institutions of the extended family, clan and kinship network—not to mention the celebrated rites of 'ancestral worship'. For corporate leaders in Chinese enterprises, such an orientation is the key mental factor explaining the moral discipline of the aristocratic 'self' (that is, the leader) and its interrelatedness with 'important others' (that is, all those who are embraced within its networks of work, business and other connections). As Kao and Ng (1988: 256) discuss its ramifications, it instils in the individual an affective concern for the welfare of the related 'others' as well as a desire (or motive) to maintain harmony and a stable web of reciprocity with them.

Conceivably, several features of the common 'personality' configuration arising from these Chinese propensities towards 'minimizing' the 'self' are relevant in helping explain the industrial discipline and commitment which are recognizable in the leadership found among Chinese businesses and which tend to render them 'statesman-like'. These properties include, *inter alia*, such attributes as:

> ...the first outstanding quality is an explicitly submissive attitude towards authority, an awareness of the necessity for orthodoxy. ...The second outstanding quality is a strong drive towards success. In this connection, fate and fatalism serve as a socio-emotive mechanism to tide over any frustration caused by failure. The notion of 'fate' is also accorded a 'situational' or 'cyclical' interpretation, with a distinction drawn between 'lifelong fate' and 'periodic fate'. ...The contradiction between authority submission and competition has led to ambivalence in the orientation of the individual towards his achievements and success. One way of coping is for him to adopt an effacing attitude, to attribute such positive outcome to his 'related' others (Kao and Ng, 1988: 260).

Such a psychology of legitimating the individual's motive and judgement with an altruistic rationale perhaps in turn helps shape and vindicate the almost typical 'unitarist' preference elected by Chinese business leaders in opting, for instance, to secure and achieve 'integrative harmony' in the firm. Here, it is morally imperative for the leader to ensure that the logic of everyone's activities is to not impair others' well-being in order to advance one's own. In a metaphysical dimension, such a secular stance of 'self-restraint' in fact implies harmony with nature— echoing the Buddhist belief in the natural balance between 'cause' and 'outcome', between 'sacrifice' and 'reward', as well as between 'affliction' and 'relief'.

Also consistent with the thesis of the 'minimal self' are the widely cherished norms of reciprocity, forming an integral aspect of workplace ethics. Psychologically, such a mental propensity is due more to the individual's anxiety in seeking to maintain among his mutual ties a tranquil state of harmony and fairness, and less to the self-centred concern to satisfy one's 'ego' or desire.

The 'minimal self' thesis offers a perspective for interpreting the 'low-key' and quiescent appearance of many Asian business leaders who have won conspicuous admiration and support from their subordinate staff in spite of their self-effacing posture. On most occasions, such a sentiment of mutual identification across the 'employment' divide has rendered such industrial defensive combinations as the workers' union irrelevant or even obsolete. Again, Kao and Ng (1988) provide an explanation of this phenomenon by referring to the 'minimal self' concept. It is argued that the 'minimal self' emanates from the religious-moral dicta of individual behaviour as directed towards interpersonal relationships in a multiplicity of settings in the work situation. In addition, it is meaningful in activating the individual's behaviour only inasmuch as such webs of obligations vis-à-vis the related others are given appropriate recognition, implying a harmonious state of one's social integration at work. In a sense, it epitomizes an altruistic inclination of the individual—but in a holistic order rather than a segmental approach.

Therefore, while negating the 'we–they' industrial divide for its rupturing effects on 'harmony with others', such an ethos, by emphasizing integration with the 'related others' in the hierarchy, contributes to the expansion of trust which helps cement together both the manager and managed by instilling in them a unity of purpose, a positive attitude and commitment towards work. Indicative of an altruistic and prudent leadership at the helm, such a harmonious and integrated workforce is likely to excel as a satisfied and well-motivated human enterprise displaying high morale and productivity.

CORPORATE STATESMANSHIP AND THE ORIENTAL (CONFUCIAN) NEXUS: THE TALE OF TWO ENTERPRISES

This section presents empirical illustrations of how a flair for 'corporate leadership', reminiscent of the qualities discussed earlier, are appreciated in the workplace. Profiles of two leading corporations run by Chinese capital and management, one in Hong Kong and one in Taiwan, are described briefly as exemplifying those corporate and governance features which have been identified earlier in the concept of 'corporate statesmanship'.

CASE I: A MACHINE WORKS AND ITS GOVERNANCE

This is the largest and leading mechanical engineering plant in Hong Kong producing fully assembled machinery and parts, catering essentially to the East Asian markets and other Third World economies. It commenced as a petty machine shop, housed in a temporary shed, in the early 1950s shortly after the War of Liberation in China. Its success and spectacular expansion to its present scale of business operation is a typical case of the industrial dramas featuring the enigma of 'legendary' entrepreneurship of 'refugees' fleeing from the socio-political upheavals of the mid-century Mainland and seeking a transient shelter in the 'colonial' territory. The features underlying the phenomenal development of the enterprise, making it a 'standard-bearing' piece of business administration, provide insight into what has here been called 'corporate statesmanship'.

What appears to be distinctive, in the first instance, is the nurturing of this enterprise through a patient process of gestation chaperoned by its founder-cum-owner-manager, who has hitherto viewed his headship more as an enlightened regime of benevolent governance than one of technocratic (if not bureaucratic) management. Such a characterization is evident in several dimensions, viz., (a) his corporate philosophy; (b) his imagery of the world, including business, economics, politics and society; (c) his interface with his staff members throughout the ranks, as well as industrial networking in both his professional and business partnerships (for instance, the buying and supplying outlets); and (d) his vision about the time horizon of commitment, especially in differentiating between short-term cyclical crises and long-term propensities and trend.

What was espoused in the corporate philosophy of this engineering plant, inspired heavily by the personal conviction of the chairman, was its prudent rather than idealistic nature. It featured in essence a 'grass-roots' type of mentality cherishing the importance of 'austerity'—yet vaguely reminiscent of the 'scientific management' rationalism as well as the 'human relations' ethos in cherishing a holistic orientation towards the people. It was typical of the celebrated Chinese paradox mixing both the 'soft' and 'hard' properties, the enchanting 'yen–yang' dualism, conceivably made possible because of the Chinese 'plastic' temperament which tolerates non-specificity, implied subtlety and the obscure 'rule' of hidden agendas which are admirably effective in masking conflicts and contradictions. Translated into action plans, such a philosophy purportedly gave rise to the strategy of this machinery plant to prescribe a set of ambitious yet interesting operational goals, viz., striving to produce at costs as cheap as in Mainland China yet at a level of quality comparable to the Japanese. It follows that a zealous philosophy was adopted in inculcating both productivity and quality excellence, in instilling a corporate-wide belief that it pays off (a) to commit to industrious, dedicated, vigorous and disciplined performance able to win the customers'/buyers' approval and compliments; and (b) to invest in human resource upgrading (i.e., by way of training and education in technical know-how, including self-learning and institutional instruction as well as 'on-the-job' osmosis), in order to enhance the individual's capabilities for accomplishing the first goal.

In other words, the philosophy propagated was in large measure a Confucian 'recipe' for normative and superstructural construction of a 'secular' entity (i.e., the factory) for achieving materialistic excellence through performance in business. Reminiscent of the Confucian prescription of governance, the ordering of priorities in rating the beneficiaries' claim and entitlement to the firm was unequivocal and associated with, in descending order (like a series of concentric circles radiating from the nucleus), their relative importance as the primary, secondary or tertiary stakeholders. At the core of the corporate mission was the advancement of the shareholders' (owners') interests; next came the protection and betterment of the 'commonwealth' of the workforce, also reckoned as the appointed membership of the firm; and at the periphery was the tertiary interests of such outside parties as the vendors or competitors (i.e., one's trading partners and industrial counterparts). The moral dictum observed in dealing with the tertiary class of peripheral 'stakeholders' was to abide by the 'rules of the game'—not to abuse, exploit, nor to act injuriously and viciously to harm these 'others'. Such a 'quasi-parochial' corporate philosophy was a 'micro' manifestation of the Chinese logic of prudent governance: to reign and perpetuate a state of decent prosperity, rather than to strive for the visionary utopia of attaining a global realm of 'communist' and 'egalitarian' commonwealth.

Such a corporate orientation can hardly be appreciated in isolation without reference to the leadership's core assumptions about life, society and work. These cornerstone social values and attitudes constitute and help shape the frame of reference of the governing echelon of management. Such a perspective is inspired by the social imagery which anchors the individual in his perception as an outgrowth from his class background, as well as by his subjective experiences of childhood, family, schooling and work history. These life experiences, through various stages of the individual's career, tend to consolidate into a cognitive structure in his mind with which social events and actions are interpreted. In this case, the founder's life experiences of the vicissitudes of socio-political upheaval in Mainland China nurtured in his imagery of the 'world' a mild degree of 'optimistic' fatalism.

Such a social imagery of this 'patron' founder of the plant entails inter-esting contrasts with the ideological profile portrayed by Wong (1988) in his 'benchmarking' study of the legendary 'emigrant entrepreneurs' mov-ing from Shanghai to settle in the territory's 'veteran' cotton-spinning trade in the early 1950s. The latter seem to betray, instead, a more sec-ular, pragmatic yet ideologically equivocal mentality—a representation of the 'world' which is readily understandable in the fluid context of the 'refugee'-dominated society of the mid-20th century. Wong observes that 'many of the industrialists did not see a clear distinction between long-range interests and social responsibility'. The reason why the spinners provided dormitories for the workers and protected them against redun-dancy is seemingly rational rather than ideological. It is not because these measures were intrinsically right, but 'because these would be to their advantage in the long run'.

In the wake of the inflation-cum-labour shortage syndrome which beset the manufacturing economy at the turn of the last decade of the 20th century, the mixed forces of the attractive pull of real estates price boom as well as the prohibitive cost-push of escalating labour outlays caused by the intensifying menace of industrial manpower shortage, have been suffi-ciently lucrative and formidable in inducing most textile mills to rescind their established production activities either (a) to make way for new property development on the spacious sites they used to occupy, or (b) to relocate their processing work northwards across the border, in order to substitute expensive Hong Kong labour and land for the much cheaper resources available from the Mainland. By contrast, the machine shop in our casestudy was resolved to withstand these 'odds' and 'attractions': it elected not only to sustain uninterruptedly its local operations, in spite of such adversities and alternative opportunities, but also to enhance its investment in modernizing and automating its plant, on a remarkable scale of rationalization in emulation of the Japanese managerial practices (like the 'Just-In-Time', 'Work Excellence' and 'Total Quality' techniques and methods).

Such a 'proactive' strategy of the mechanical engineering plant is indicative of the altruistic horizon of its leader in his commitment, faith and attachment to his industrial establishment and its workforce in Hong Kong, whom he viewed as members of his governing 'constituency' with a moral duty of guardship and stewardship over its fate and well-being. This affective identity explains his reluctance to withdraw from Hong Kong as his industrial bastion, backed simultaneously by his opti-mistic assessment of the profitable pay-off from sustaining industrial investment in Hong Kong.

The owner-founder has in this context demonstrated his aptitude of 'statesmanship', imagination and governing wisdom by developing a 'mixed bag' of 'self-strengthening' devices on both 'hardware' as well as 'software' frontiers. Equally far-reaching in his prescriptions of 'directorship' are his concern to update the technical know-how of his staff members and strengthen their 'knowledge' nexus in order for them to handle efficiently an increasingly complex production apparatus, which had become highly automated as a result of the hardware innovations mentioned earlier. Furthermore, what has given a 'humanized' impetus to such a 'technocratic' enhancement of the 'man–machine' capabilities of the plant is his insistence on being just 'one of them'—an 'ordinary' member among the 'rank and file' on the shopfloor. By chatting and dining regularly with his staff members and by indulging habitually in these patterns of personalized contacts and interactions, he takes pride in having been able to transcend the 'status distance' in the work hierarchy. Such a 'personalized touch' in penetrating the 'shopfloor' has earned for him a high level of charismatic appeal, enabling him to cultivate a corporatewide *esprit de corps* under his inspiration as the 'enlightened old guard'.

Ironically, all these qualities have acted together to make the long-term prospects of his enterprise and its capabilities of corporate survival both more tenable and realistic as well as more problematic and fragile. The key issue in this connection is the subtle and intricate agenda of managerial succession, a process which is being mapped out steadily under the founder's meticulous engineering and yet has to be made explicit in design and tested for its resilience. The mentor-founder is purportedly grooming his daughter, a doctoral graduate in engineering from a Hong Kong university, to evolve as his heir designate. However, what is most crucial and often proves to be perverting in any attempts to perpetuate an administrative regime of personalized 'governorship' for an enterprise or for any collectivity, is the transfer to and cultivation in 'posterity' of the same degree of and flair for 'personalized' charisma which has served strategically to buttress the reign of the old leader in his 'statesmanship'. In fact, a highly effective and popular regime of charismatic leadership enshrined under an earlier administration—in the context of either a nation-state or a business corporation—always engenders the paradoxical effects of emasculating, if not pre-empting, the charismatic basis of the next incumbent in the succession chain, especially if the 'patron' and the 'patronized' leaders belong to the same family and are linked by hereditary descent.

Perhaps the dilemma can be answered in part by a succession strategy of choosing and installing an heir outside the network of consanguine/ patrimonial ties. However, the negative implication for what is essentially a 'leader-centred' type of family bureaucracy is the 'alienness' which such discontinuities in succession would generate. This may instigate the parochial and unpopular argument that corporate statesmanship has in its gestation to be associated with an authentic reign of proprietorship or ownership—i.e., a sense of 'property' right which will engender intrinsic involvement and identity with the property.

The strategy which the owner has adopted in such an almost 'impossible' situation of conserving his corporate 'estate' has yielded, in spite of the 'Chineseness' of his style, a relatively unconventional formula of 'socializing' the ownership of his company by assigning it to a 'trust' foundation he has established for furthering education in China. This decision of donating a piece of industrial estate to the pursuit of a social cause is noble and altruistic, attesting again to the manifestation of a 'selfless' flair for statesmanship. Besides detaching the industrial concern and its asset from the equity holding of his family, such an act of 'de-privatization' was extended further by having the company listed on the open stock and share market—by re-constituting and incorporating the firm into a public limited company. The intention was to 'de-personalize' the ownership and control of the factory, so as to institutionalize its governance with the appointment of a board of directors to eventually take over the collective rein of its administration. Yet such a manoeuvre in transferring and rationalizing the exercise of the governing prerogative is again at best partial in addressing in its entirety the problem of transition from the regime of the old leadership to that of a succeeding one.

Here, the reasons are manifold and compounded by the owner's own ambivalence and indecision about the future configuration of his succession plan. The first factor is his vague yet 'statesmanly' vision of not perpetuating an 'in-house' family dynasty of control, but converting it into an enlightened system of a quasi-public estate devoted to a public cause. The second constraint is his unexpressed yet implicit assumption that he always remains the most resourceful personality in the enterprise to pilot and steer its development, even after his nominal retirement from any managerial portfolio. The third is the expectation, which he and his family harbour, that he still owes the latter a native duty of sponsoring capable members of his posterity for key positions of responsible participation in the enterprise. In other words, such normative inconsistencies stemming from the difficulties of divorcing totally his succession decisions from, first, the constraints of hereditary inheritance norms and, second, his egocentric propensities of self-indulgence in his own charisma, are likely to leave the prospect of his future succession trapped in a relatively fluid, oscillating and staggering state, unless he is able to inspire his daughter to consolidate promptly a new regime of effective leadership comparable in rigour and strength to his 'corporate statesmanship' which crystallized under his 'entrepreneurial'-cum-'governing' accomplishments in the enterprise.

CASE II: A STEEL PLANT AND ITS IDEOLOGY

In contrast to the foregoing case, which essentially epitomizes a 'homegrown' ideology of governance betraying the personalized nature of the founder's statesmanship which, paradoxically, creates for him an impending dilemma of succession, this second case illustrates how, in Taiwan's leading steel works (the China Steel Corporation), the orthodox prescriptions of classic morals like 'Confucianism' have been successfully applied in helping its leadership to consolidate a sustainable *cultural* regime of corporate statesmanship, which is able to survive the rupturing effects of managerial succession. It is a classic example of how, in an oriental context, 'corporate culture' serves as an efficacious ideological instrument in fashioning both structure and behaviour in a Confucian bureaucracy and rendering it similar to what Mintzberg (1983) in his *Structure in Fives* has labelled the Sixth 'Missionary' form.

The case of the China Steel Corporation and of its leadership is worth exploring as a lesson in corporate statesmanship, inasmuch as it represents the secular yet suprahuman 'corporatist' vigour of large-scale Chinese capital and its custodian (who is the 'Renaissance' manager, in the language of Kanter [1992], rather than the founder-owner per se) in steering the business for planned growth and innovations through a host of 'natural intervention' processes drawing upon Confucian teaching as the key dosage in its human enterprise for spiritual enhancement. Such a 'prescription' has enabled the works to transform itself successfully into a modern 'paternalistic' industrial corporation. Through its history of remarkable growth in recent years, this steel works has become 'the third most productive steel company in the world'. Much of the achievement is attributable to the resourcefulness of its manpower, as engendered in such salient corporate human resource properties as its 'organizational cohesiveness and stability, as well as the morale, satisfaction and productivity of its staff' (Kanter, 1992). China Steel has achieved such an 'estate of the realm', its harmony being 'corporate-wide' as a result of a patient, vigorous and carefully nurtured process of organizational experimentation.

It has apparently excelled at 'institut[ing] a seriously designed system of corporate attitudes, values and philosophy' (ibid.), notably in the shaping and subsequent growth of its corporate culture.

Several of the key features which the present leadership has instituted in advancing and consolidating commitment and performance within the corporation attest to a realm of a highly efficacious 'psychological contract' that characterizes the governorship of its chairman, with his half-scholarly and half-pragmatic flair for 'statesmanship'. The first of these features is the distinctive dosage of Confucian and Chinese traditional values which it has adopted to constitute the fundamentals of its corporate culture. The second is in the area of staff motivation, where it systematically propagated the Chinese traditional orientation to work. Under such an approach, the individual's obligation to perform one's role is exalted, as distinct from the satisfaction which is expected to emanate from the job for the incumbent. Enshrined in the mind of the workforce—for every staff member in the hierarchy from top to bottom—is a moral assumption obliging every job-holder to involve himself and be dedicated to his job as an intrinsic duty: 'his performance [could] stay high despite the hardship of obnoxious tasks, onerous working conditions or even unsatisfactory level of remuneration' (Kanter, 1992). This propensity to endure short-term sacrifices and privations reflected a high level of mutual trust and affective commitment cementing together the rank and file employees and their superiors in the managerial echelons. Such solidarity is attributed in part to the leadership's humanistic stance 'to assist individual staff in the company to achieve tranquility, self-strength and excellence' (ibid.).

In contrast with the previous case, the approach of the corporate leadership in building up such a normative regime of integrative trust among its staff members appeared to take on a more structured and institutionalized rigour than in the instance of the machinery manufacturing company in Hong Kong. Central to its 'OD' (i.e., 'Organizational Development') activities in China Steel, top management exalted, as the core of its corporate ideology, such values as (a) the virtue of 'sincerity' which implied not only the individual's dedicated involvement in his job but also his abilities to sustain and nurture 'interpersonal' trust; and (b) a creed for humanity which, as a Chinese notion, was closely associated 'with the norms of loyalty (chung) and reciprocity (shu). To reinforce and consolidate such an enterprise culture, China Steel has bred a group of corporate leaders which '[was] able to display its concern for its staff members, to set examples, and to nurture among the staff a sense of corporate altruism and identity—by deflating the self and strengthening concern with others whilst appealing to the moralistic support of the subordinates' (Kanter, 1992). Concomitantly, the 'we–they' class divide was de-emphasized. By virtue of their work contacts and mutual association in after-work interactions, the seniors were always able to set a 'referent' model for cherished emulative behaviour at the subordinate levels. Adding to this was the 'staff protocol' which, having been sponsored actively by its leadership throughout these years, has proved its efficacy in governing the normative conduct of authority and work relations on the shopfloor. The *raison d'être* provided was again ostensibly Confucian in nature. The 'core' virtues cited were 'loyalty and reciprocity' to constitute the corporation's ethics of propriety propagated by its leadership. In the work situation, loyalty was conscience-inspired and duty-bound, implying a sacrosanct commitment to one's existence in the organization which constituted a strong motivation for joint effort, task involvement and excellence in order to give effect to the collective goal and common good. In parallel, reciprocity demanded that kindness, benefits, affection and care from the paternalistic manager ought to be duly reciprocated. 'Such an obligation is, however, always tacit and not explicit' (Chao, 1994).

The China Steel Corporation represents a case of corporate leadership which attempts to institutionalize a normative infrastructure of Confucian ideology, which is, however, given detailed interpretation and prudent elaboration to serve as an invisible yet penetrative body of ethical guidelines or codes of practice for directing the activities of corporate governance. The renewed vitality in the performance and productivity of the enterprise is reminiscent of Kanter's (1992) model of 'Corporate Renaissance' engineered by the 'change masters' in the top management echelon. However, it is demonstrably a role beyond just that of 'corporate entrepreneurs' that the latter has played in China Steel, because it is more than just innovations and changes that the leadership has introduced. Instead, it is a regime of corporate statesmanship which not only features the legitimacy of change and a corporate-wide endeavour in organizational re-structuring but also epitomizes a civilized, intellectually inspired and solidaristic spirit in its patently Confucian-ordained enterprise culture, upholding the normative importance of mutual trust in work relations, dedicated excellence in performance and *esprit de corps* in sustaining a sense of corporate community beyond the administrative reign of the present chairman. It has enshrined, therefore, a superstructure of Confucian discipline prescribing corporate governorship under present and future chairmen. And the resilience and continuity of this moral code of etiquette, constituting a consensual body of the 'rules of the game', will presumably better insulate this corporation from the frictions and trauma of managerial succession endemic in the personalized regime of 'charismatic' statesmanship documented in the first case study of the machine shop.

CONCLUSIONS

This paper explores a notion intended to supplement and amplify our existing knowledge about the logic of enterprise management in its strategic aspects which is largely neglected in the mainstream management literature. This notion, inspired by the political scientist, relates to the scope and tenacity of 'statesmanship' in enterprises and corporations. The appeal of such a 'hybrid' idea of 'corporate statesmanship' lies in its ability to integrate what have so far remained relatively fragmented yet popular issues of management, viz., entrepreneurship, the governance of enterprise, the succession of managerial regimes, and the normative instrument of 'corporate culture'. This 'holistic' idea of 'corporate statesmanship' is in harmony with the analogy now increasingly drawn between the nation-state and the corporation in their *raison d'être*, as evidenced in such terminology as the 'corporate state' and, vice versa, 'corporate citizenship' and 'corporate nationality'.

'Corporate statesmanship' commences and in part coalesces with 'entrepreneurship' in order to lay the foundation of the corporation as a 'nation-state' writ small. However, it does not stop short at corporate building or renewal alone. The nexus of 'statesmanship' is and needs to be tested further at the point of maintaining, organizing and managing the collectivity (i.e., the enterprise or its macro counterpart, the nation-state) often under the emblem of an inspiring and altruistic vision of the leaders. The agenda here is an issue of constitutional reign, or what is labelled popularly as that of 'governance', which deals with the relationship between the manager and the managed, the ruler and the ruled, as well as the generic code of conduct pertaining to the behaviour of all interested parties (i.e., the key stakeholders, including the owner/shareholder, the staff and employees, and other salaried or honorary lay appointees like directors on the board). In the orthodox approach, Western prescription has always placed almost total reliance upon the board of directors as the governing body at the apex. However, it is suggested that there is hidden a supplementary, if not an alternative, normative mechanism which determines strategically the efficacy of corporate governance. This is the style, philosophy, assumptions and ethos espoused by the corporate leadership—inasmuch as it can set a role model for emulation by its staff and contribute to the consolidation of a body of business and work ethics and etiquette, as the inner logic or 'invisible hand' of corporate governance. In our case studies, it appears that corporate statesmanship has been attested to, in varying degrees in the two enterprises investigated, by such a quality of governance which is not only institutional (as epitomized structurally by the board of directors) but also normative in nature (as enshrined and embodied in the spirit and ethos of the leadership).

However, this type of personalized approach to governance, emphasizing the normative appeal of corporate leadership, raises in turn its intrinsic nature of volatility which may become exposed when (a) the leadership declines in its strength and charisma, or (b) more importantly, discontinuities arise because of management succession. The typical Chinese patrimonial approach of conserving a family regime by way of intergenerational hereditary arrangement has always provided a 'way' of coping with such succession and continuity. However, it is also commonplace knowledge that such a formula is notoriously bizarre, for it rests critically upon the calibre of the next-generation successors. Often, for want of such qualities, the tenacity of 'corporate statesmanship' is highly fragile, limited to just a 'single-generation' regime.

The machinery plant in our case studies is beset by such a dilemma. The potential risk perceived by its chairman about the emasculation of his 'statesmanship' (which is highly personalized) in the event of his abdication of power and control, has induced him to institute a hybrid arrangement of (a) 'socializing' part of his estate; (b) grooming his daughter as the heir 'apparent'; and (c) persisting in his own regime of 'rule by the person', in spite of his impending 'self-pronounced' retirement. In this context, the continuity of a statesman-like governance of his highly reputed machinery plant is questionable or even haphazard, apparently because of the innate conflict within the mind of the 'old guard' between his ego and his altruistic tendencies, which in the long run may undermine his trust in others and that of others in him.

Such a potential crisis of rupturing an established personalized regime of 'corporate statesmanship' is less conspicuous in the other case study. While the first case probably represents a highly popular 'personalized bureaucracy' which is relatively ill-equipped to perpetuate such 'statesmanship' by succession, it has been observed that the notion of 'corporate culture' has been captured with a remarkable degree of imagination and resilience in the second case, that of the steel plant. In either case, the tactful cultivation and insightful nurturing of a schematic corporate superstructure, anchored upon a successfully propagated 'normative consensus' which transcends the hierarchy, has enabled the corporation to tackle a two-fold issue with apparent effectiveness in:-

1. consolidating a normative structure of corporate governance parallel to the 'legalistic' board of directors system, which lays down an invisible framework for behaviour of trust, property and fidelity; and

2. addressing the problem of succession since the next generation of leadership has been groomed in advance within the 'embrace' of such a corporate culture which is directed, *inter alia*, towards the Confucian ideology of statesmanship in governance.

By comparison, the second case of the steel plant seems to be of stronger instructional value in our present exploratory inquiry into 'corporate statesmanship', because it is anchored upon a case of 'technocratic bureaucracy', yet humanized by a Confucian regime of corporate culture and leadership. Its chairman has been consistently cautious in detaching himself from any tendencies towards the aggrandizing personalized cult that could otherwise enshrine him as the 'immortal' helmsman of the enterprise. Instead, he has patiently and systematically engineered the orderly and holistic codification of a highly prudent yet altruistic code of practice—crystallized into a normative institution of governance which can readily be inherited by any future incumbents appointed to the 'Chief Executive' office after him.

The paper is exploratory and deals with the concept of 'corporate statesmanship' as underlying the effective functioning of organizations, their leadership, culture and succession issues. It is hoped that it will arouse interest both among academics and practitioners to look beyond the frontiers of management and entrepreneurship to see how the two issues converge to present an intriguing agenda of corporate governance, in normative as well as organizational terms that may ascend to the realm of 'statesmanship' in the reign of enterprises.

14

CHINESE CHIEF EXECUTIVE OFFICERS' EMPLOYEE CATEGORIZATION AND MANAGERIAL BEHAVIOUR

Borshiuan Cheng

CHINESE ENTREPRENEURIAL CEOs AND ECONOMIC DEVELOPMENT

Issues on the organization of Chinese enterprises have become interesting research topics in recent years. Of the many reasons for such a trend, three principal ones are: first, the four Dragons of East Asia have in the period from the 1960s to the 1980s achieved miraculously high economic growth. Taiwan, Hong Kong and Singapore are typical Chinese societies. Even Korea was once baptized in the traditional Chinese culture (Rozman, 1991). Second, Mainland China is thriving with its economic reform, and amazing success has already been achieved in the coastal areas. That is why Vogel (1989) once proclaimed that Guangdong would become the fifth dragon of Asia. Third, to many multinational corporations, investment in China has proved to be the key to upgrading their global competitiveness and the only sure way to profitability (Szterenfeld, 1994). By studying the characteristics of Chinese organizations, scholars have

The author wishes to express his sincere gratitude to Dr Yei-Yu Yeh for her assistance in revision.

attempted to gain understanding of the thrust behind economic achievement in the East Asia region.

Three approaches are usually used in the study of Chinese organizations: cultural tradition, market force, and authority system (Hamilton
and Biggart, 1989). Each approach has certain merits as well as limita-
tions. In the cultural approach, the major emphasis has been on the influence of Confucian ethics in the successful transition from agriculture to
modern industries. Though cultural differences do explain a part of the
scenario, it is to be noted that many Western countries have successfully
completed their transition without a Confucian legacy. Further, even
Malaysia and Thailand, lacking in Confucian ethics, expect to industrial-
ize by the beginning of the 21st century (Vogel, 1989). For all its possible
influences, culture is certainly not the only determining factor.

In the market approach, scholars stress the merits of free market as
the main force behind the economic achievement of Chinese societies. It
is argued that governments in these societies respect the market mechanism and leave the private enterprises alone without meddling. Therefore, capital, labour and resources can all be put to the most sensible
use for higher profits. Furthermore, those surviving the competition constitute the fittest enterprises with the most effective organization. As a
result, they grow in size through vertical integration (Chandler, 1977).
This argument explains the contrast between Taiwan's and Hong Kong's
experiences against Mainland China's economy before reform and liberalization. However, the mechanisms of free market usually lead to large
corporations with vertical hierarchy and loose inter-organizational network. Thus, the market approach fails to explain many phenomena in
Taiwan and Hong Kong where small/medium-sized enterprises are more
alive, inter-organizational network is interwoven tightly as a web, and
expansion is usually horizontal rather than vertical.

In the authority system, the state or the government plays a very important role in the process of economic development. Through policy formulation and intervention, the government can direct the development
of the economy. Take Taiwan for instance. Its government initiates
an export-oriented industrial policy while supporting the industry with
loans, subsidies, tax abatement, import control, technology transfer and
other means. The government is an invisible hand commanding economic
development. However, the merits of government dominance are debat-
able. While some attribute the economic growth to correct leadership by
the ruling Kuomintang party (C.H.C. Kao and Lee, 1991; Kuo, 1983),
others point to the negative impact of such a dominance (Chen et al.,
1991; C.C. Liu, 1975).

All the three approaches emphasize the macro and structural factors that have contributed to economic growth in the East Asian region. However, all have overlooked the contribution of individuals. As Adler and Fontana (1987) once emphasized, we must recognize the importance of individuals in the structure of society. In this respect, entrepreneurial CEOs play a key role. They do not take environmental changes passively. They take initiatives to interact with the environment and therefore play a decisive role in economic development (Schumpeter, 1934). It is the entrepreneurial CEOs who are influenced by and operate in the culture, who develop effective and profit-making enterprises in the free market, and who seize the opportunities created under the government control (Sato, 1993).

The impact of entrepreneurial CEOs on economic growth is evident in Taiwan, Hong Kong and coastal areas of Mainland China. In 1980, the coastal areas of Mainland China saw rapid economic development and this achievement was closely related to the participation of CEOs from Taiwan. It was the entrepreneurs from Shanghai who started industrialization in Hong Kong earlier than the other three dragons of East Asia (Wong, 1990). Working under the export-oriented industrial policy, the CEOs in both Taiwan and Hong Kong entered industrial sectors such as clothing, electronics, watches, and toys (Hsung and Hwang, 1992; Sato, 1993). Once contact was made with outside inter-organizational networks, they launched on production. Diversification began upstream from taking orders or export trading to the production of components downstream. An industry's operations were divided into smaller production units with the CEO in charge of each being financially independent. As a result, small/medium-sized enterprises bloomed in Taiwan and Hong Kong.

Because each production unit (or plant) has to be financially viable to survive, CEOs were market-oriented. They joined cooperative networks to form a consumer-oriented alliance, with all production and sales being focused on the needs and wants of the customers. This kind of organizational networking was highly successful (Nohria and Eccles, 1992; Powell, 1990; Snow and Miles, 1992). In fact, the consumer-oriented export network system could be the main reason for the competitive edges of both Taiwan and Hong Kong in the world market. Entrepreneurs positioned at the nodes of the network truly held the key to economic development.

THE CEO'S HIERARCHICAL STRUCTURE AND EMPLOYEE CATEGORIZATION

To run competitive market-oriented enterprises, Chinese CEOs had to raise total productivity. They were inevitably influenced by the culture in managing human resources in their enterprises. In a traditional society, power resides at the top and flows down through the hierarchies. Therefore, the Chinese tend to idolize the higher-up while belittling the lower class (Hamilton, 1984; K.S. Yang, 1988). Being high up at the vortex, Chinese CEOs hold a position of unshakeable superiority. In addition to being resource allocators like their Western counterparts, they stand for authority. Many empirical studies on the organization of Chinese enterprises have revealed great power distance, with contrasting interactions between people at the top and bottom levels (Cheng, 1993; Hofstede, 1980a; S.G. Redding, 1990; Silin, 1976). Holding power and control, the CEOs were flexible in the distribution of organizational resources, largely according to their personal likes or dislikes (Walder, 1983).

Equality not being much of a concern, Chinese CEOs categorize employees flexibly in order to manage human resources for raising total productivity. Through such categorization of employees, different roles are assigned to individuals. In view of the pivotal position of the CEOs and the subjectivity involved in employee categorization, it is necessary to understand the cognitive system and the management philosophy underlying such a practice (Brewer, 1988). Only then can the riddles of Chinese organizational life be unravelled (S.G. Redding, 1990).

The Confucianism-transformed hierarchical structure has been the essence of the Chinese social system (C.N. Chen, 1986; K.K. Hwang, 1988). As a result of a ten-year field study, Fei (1948), a comparative sociologist, emphasized that in contrast to the group structure in the West, the Chinese societal structure by tradition was hierarchical, like concentric ripples. Right at the centre was the principal figure and his relations with others in the society were like rings of ripples spreading outward one after the other. The farther one got away from the centre, interaction became less close. Thus, clear differences existed between the close and the distant, between the eminent and the humble.

Hierarchical structure is an important cultural legacy of the traditional Chinese society, and its influence on organizational structure and the CEO's employee categorization cannot be minimized. Cultural values and the context in which an organization exists mediate the nature of the hierarchical structure.

In the traditional Chinese culture, the principle of harmonious relationship among roles is highly important. Within a hierarchical relationship, a CEO demands loyalty to the authority and unreserved commitment to the organization. Thus, relationship (*guanxi*) and loyalty (*zhongcheng*) enter into the structure of employee categorization. The third element in employee categorization is related to the context in which an organization exists. An enterprise has its own goals and missions. In carrying on business activities to attain the established goal of the organization, it is only natural to expect excellent work performance from the members. Thus, competence (*chaineng*) is also an essential factor in a CEO's employee categorization.

In terms of all three aspects, employee categorization in Chinese enterprises is structurally hierarchical. A CEO can categorize employees according to three criteria, namely, whether or not they are ethnically related by kinship or parakinship (*guanxi*); whether they possess unfailing loyalty and unreserved obedience to the CEO (*zhongcheng*); and whether by their ability and motivation they can fulfil the goals assigned to them by the CEO in the organization (*chaineng*). The three basic elements in employee categorization are illustrated in Figure 14.1.

Figure 14.1
The Dynamics of CEO's Employee Categorization

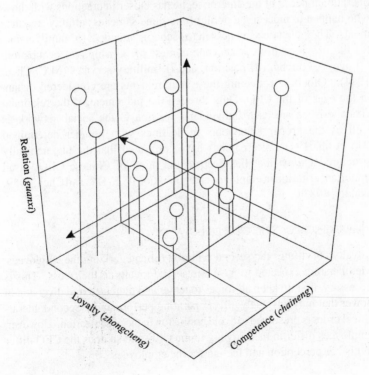

It has often been observed that the hierarchically structured relationship is the only standard for employee categorization in Chinese enterprises (C.N. Chen, 1986; K.K. Hwang, 1988). Such a view is simplistic and ignores the reality. Even in family-owned enterprises, the CEO maintains a distinction between his family and the enterprise. Different principles are utilized for running them (Pan, 1989). Though both kinship and *guanxi* have considerable influence, they are not the only factors in employee categorization. Only by considering competence and loyalty together with kinship and *guanxi* can a veridical picture of the interactions among individuals and groups in a Chinese enterprise be delineated.

HIERARCHICALLY STRUCTURED *GUANXI*

According to the tradition of hierarchical structure existing in Chinese society, *guanxi* can be close or distant. A CEO's relations with members of the organization vary from person to person. He is closer to those who are his relatives. As for 'non-relatives' recruited to meet the operational needs of the enterprise, he has closer interactions with those who happen to meet some or all of the 'nine sameness affinity' requirements. They include sameness in (*a*) schools attended, (*b*) family name, (*c*) the province from which one comes, (*d*) kinship, (*e*) occupation, (*f*) age, (*g*) hobby, (*h*) position, and (*i*) military services (M.C. Chen, 1984). Others not meeting these requirements are considered distant in the eyes of the CEO. Only through the judgement of the relational characteristics are each individual's position in the social network as well as the proper behaviours in dealings with him/her determined (Ho et al., 1991). Researches have confirmed that the hierarchically structured *guanxi* that lies deep in the mind of Chinese CEOs is an important criterion in employee categorization (C.S. Kao and Chen, 1989; Walder, 1983).

HIERARCHICALLY STRUCTURED LOYALTY

Loyalty constitutes the second criterion for categorizing the employees. Members are expected to have unreserved loyalty to their boss. This is necessary, first, to keep all forces together and thereby avoid diversion in power that may adversely affect operating performance. Second, hierarchical order is preserved to avoid confusion in the organization. However, employees differ in their loyalty to the CEO and so does the CEO differ in his/her perception and feeling for the employees.

Basically, loyalty reflects a faith in the organization or its CEO (C.Y. Liu, 1982). Unreserved devotion and unswerving loyalty that are required of all members of the organization are based on the linkage between patronage and gratitude, with the boss patronizing as the benefactor. In whatever way loyalty may be interpreted by various chief executives, the fundamental requirement remains the same. All members are expected to be receptive to the CEO's beliefs in the company's goals and values and to stand ready to put in extra efforts whenever required.

HIERARCHICALLY STRUCTURED COMPETENCE

An organization has its goals. Adequate performance on the part of the members is required to keep the organization alive and growing. Due to differing circumstances in the organization, work performance may vary. However, a degree of consistency between a member's work behaviour and his/her performance does exist (Fleishman, 1967) and is used in employee categorization.

Competence is a function of the member's work ability and his/her motivation. Since ability and motivation are difficult to observe, CEOs judge their employees by objective criteria like work performance, work quality, and work efficiency. Alternatively, some subjective indicators of performance are also utilized (Reitz, 1977; Vroom, 1964). As a result of long interaction between the CEO and the employees, members of the organization gradually get categorized according to their competence.

Based on the foregoing criteria, a CEO may categorize employees into eight prototypes. As depicted in Figure 14.2, they are designated as (a) Management Apex (close/loyal/competent), (b) Business Assistant (close/loyal/mediocre), (c) Haughty Guy (close/rebel/competent), (d) Unworthy Scion (close/rebel/mediocre), (e) Career Partner (distant/ loyal/ competent), (f) Message Informer (distant/loyal/mediocre), (g) Monitored Target (distant/rebel/competent), and (h) Peripheral Personnel (distant/rebel/mediocre). These eight prototypes play different roles in the organization. Consequently, the rules of the CEO's interactions with these eight prototypes constitute the operating basis for organizational behaviour in Chinese enterprises.

Prototype A (Management Apex) is the soul of the organization and enjoys a high position with a lot of power, and constitutes the core of decision-making. Prototype B (Business Assistant), though lesser in ability, receives a lot of care and attention because of his/her close *guanxi* (interrelatedness) with the boss. This person may spend time idly

Figure 14.2
Employee Categorization and Prototypes

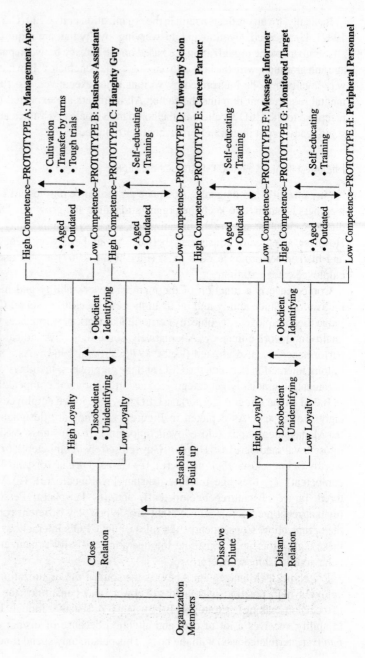

while handling only confidential matters like internal accounting and auditing.

Prototype C (Haughty Guy) has a close relation with the CEO and is highly talented. But he/she is not obedient and often clashes with the CEO. The latter adopts a conflict-avoidance approach in dealing with such an employee. Prototype D may be called the Unworthy Scion because, except for his close relations with the CEO, he/she lacks in loyalty as well as competence. Whether such an employee is allowed to occupy an important position in the company is a moot question for the CEO.

Prototype E (Career Partner) is a key figure in the organization and a principal managerial talent. Though not closely related with the boss, this person is heavily relied on by the boss and is his right-hand man due to both his competence and loyalty. However, since Prototype E lacks in kinship or parakinship relations, he/she is unable to become the key person in the organization despite having a position of importance and responsibility. Prototype F (Message Informer) is a monitor working as the CEO's eyes and ears. Owing to unswerving loyalty, he/she has the boss's trust; but his/her incompetence restricts the person to petty roles only. He proves helpful in monitoring Prototype G against clique formation for self-interest. He helps the boss in collecting information on the employees about their daily lives and work. The main role is to keep the CEO always informed about the employees.

Prototype G (Monitored Target) is the last person with whom the boss feels safe. Despite competence and performance, Prototype G lacks in *guanxi* and is unwilling to pledge his/her allegiance to the boss. Therefore, the boss remains suspicious and is on his guard at all times lest the person divulge highly confidential information. Prototype H is peripheral. Incompetent, distantly related, and unable to show his loyalty to the boss, he/she remains only a temporary worker in a low position. If the organization decides to lay off, such a person is the first to get the axe. Studies on Taiwanese enterprises have demonstrated that all the prototypes are to be found in the real setting (Cheng, 1993; C.H. Lin, 1993).

THE DYNAMICS OF EMPLOYEE CATEGORIZATION

The dynamic nature of employee categorization has often been overlooked by researchers who consider relationships (*guanxi*) to be steady and static (Fei, 1948; K.K. Hwang, 1988). Change in categorization is not a gradual and continuous process. Consistent with the catastrophe theory, there are shifts and changes in both forward and backward directions. Though the impressions already formed by the CEO about employees display a kind of inertia and resist change, shifts in categorization occur when an employee's behaviour is inconsistent and repeatedly deviates from the expectations. What exactly makes an executive recategorize the employees?

POSITION CHANGE IN CLOSE/DISTANT *GUANXI*

The structure of an organization based on employee categorization as close or distant is dynamic and often changes over the years (Chiao, 1982; C.H. Lin, 1993). A distant *guanxi* may become close if new relationships are acquired. The opposite may also happen. Generally speaking, newly developed *guanxi* (relationship) may comprise marriage, adoption, and sworn brother/sisterhood. Further, with regular effort, employees may also change the relationship with the CEO. Such acquired and cultivated *guanxi* are not only common but widespread in Chinese society (Chiao, 1982). Common practices in this respect are claiming kinship, seeking personal ties, worming one's way through, doing favours, keeping contact and sending gifts.

On the other hand, *guanxi* may also get diluted or dissolved. The dissolution of *guanxi* includes divorces between close relatives, and breakups between parents and sons/daughters. As for dilution, it ranges from reducing dealings, making no gift or favour, not yielding to appeals for favour, to be coldly disowning of all one's relatives and friends. Thus, for the CEO there is no 'permanent friend or foe', as relationships with employees may shift from close to distant.

POSITION CHANGE IN LOYAL/REBEL QUALITIES

In the eyes of the chief executive, employees' loyalty varies with changes in behaviour. However, keeping the CEO's needs in mind, they are expected to conform to their proper roles (Hamilton, 1984).

An 'obedient' or 'identifying' employee wins the boss's heart, and vice versa (Cheng, 1993). Compliant subordinates are apt to lay emphasis on the interpersonal harmony between the higher-ups and the underlings. Hence, they openly echo the CEO's views, acknowledging the power distance in the pecking order and appreciating what the boss may have in his mind. They always try to create an impression and defend the CEO's face and prestige. Being sensitive to words and facial expressions, they are adept at understanding the intentions of the boss, and they seldom raise demands for resource-sharing. Further, 'identifying' consists of loyalty, accommodating behaviour, embracing the CEO's concept of management, and performing duties honestly. These employees cater so much to the boss's intents and wishes that they tend to take 'all slanders themselves while crediting all honors to the top' (Cheng, 1988).

When an employee repeatedly disobeys and fails to be 'identifying', he/she is degraded and the position on the dimension of loyalty is accordingly shifted. In the eyes of a chief executive, disobedient behaviour is usually found among those who are individualistic, ready to show off, openly oppose the boss, demand equality, display egoistic tendencies, and are blunt, inconsiderate, likely to embarrass the leader, and haggle for sharing resources (Cheng, 1993). Those who challenge the CEO's authority, criticize the management, pursue profit at the cost of honour, or try to outshine the boss with their high achievements, are more likely to get downgraded in loyalty by the chief executive (Chou, 1984).

POSITION CHANGE IN TALENT/MEDIOCRE ABILITIES

The chief executive does not hold a fixed opinion about subordinates when their actual performance changes consistently. Subordinates can improve their professional experience through self-training or discipline. Other methods to change their position on the dimension of competence include devotion to work, willingness to go in for training, and not shying away from trials and tribulations or from self-disciplining. Thus, an attitude of 'You do the job and I feel okay' can be firmly established (C.H. Lin, 1993). Eventually, the actual achievements may alter the CEO's previously formed impressions.

With rapid advances in science and new innovations, existing technology soon becomes out-of-date. Similarly, with changing external environment, organizations transform themselves, and existing knowledge about the management and organizations becomes obsolete (P. Drucker, 1989). A practice successful in the past may not guarantee success in the future (Zelikoff, 1969). Thus, those members of the organization who stay in the rut are doomed to fall behind. Further, slow learners are unable to catch up with new knowledge and technological innovations. Advancing age also acts as a factor in their willingness to learn and change. All these lead to reduced performance, and a lowering of the CEO's impression about their competence. The dynamic processes involved and the various influences operating on shifts in position are depicted in Figure 14.2.

INTERACTIONS AMONG THE CEO
AND PROTOTYPICAL EMPLOYEES

THE CEO'S VALUES, TRUST AND/OR IN-GROUP BIAS

Studies have confirmed the influence of the CEO's values on organizational design and behaviours (Eisenhardt and Schoonhoven, 1990; Hambrick and Brandon, 1988; Mintzberg, 1989). The CEO's preference for and emphasis on a particular categorization standard lead to differences in the degree of trust in and/or in-group bias against the eight prototypes of employees, or in in-group consciousness.

Table 14.1 shows how a CEO would rate his trust in employees among the eight prototypes by differential weighing of the three aspects (i.e., relationship, loyalty and competence) in employee categorization. When a CEO considers *guanxi* to be more important than loyalty, which in turn is regarded as more important than competence, the weighing follows 'R > L > C'. Consequently, the eight prototypes of employees would be rated in descending order of degree of trust as: A-B-C-D-E-F-G-H. For a weighing rank of 'R > C > L', the order of trust is A-C-B-D-E-G-F-H. With the weighing rank being 'L > R > C', the order of trust is A-B-E-F-C-D-G-H. For 'L > C > R', A-E-B-F-C-G-D-H would be the order of trust the CEO places on employees of different prototypes. For 'C > R > L', the degree of trust among eight prototypes is in the order of A-C-E-G-B-D-F-H. With weighing of 'C > L > R', A-E-C-G-B-F-D-H is the order in which a CEO would trust an employee by categorization.

In summary, a CEO's trust in the prototypes and the in-group bias varies because of his/her own values or preferences for the three categorizing standards. All CEOs would trust Prototype A the most with the highest in-group consciousness. Such differences in trust and in-group consciousness in turn produce far-reaching influences on organizational behaviour.

IN-GROUP BIAS AND MANAGEMENT BEHAVIOUR

Since CEOs categorize their subordinates and hold varying degrees of trust and in-group feeling for each prototype, bias is inevitable and is reflected in managerial behaviour (Chang, 1995; Wilder, 1986). The CEOs divide employees into in-groups and out-groups, and respond and treat the two differently.

Table 14.1
Relationship among CEO Values, Employee Categorization, In-group Consciousness and Trust Formation

Trust	Relation Weighing		Loyalty Weighing		Competence Weighing		In-group Consciousness
	Loyalty	Competence	Relation	Competence	Relation	Loyalty	
High	A	A	A	A	A	A	In-group
↑	B	C	B	E	C	E	↑
	C	B	E	B	E	C	
	D	D	F	F	G	G	
	E	E	C	C	B	B	
	F	G	D	G	D	F	
↓	G	F	G	D	F	D	↓
Low	H	H	H	H	H	H	Out-group

A: Management Apex   B: Business Assistant   C: Haughty Guy
D: Unworthy Scion   E: Career Partner   F: Message Informer
G: Monitored Target   H: Peripheral Personnel

Emotional Attachment

The emotional relationship that develops between the CEO and out-group subordinates results from work and work contracts. Since both sides are related by contractual rights and obligations, the relationship is neither close nor affectionate. In such a situation, one can hardly expect congeniality, intimacy and feelings of mutual trust to develop (Tsui and O'Reilly, 1989). As such, there is no feeling of obligation on the part of the CEO to look after out-group employees. The relationship with the in-group subordinates is different. Apart from the feeling of mutual closeness, both sides are attracted to and trust each other, and the CEO feels obliged to look after these subordinates. Moreover, in terms of management philosophy, the CEO tends to apply Theory Y to in-group subordinates and Theory X to out-group subordinates.

This differential in trust results in differences in perceptions of the behaviours of in-group and out-group subordinates. In-group and out-group subordinates in their turn interpret the decisions of the CEO differently. Thus, similar behaviours are interpreted differently by the two groups. With in-group subordinates, a benign cycle is likely to be produced. With out-group subordinates, a vicious cycle is more likely (Graen and Scandura, 1987).

Leadership Style

The CEOs also deal differently with in-group and out-group subordinates. Generally speaking, in-group employees hold a more congenial hierarchical relationship with the CEO, with each understanding what the other thinks and feels. As such, in-group employees participate more frequently in decision-making. A CEO may privately ask in-group employees for their opinions, thereby allowing them to influence his decision (Silin, 1976). Apart from formal occasions, in-group employees can make informal contacts with the CEO (C.H. Lin, 1993), and express their comments and recommendations informally. Further, CEOs tend to delegate greater power to in-group subordinates for a wider range of business activities. As for out-group employees, they can expect, if at all, only limited delegation (Chang, 1995). The CEOs also tend to treat in-group employees in a liberal manner, and are more considerate and human-relation-oriented. On the contrary, they are strict, demanding and task-oriented towards out-group subordinates. In other words, the CEO acts as a benevolent autocrat toward in-group subordinates and a complete autocrat toward out-group subordinates (Cheng, 1993).

Organizational Structure

An organization is like a conical pyramid, with more people at the bottom but only a few at the top. Its characteristics can be described along three dimensions: vertical differentiation, horizontal differentiation, and central differentiation. Vertical differentiation represents hierarchy in the organization; horizontal differentiation divides all the hierarchy functions and jobs into various departments. As for central differentiation, it distinguishes each individual employee by the importance of his/her role in the organization, or by his/her distance from the decision-making centre (Van Maanen and Schein, 1979).

Given the CEOs' differentials in trust, in-group employees are likely to be at high or middle levels of management and operation, while out-group employees tend to be at a low level of execution and implementation. In terms of horizontal differentiation, the work of in-group employees is mostly concerned with functions vital to the company, like the business department of a trading company, with taxation, accounting and matters confidential to the company, and with the company's personnel and auditing (Cheng, 1993). As for out-group employees, they carry on jobs of lesser importance to the company. In short, in-group employees play key roles in the organization while out-group employees' functions are peripheral and they are easily replaceable.

Job Design

To facilitate close control over out-group employees, they are usually assigned jobs that are clearly structured and determined by objective criteria. Thus, out-group employees have less flexibility and have to work strictly according to job specification or description. Conversely, the jobs assigned to in-group employees are less structured and they enjoy greater flexibility. As a result, performance control is relatively lax.

Employment

In terms of longevity, a CEO often plans for long-term employment for the in-group and accordingly arranges for their career development. They are provided with more opportunities for education and training with the expectation that they would prosper with the enterprise (K.T. Lin, 1987). Consequently, in-group employees get faster promotions. On the other hand, out-group employees do not enjoy such advantages and are often employed on a temporary basis. As such, when the economy is booming, a great number is hired; but once recession comes, they are laid off or dispensed with on some excuse or other.

Resource Allocation

In-group employees have more opportunities to be rewarded and in greater amounts (Bond and Hwang, 1986), and the reverse is true for out-group employees. Outwardly, a company's wage and incentive systems seem to follow the objective criteria of greater rewards for better performance. In reality, this is not always the case. Social responsibility and equality principles apply to in-group employees, while for out-group employees, equity principles with greater rewards for better performance and vice versa prevail. Moreover, in-group employees have more opportunities to use production and service resources such as budget, personnel, or other facilities. As a result, there is a benign cycle between in-group employees and their performance (Pfeffer, 1981).

Job Attitude

The foregoing discussion would indicate that CEOs differ substantially in their interactions with in-group and out-group employees, resulting in the development of different work attitudes. Not many studies on attitudinal differences are available. However, there are indications that where mutual trust exists between the leader and the employees, the latter are more willing to work hard and meet the leader's expectations (Cheng, 1993; Graen and Scandura, 1987; Katz and Kahn, 1978). In

Table 14.2
Relationship between In-group Bias and Organizational Behaviour

Organizational Behaviour	In-group	Out-group
1. Attachment:		
Management philosophy	Y	X
Intimacy	High	Low
Obligation	High	Low
Attractiveness	Strong	Weak
Trust	High	Low
2. Leadership:		
Hierarchical relationship	Fit	Unfit
Decision-making participation	More	Less
Two-way communication	More	Less
Delegation	Great	Little
Treatment	Kind	Harsh
3. Organizational structure:		
Hierarchy	High	Low
Centrality	Central	Peripheral
Function	Important	Unimportant
4. Job design:		
Work structure	Obscure	Clear
Role flexibility	Greater	Less
Performance control	Loose	Tight
5. Employment:		
Employment condition	Lifetime	Short-term
Promotion speed	Fast	Slow
Promotion latitude	Greater	Less
Training	More	Less
Career planning	With	Without
6. Resources allocation:		
Reward criterion	Non-performance	Performance
Reward size	High	Low
Other resources	More	Less
7. Job attitude:		
Job satisfaction	High	Low
Role compliance	High	Low
Organizational commitment	High	Low
Organizational citizenship behaviour	High	Low
Turnover	Low	High

addition, recent studies on kindness-repaying behaviours inside Chinese organizations display a positive relationship of kindness-giving and -repaying between a superior and his employees and their performance (C.M. Liu, 1994).

Being trusted, it is only natural for the in-group employees to develop a feeling of gratitude. Consequently, they are not only more willing to devote themselves to work but also show compliance, work satisfaction, and higher commitment to the organization. Besides, they are more likely to volunteer for extra work whenever beneficial to the organization. Their turnover is also relatively low. On the other hand, out-group employees perceive relations with the CEO and the organization as purely formal. In the absence of affectional bonds, their work satisfaction and organizational behaviour are likely to be relatively low. Possessing an unfavourable attitude toward their job, they show higher turnover (Chang, 1995; F.S. Hwang, 1977). Possible relationships between in-group consciousness and organization behaviour are summarized in Table 14.2.

CONCLUSION

For a long time, studies on the economic development of Chinese enterprises have focused on macro factors that are external to the organization, such as Confucian ethics, government role, and market mechanism. They have overlooked the role of the chief executives in Chinese enterprises, who have been the key factors in making these structural factors work successfully.

Joining the enterprise, CEOs develop a cooperative network of mutually complementing organizations forming a consumer-oriented alliance. Having the power and authority to manage human resources and to raise productivity, they set up a vertically integrated cooperation system. Developing a cooperative network with many organizations attending to consumers' needs is a major reason behind the excellent achievements of the Chinese enterprises in Hong Kong, Taiwan and Singapore from around the 1960s to the 1990s. The chief executives, who manage human resources with unquestionable authority to fulfil the missions of the organizations, constitute the nodes of this network.

Besides being the owner-manager of an enterprise, a Chinese CEO also plays the role of the head of the family. He is not only the information centre and the resource allocator but also responsible for the success and failure of the enterprise. Hence, he exerts a decisive influence on the enterprise (S.G. Redding et al., 1994; Silin, 1976). The key role of the CEOs has largely gone unnoticed and needs to be explored systematically.

To understand the CEO's managerial behaviour, the author contends that it is essential to analyze the key role of the underlying cognitive structure in categorizing the employees. It has been pointed out that, mediated by reasonable resource allocation, uncertainty reduction and vertical goal congruence, employee categorization has a positive effect on organizational effectiveness (Cheng, 1995; Graen and Scandura, 1987). It is contended that the Chinese CEOs place all their employees in eight prototypes according to the degrees of *guanxi*, loyalty, and competence. By analyzing the differentials in the nature of a CEO's employee categorization, interactions between the CEO and each prototype can be understood, and the complex, diversified, and characteristic organizational behaviour inside Chinese enterprises can be appreciated.

Many scholars conducting cross-culture studies on Chinese enterprises consider familism and kinship as the only important characteristics (C.N. Chen, 1986; S.G. Redding et al., 1994). This is a simplistic view. Though the loyalty and competence of the employee are still considered important and cannot be ignored (C.S. Kao, 1990), one has to take into account the dynamics of employee categorization, which most people believe to be static with hierarchical order remaining unchanged. Such a view ignores the common phenomenon of inter-prototype shifts due to position changes on each dimension: between close and distant, loyal and rebel, talented and mediocre. It is only by understanding the dynamic nature of employee categorization and prototype shifts that one can gain insight into the functioning of Chinese enterprises.

The importance of the interactions between external structural factors and the managerial behaviour of the chief executives is first emphasized. Following Fei's view that 'society and individuals are two inseparable identities always complementing each other' (H.T. Fei, 1994: 21), the systematic exploration of CEOs' managerial behaviour by analyzing their cognitive structure of employee categorization is stressed. Second, the vital influence of the CEOs in shaping organizational culture—which is itself an important research topic (E.H. Schein, 1985; 1990)—is also emphasized, particularly in the context of employee categorization and the linking of loyalty and competence with interrelatedness (*guanxi*). Only through such knowledge can one penetrate deep into the relationship between organizational culture and organizational behaviour in Chinese enterprises.

Further, being the key figure, all human relations and power in the organization revolve around the CEO. This is the reason why succession struggle inside Chinese enterprises is so intense. Since human relations inside an organization are built around its CEO, once he/she retires or passes away, all existing power relationships in the organization dissolve. The person who assumes the position of the new CEO has the supreme power to recategorize the employees and reallocate power. Therefore, in the process of the transition, sibling fights, duels for the 'throne', emergence of factions, meddling by the relatives of the erstwhile boss, grudges between the new boss and former executives, and disputes between in-group and out-group members develop (S.C. Hsu, 1993). In conclusion, the role of the chief executives in the functioning of the organization holds the key to the mystery of rapid growth and success of Chinese enterprises.

15

The Role of *Chin-Shins* of Top Managers in Taiwanese Organizations: Exploring Chinese Leadership Phenomena

Shu-Cheng Chi

The increased interest in understanding organizational behaviour across different cultures in recent years has been helpful to both management theorists and practitioners. Japanese practices have probably received the most attention. Ouchi, who proposed the well-known Theory Z, has suggested that Japanese companies operate with unique systems of incentives and control (Ouchi, 1981). Understanding the effects of such systems (e.g., lifetime employment policy) can be beneficial both to managers in other countries and to the development of a comparative theory of behaviour in organizations. Similarly, the recently booming economies of China and other nations of the Pacific Rim have become a major recent focus of international interest that has stimulated interest in the management styles of Chinese organizations.

This paper focuses on an important leadership phenomenon in Taiwanese organizations: the role of '*chin-shins*' (or confidants, the equivalent term in English) of top managers. *Chin-shins* (confidants) hold special positions in their superiors' relational networks. The concept of *chin-shin* is composed of two subconcepts: *chin* and *shin*. *Chin* has the meaning of closeness, while *shin* signifies trustworthiness. In other words, a *chin-shin* refers to a subordinate who is close and trustworthy to a superior. Often times, a *chin-shin* is more than an ordinary subordinate to a superior; in some cases there can be pseudo-kinship. A *chin-shin* relationship will, however, gradually fade away when employment relationships end.

Examples of *chin-shins* are found throughout Chinese history. Historically, many political figures have become widely known as successful *chin-shins* of their superiors/emperors. And the roles of *chin-shins* continue in contemporary Taiwanese organizations where they are crucial to managers' decision-making practices. In this paper, we shall examine the various roles of top managers' *chin-shins* in Taiwan. Drawing on the author's studies, a general description of the *chin-shin* phenomenon will be developed and discussed.

SOCIAL NETWORKS IN TAIWANESE SOCIETIES

Taiwanese societies are traceable to Chinese ancestors. Having been separated from Mainland China since 1949, Taiwan has been moving toward political democracy as well as functioning as an independent economic entity. But, despite the significant difference in political systems between Taiwan and communist China, their complex social networks are similar. *Guan-shi*, for instance, as has been suggested by many theorists, is an important social mechanism in Chinese societies (e.g., Huang, 1985). Both in Taiwan and China, to have 'connections' with someone is helpful in conducting business activities. *Guan-shi* exists in different degrees, and individuals belong to sets of overlapping social networks.

Fei (1948) has used the notion of 'differential order' to describe Chinese societies, arguing that Chinese people do not perceive themselves as related to each other on unequal bases. Metaphorically, Fei explains, a person can be thought of as being at the centre of a set of concentric circles: the closer the circles the stronger the relational ties. Rights and obligations are understood differently depending upon the relative positions of people and the terms of their relationships. Family is the basic unit in Chinese (and in Taiwanese) societies. Circles of outsiders normally take the second place to kinship (G. Redding and Wong, 1986). *Guan-shi* derived from employment relations usually does not supersede family origins. A *chin-shin*, however, often holds a special status locating near the centre of differential order of his/her leader. Compared to other members, the *chin-shin*'s *guan-shi* with the superior is very unique.

CHIN-SHIN VS IN-GROUP

In the Western leadership literature, it is commonly suggested that leaders maintain homogeneous relationships with their subordinates (e.g., Fiedler, 1967). Graen and his associates have argued, however, that leaders develop differential exchange relationships with individual subordinates (Dansereau et al., 1975; Graen and Cashman, 1975). Indeed, leaders generally establish special relationships with a small number of trusted subordinates (an in-group). They may pay relatively more attention to these members, and less to their remaining subordinates (the out-group). Graen and Cashman argue that the in-group or out-group relationship is established through a pattern of dyadic interaction between a leader and particular subordinates. Selection of in-group members is made on the basis of experience with their competence and dependability. Dyadic exchanges with in-group subordinates follow a different developmental path from that for out-group subordinates. Members in an in-group are given high levels of trust, interaction, support, and formal/informal reward, while members in an out-group receive low levels of trust, interaction, support, and reward.

These ideas may help to explain the phenomenon of chin-shins. Chin-shins may be regarded as an 'in-group' or, more exactly, the 'core' of an in-group. They are very close to the centre of a differential order owing to a strong exchange relationship with a leader. This relationship makes a chin-shin important to the roles played by superiors in social networks. In a sample of 62 Taiwanese high-level managers, we (Chi and Lin, 1994) found significant differences in their perceptions of closeness and trustworthiness across three categories of subordinates: (a) chin-shins, (b) in-group members (but not chin-shins), and (c) out-group members. The relationship between chin-shin and superior goes beyond instrumental social exchange. A chin-shin may perceive his/her superior as someone who deserves true-hearted gratitude. Such feelings toward a superior are expressed as a sense of 'pau-en' which, in Chinese, means unreserved repayment to someone else. (The meanings of chin-shin in relation to pau-en originated in Confucius' teachings about the kinds of relationships between emperor and subordinate. If a subordinate demonstrates loyalty towards his/her emperor, an emperor will correspondingly treat the subordinate with sincerity.)

As a further exploration of chin-shin relationships, the author (Chi, 1995) studied 58 manager/chin-shin dyads for their perceptions of each other. The results showed partial, and negative, correlations between *chin-shin* relationships and instrumental *ren-chyng* between them, but were positively related to affective *ren-chyng* between them.[1] Hence, it would seem that exchange theory may explain early stages of *chin-shin* relationships but not its maintenance. As a *chin-shin*'s roles become well-established, the relationship shifts from a transactional basis to an affective one; and it seems likely that, as superior and *chin-shin* draw each other closer to the centre of differential social matrices, their relationships are transformed into a different status and, the more central the circle, the more a person needs to maintain an unreserved attitude.

EXAMPLES OF *CHIN-SHINS* IN CHINESE HISTORY

There are numerous examples of *chin-shins* in Chinese history. Some of them were strategists, some militarists, some politicians. These people approached the power centre of their time and lent support to their superiors. Yen (1987) identified four major types of historical *chin-shins*: Officer of Interior, Head of Intelligence Office, Key Government Officer, and Servants. The first type, Officer of Interior, started in the West Han Dynasty where the *chin-shin* role was first institutionalized. Emperors subjected their major decision power to the interior majesty. With the East Han Dynasty this office became the office of the emperor.

The second type of *chin-shins* is called Head of Intelligence Office. This office was established because of the emperor's dominance. It served as an information-gathering source from both domestic and foreign sources. This office later became the means to strengthen the empire and even to destroy nonconformers. Third, owing to their special relationships with their emperors, Key Government Officers often possessed more power than other people. Finally, Servants close to the emperors knew clearly what those emperors wanted, and so could exhibit authority that others could not.

Since *chin-shins* held key positions and became extremely influential, emperors had to choose them with care. Western leadership theorists have suggested that superiors consider in-group members on factors such as task competence, loyalty, shared values, and friendliness (Yukl, 1994). Many Eastern scholars, however, emphasize a different set of criteria,

---

[1] P.C. Yu (1993) distinguishes between instrumental *ren-chyng* and affective *ren-chyng* in Chinese societies. Instrumental *ren-chyng*, he argues, means that a person establishes a relationship with another person for the purpose of his/her own self-interest. On the other hand, affective *ren-chyng* means that a person maintains a relationship with another person with a goal of interpersonal attachment.

which were originally proposed by Emperor Tang Tai-Chung as the Six Good and Six Evil Principles. The Six Good Principles refer to a saint subordinate, a kind subordinate, a loyal subordinate, a wise subordinate, a virtuous subordinate, and a straightforward subordinate. The Six Evil Principles refer to a lazy subordinate, a flattering subordinate, an evil subordinate, a talkative subordinate, a rebellious subordinate, and a subordinate who ruins the country. Basically, the Six Good Principles are about virtue, wisdom, loyalty, industry, frankness, and foresight, while the Six Evil Principles denote greed, flattery, talkativeness, evil-heartedness, destructiveness, and misplacement of good and evil. In sum, then, a successful *chin-shin* should possess the moral assertiveness to tell good and evil apart, a wise and strategic sense, and moral integrity so as not to be afraid of the consequences of speaking up. Those who run contradictory to these principles bring distrust, conflict, and disaster to the empire.

Based upon some famous examples in the history of China and Japan, Sakaiya (1993) argued that the most precious persons in organizations are the ones who help the leaders build their heritage. He suggested three things that are necessary for these persons' effectiveness: unselfish passion, upholding the fundamental goals of the leader, and having no thought of becoming a successor to the leader. In other words, *chin-shins* do not seek credit for themselves or personal pride. They are satisfied with their role without receiving overt credit. Second, *chin-shins* hold steadfastly to the guidelines of their leaders. Only when their goals are in line with those of their leaders can their talents and wisdom be discovered and fully utilized. Finally, *chin-shins* must not have thoughts of becoming successors to their superiors, at least not when their leaders are still in power. Thus, they can be successful because they hold firmly to their 'left-right' hand role.

THE FIVE ROLES OF *CHIN-SHINS* IN TAIWANESE ORGANIZATIONS

We now turn to a discussion of the operative roles of *chin-shins* in Taiwanese organizations: (*a*) decision aide, (*b*) public relations agent, (*c*) black/white face, (*d*) information gatekeeper, and (*e*) resource controller.

DECISION AIDE

One of the most important roles of *chin-shins* is that they may serve as decision aides to superiors. What this means is that they facilitate superiors' handling of various tasks. *Chin-shins* help by making routine decisions when their superiors are absent. *Chin-shins* take over tasks for them, thereby leaving managers more time to handle other more important ones. In addition, *chin-shins* often serve as advisors, giving valuable suggestions to their superiors, coming up with ideas for their superiors, or acting as devil's advocates so their superiors do not rush too fast into decisions. In Taiwanese organizations, a manager's personal stamp often stands for the person himself/herself. Therefore, a *chin-shin* is one who has the authority to use the manager's personal stamp and sign documents on his/her behalf.

In the old teachings by Tang Tai-tsung, a *chin-shin* needs to have moral integrity and straightness. To be a good facilitator, a *chin-shin* must give proper advice to the superior without fear for his/her safety. (In olden days, *chin-shins* might have been executed because they said something that superiors did not want to hear.) Still, an important task for a *chin-shin* is to give personal suggestions to the superior, and let him/her evaluate alternatives.

PUBLIC RELATIONS AGENT

The second role of a *chin-shin* is as 'public relations agents'. In Chinese societies, personal connections and relationships are very important. *Chin-shins* may help managers maintain relationships with people outside the company. Social networking often is in a context of differential social status. People in different statuses build relationships with others of similar social class. Through *chin-shins*, managers may extend their informal ties with people in different social classes. Also, as already mentioned, individuals have their own differential matrices and managers may use their *chin-shins'* *guan-shis* to expand their own relational matrices.

Chin-shins may also help managers establish closer relationships with other subordinates. There is relatively high power distance between top managers and subordinates in Taiwanese organizations (Hofstede, 1980a) and managers at the top maintain a paternal role which makes them remote from subordinates at the bottom. *Chin-shins* can serve as an intermediary mechanism to facilitate information flow and also better human relations. *Chin-shins*, in short, can be friends to other subordinates, and it is easier for friends to talk about their feelings toward the company to a *chin-shin* than to a high-level manager, provided of course that the *chin-shin* is trusted by subordinates.

BLACK/WHITE FACE

The third role of *chin-shins* is the 'black/white face'. Theorists have argued that individuals are managers of others' impressions in their everyday activities (e.g., Tedeschi, 1981; Tetlock and Manstead, 1985). Relatedly, Huang (1985) speaks of 'face-making' as an important mechanism that affects individual behaviour in Taiwanese societies. That is, a person may purposely construct impressions in order to justify his or her social position or prestige to others. Goffman (1955) classifies human behaviour into two aspects: front-stage and back-stage, and Huang argues that 'face-making' is the front-stage behaviour for those people in mixed relationship networks, while 'sincere behaviour' is the back-stage behaviour for only those people in the affective networks. Thus, individuals may purposefully arrange the settings of interaction with others and manage their managers and appearances so as to convey some particular images.

Having *chin-shins* facilitates such face-making play. Superiors and their *chin-shins* can work together taking varying parts. In one situation, for instance, a superior may play a nice guy (white face), while his/her *chin-shin* plays the devil (black face). In another situation, their roles may be reversed. In one case that the author has observed, a manager wanting to give warnings to his subordinates concerning their work performance might do it indirectly. That is, he used his *chin-shin* as a kind of sacrificial lamb, scolding the *chin-shin* in front of everyone in a thoroughly prearranged performance.

INFORMATION GATEKEEPER

The third role of a *chin-shin* is as information gatekeeper. Mintzberg (1973) has proposed ten roles of managers, which can be categorized into three groups: interpersonal, informational, and decisional. A *chin-shin* serves as a superior's important assistant. Hence, information that is passing to the superior may be reviewed by the *chin-shin*. One purpose of a *chin-shin* serving as an informational gatekeeper is to assure that the superior is not overloaded. In other words, the *chin-shin* screens and rules out unimportant communications so that superiors may spend time on crucial decision-making.

Some possible unintended consequences may result from this role, however. A *chin-shin* may develop great power because he/she controls information channels. Brass (1984) has argued that a person's structural position in an organization may have strong implications for power acquisition. In his study, he found that measures of the relative positions of employees within work flow networks were strongly related to perceptions of influence by both superiors and subordinates. In our earlier discussion of *chin-shin* roles in history, it was noted that they sometimes serve as spies or intelligence agents. Emperors sometimes used *chin-shins* to collect information from the bottom and, in some cases, utilized the information to eliminate those who were against them. The role of *chin-shins* as information gatekeepers may result in subordinates' bad impressions of them. Subordinates may become watchful of them, and relationships may deteriorate.

RESOURCE CONTROLLER

The fifth role of a *chin-shin* is as resource controller. Organizations acquire resources and transact with their environment to sustain their operations. The ability to control the supply of resources to others means power (Pfeffer and Salancik, 1978). Managers generally possess a certain degree of resource control and have the right to allocate resources according to their assigned positions. This is often called the 'formal' source of power in organizations. *Chin-shins* do not have the formal authority to exercise power on behalf of managers. However, since *chin-shins* are located close to the centre of the superior's differential matrices, they are, informally speaking, a surrogate for their managers. Thereby, *chin-shins* may gradually gain power over certain resources. The derivation of such resource control is due partly to their handling tasks for superiors. The more a *chin-shin* can manoeuvre resources, the more he/she can facilitate a superior's decision-making or help him/her in relationship-building.

This also may have negative consequences. Other subordinates may perceive the *chin-shin*'s power enlargement as threatening. They find that they may need the *chin-shin*'s approval to utilize resources. There may be a sense of unfairness perceived by subordinates. The increase of a *chin-shin*'s resource-controlling power creates a dependent relationship for others. Subordinates have to submit themselves to the orders of *chin-shins*. Gradually, such privileges of *chin-shins* become institutionalized and may be perceived as rightful. If *chin-shins* do not handle their relationships with other subordinates well, conflicts may derive.

DEMOGRAPHIC DISTRIBUTION OF SUPERIOR AND *CHIN-SHIN* IN TAIWANESE ORGANIZATIONS

To better understand the *chin-shin* phenomenon in modern Taiwanese organizations, the author (Chi, 1995) has collected a sample of 137 managers in 137 different companies. These respondents were asked to respond to questions in terms of a high-level manager and his/her *chin-shin*. The questionnaire included four types of questions: perception of leadership behaviour, *chin-shin*'s roles, perceptions of leaders and *chin-shin*, and demographic data on leader, *chin-shin*, and the informants themselves.

GENDER

In our sample of 137 high-level managers, 117 were male, and 18 were female. This proportion reflects the fact that high-level managers in Taiwan are predominantly male. Among the male managers, 80 chose male *chin-shins* while 36 chose female *chin-shins*. Among the female managers, 11 chose female *chin-shins* while 6 chose male *chin-shins*. Thus, although same-gender superior/*chin-shin* pairings were more common than different-genders pairings, about one-third of the managers chose opposite-sex *chin-shins*, regardless of their own sex. This does not mean that gender has a strong effect on the choice of *chin-shin*. What it suggests is that among the possible reasons for choosing a *chin-shin* are factors like ability, personal attributes and character, factors that have greater effect than gender on such decisions.

AGE

The cross-table of managers and *chin-shins* in terms of age is shown in Table 15.1. We can see from the table that many managers were older than their *chin-shins* by about 10–20 years. For Taiwanese managers, a 10-year to 20-year age difference may be the easiest age gap between superior and *chin-shin*, because Taiwanese managers generally hold to the Confucian idea of respecting elders. Hence, in company settings, age often plays an important role in promotion and social status. Although there has been great change toward Western concepts of performance and ability in recent years, the effects of age still exist. Most young workers have to wait for years to climb up an organizational ladder, and it is relatively difficult for a younger manager to manage his/her relationship with an elder *chin-shin*. Such cases in our sample are few (i.e., 4 in 10-year gap and 1 in 20-year gap), and these exceptions might be due to their either being the successor of the company's original owners, or a start-up entrepreneur.

Table 15.1
Cross-table of Age between Superior and *Chin-shin*

Chin-shin Superior	Below 30	30–39	40–49	50–59	Above 60	Total
Below 30	2					2
30–39	16	13	3	1		33
40–49	9	27	9	1		46
50–59	3	15	21	2		41
Above 60		2	1	3	4	10
Total	30	57	34	7	4	132

Note: Unit: person.

TENURE

A similar tendency as for age was found for tenure; but it was less obvious. The most mentioned tenure for managers was over fifteen years in the company and, similarly, the *chin-shins* of these managers had also worked in the company for more than fifteen years. This result may reflect the fact that superior/*chin-shin* relationships do not evolve in a short period. The parties need time to test the *chin-shin* relationship. On the other hand, for managers, it may not be easy to find and establish a good long-lasting relationship. Therefore, they need to have a longer period of time to develop mutual compatible relationships with a *chin-shin*.

EDUCATION

The cross-table of education between superior and *chin-shin* (Table 15.2), shows that the most common situation was that in which both are college graduates (48 cases). Situations in which one was from college and the other from a technical institute came second, and those in which one was a graduate and one from college came third. In other words, in most situations, superior and *chin-shin* had a similar educational background, with some cases of superiors having slightly higher education. This may reflect the fact that *chin-shins* serve in supporting roles. Superiors may want to have capable persons to be their aides, but may not wish to have a person with higher abilities than their own which would threaten their status.

Table 15.2
Cross-table of Education between Superior and *Chin-shin*

Superior \ Chin-shin	Below Junior High School	High School	Technical Institute	College	Graduate School	Total
Below Junior High	1	1				2
High School	2	2		1	2	7
Techincal Institute		5	8	5		18
College	1	7	19	48	3	78
Graduate School		5	2	13	8	28
Total	4	20	29	67	13	133

Note: Unit: person.

ORGANIZATIONAL LEVEL

Finally, we look at the organization level of both superior and *chin-shin*. For this, distribution is scattered. Nevertheless, there is a general tendency for a one-level difference to exist between the two persons, with the superior one level higher than his/her *chin-shin*. This result fits our general expectations. Difficulties may arise if the cases are opposite. A *chin-shin* may be two or even more levels lower than the superior, which cases do exist, that result in making other subordinates feel uncomfortable because of the somewhat complicated relationships.

PERCEPTIONS OF SUPERIOR AND *CHIN-SHIN* BY SUBORDINATES

In order to understand subordinates' perceptions of superior and *chin-shin* relations, we used a questionnaire modified from the Job Description Index developed by P.C. Smith et al., (1969). The original JDI includes five parts: task, salary, promotion, work partner, supervisor. The author chose the supervisor dimension and modified the work partner dimension into an evaluation of a *chin-shin*. Respondents were asked to rate superior and *chin-shin* separately. Negative items were recoded before calculating a total score. The total score indicates the extent to which respondents rate superior and *chin-shin* favourably or unfavourably. Overall ratings of superior and of *chin-shin* were each around the median range.

The author also did a correlation analysis between these two scores, which showed that they were significantly correlated. In other words, when respondents rated the superior positively, they also rated the *chin-shin* positively, and vice versa. Hence, it seems that superior and *chin-shin* form a unit. Their joint leadership styles toward subordinates are interlinked with each other. If subordinates hold good impressions of superiors, they also seem to view *chin-shins* favourably, and, if subordinates hold good impressions toward a *chin-shin*, they see their superiors favourably as well.

CONFLICTING ROLES PERCEIVED BY SUBORDINATES

In a further analysis, complex relationships were found among *chin-shins'* five different roles. The roles of decision aide, public relations agent, and resource controller were all correlated positively. Also, the public relations agent role was positively related to black/white face, and negatively related to the role of information gatekeeper. In addition, information gatekeeper was positively related to black/white face and resource controller.

These results show that, for subordinates, the *chin-shin's* roles are not complementary to each other. A *chin-shin* who demonstrates a decision aide role may facilitate his/her being the superior's public relations agent, and this *chin-shin* may thereby become a resource controller and possess extra power. On the other hand, a *chin-shin* who is a good public relations agent may also need to play the role of black/white face, although a good public relations agent can help to reduce the impression of being an information gatekeeper. Moreover, the role of information gatekeeper is associated with the *chin-shin's* role of face-play.

Thus, to play the role of information linking-pin is hard. Subordinates may doubt the *chin-shin's* intention and suspect that he/she has a double face. Further, being an information gatekeeper makes a *chin-shin* a power centre, extending his/her personal power by holding crucial information (such as rumours or secrets). Subordinates do not prefer a *chin-shin* with too much power. They also do not want him/her to be too sophisticated to deal with.

An interesting finding from another of the author's samples of 45 *chin-shins* suggests different perceptions by *chin-shins* themselves. *Chin-shins* perceive their roles as mutually supporting one another. Unlike subordinates' perceptions, *chin-shins* see themselves playing various related roles with a single ultimate goal—supporting their superiors.

FINAL REMARKS

The *chin-shin* phenomenon is a historical legacy in Taiwanese society. The 'role' perceptions of *chin-shins* are at least somewhat institutionalized. People expect to 'see' *chin-shins*. In many cases, their roles are mystified and their characters are blended with myth and legend. When a leader is idealized, even idolized, this person's second hand (the *chin-shin*) will also enjoy similar adoration. This *chin-shin*'s stories will be immediately heard and carefully honoured. Serving a leader unreservedly without complaint is considered an honourable act of integrity and loyalty.

But there is another extreme, suggesting that a *chin-shin* may be viewed as a selfish, flattered person. Their behaviours are seen as having evil intentions. But acts or even desires of overthrowing their leaders are not accepted as appropriate deeds by a subordinate, and, therefore, a *chin-shin* may either be accorded high regard as a loyal servant, or be seen as a detrimental subordinate of low reputation.

The 1990s have seen tremendous changes toward economic globalization. Managers need to appreciate differences among cultures and learn to manage diversity successfully. Traditional management training is no longer enough: people must become artful in cross-cultural affairs. The case of *chin-shins* in Taiwanese organizations is illustrative. Management theorists have increasingly recognized the need to examine organizational behaviour in a global context (e.g., Boyacigiller and Adler, 1991). Cross-cultural comparative studies are important to exteneded theory-building. The roles of *chin-shins* may have culture-specific aspects, but they are not altogether unique. As noted earlier, for example, the superior–*chin-shin* exchange processes can be explained by Graen's role-making model (Graen, 1976); and the idea of mentoring (Hunt and Michael, 1983; Kram, 1985) can be extended to the kind of coaching and training done by superiors with *chin-shins*. Thus, comparative analyses of such quasi-formal phenomena as *chin-shins* may be a useful means of better understanding the convergence and divergence of organizational phenomena and managerial behaviour across nations and cultures.

16

THE THAI CONCEPT OF EFFECTIVE LEADERSHIP

Suntaree Komin

In today's globalized economy, managers no longer manage their own cultural groups. Rather, they have to manage employees of different cultural backgrounds. The question is, can their leadership/managerial style largely derived from the West be effective regardless of different cultural contexts? Can the existing conceptions of leadership theories sufficiently provide an explanation for effective cross-cultural leadership? More and more empirical research evidence in recent years has demonstrated otherwise. Substantiated with empirical evidence from data on various managerial aspects, this paper aims to explore the indigenous concept of effective Thai leadership, and presents a Thai cultural leadership model.

LEADERSHIP CONCEPTION

How to manage and lead people for maximum performance is the core issue of effective leadership. What is leadership? How adequate are the existing conceptual frames to incorporate the cultural element to explain effective leadership for different cultures?

For definition, it is generally agreed that leadership plays a central part in understanding group behaviour, for it is the leader who usually provides the direction as well as extracts maximal effort from his subordinates, to work toward goal attainment. Being part of common vocabulary, the term 'leadership' is infused with many meanings and approached from many perspectives. Its definitions appear to have moved along the following scale, with the more recent views at the bottom of the list often encompassing prior definitions:

1. Leadership as a focus of group processes
2. Leadership as personality and its effects
3. Leadership as the art of inducing compliance
4. Leadership as the exercise of influence
5. Leadership as a form of persuasion
6. Leadership as a power relation
7. Leadership as an instrument of goal achievement
8. Leadership as an emerging effect of interaction
9. Leadership as the initiation of structure

Drawing upon this scale, the *Handbook of Leadership* broadly defines it as:

> an interaction between two or more members of a group that often involves a structuring or restructuring of the situation and the perceptions and expectations of the members. Leaders are agents of change, persons whose acts affect other people more than other people's acts affect them. Leadership occurs when one group member modifies the motivation or competence of others in the group (Bass, 1990: 19–20).

EXISTING THEORETICAL FRAMES FOR LEADERSHIP

Like the definitions, there is no shortage of leadership theories in the field. It is not possible to evaluate every theory; it would suffice to scan the contributions in different phases of leadership theoretical development. Historically, modern leadership research and theories can be categorized according to a time-line analysis (Clinton, 1985) into five development phases, with each phase marked by some major research work (see Appendix A for an overview of leadership history):

1. Phase I: Great Man Era (1841–1904)
2. Phase II: Trait Era (1904–48)
3. Phase III: Behaviour Era (1948–67)
4. Phase IV: Contingency Era (1967–80)
5. Phase V: Complexity Era (1980–86)

Without getting into the details of these theories, a few general observations are pertinent. First, it seems that leader behaviour can be reduced to two dimensions—'task' and 'people'—but researchers continue to differ as to whether the orientations are two ends of a single continuum or two independent dimensions. Although many theories address the issue of degree of decision-sharing with subordinates (autocratic–participative continuum, leadership–participation model, etc.), the task–people dichotomy appears to be far more encompassing.

Second, leadership theorists do not agree on the issue of whether a leader's style is fixed or flexible. In fact, both are probably right. It might depend on the leader's personality. From the concept of 'self-monitoring'—a trait which measures an individual's ability to adjust his or her behaviour to external situational factors—individuals differ in terms of behavioural flexibility (Snyder, 1987). Some people show considerable adaptability in adjusting their behaviour to external, situational factors. Others, however, exhibit high levels of consistency regardless of situations. A person who is high on self-monitoring should be more able to adjust his or her leadership style to changing situations.

Third, it is evident that there is no place for national culture to be indicated in any of the existing theoretical frames.

NATIONAL CULTURE AS AN IMPORTANT CONTINGENCY VARIABLE

A significant fact that emerges from the overview of leadership literature is that existing theoretical frames do not consider cultural difference as a variable in leadership process and effectiveness. In the 1990s, empirical research has shown considerable evidence of cross-cultural differences in management studies. The most significant among them is Hofstede's large-scale cross-cultural study, using 116,000 employees of a multinational corporation located in forty countries (Hofstede, 1980a). He shows that managers in different cultures apply very different values to their organizational responsibilities and preferences, along four universal dimensions (Hofstede, 1980a; 1983; 1991). They are:

1. Individualism vs Collectivism: How loose or tight is the bond between individuals and societal groups?
2. Power Distance: How much do people expect inequality in social institutions (e.g., family, work organizations, government)?
3. Uncertainty Avoidance: To what extent do people seek to avoid unstructured situations through laws, rules, and procedures?

4. Masculinity vs Feminity: To what extent do people embrace competitive masculine traits or nurturing feminine traits?

Hofstede's study provides clear evidence of across-culture differences in management. It demonstrates that cultural differences can no longer be ignored or taken for granted for effective management.

How does national culture fit into the managerial and leadership conceptual frame? National culture affects leadership style by way of subordinates. Leaders cannot choose their style at will. They are constrained by the cultural conditions that their subordinates have come to expect. For example, a manipulative, autocratic leadership style is more likely to be compatible with cultures of high power distance scores, like in Arab and Latin countries. Participation is more likely to be effective in low power distance cultures, as in Norway, Sweden, and Denmark. Furthermore, this may explain the fact that a number of leadership theories (the more obvious ones like those of the University of Michigan Behavioural Studies: the autocratic–democratic continuum, and the leader–participation model) implicitly favour the use of a participative style. One should bear in mind that most of these theories were developed using North American subjects who value smaller power distance. These theories reflect to a considerable extent the cultural bias of the theorists themselves.

The general conclusion that emerges is that effective leaders do not use any single style. They adjust their style to the situation. National culture is an important situational contingency variable determining effectiveness of leadership style.

THAI CONCEPT OF EFFECTIVE LEADERSHIP

Conceptually, an organization does not exist in a vacuum, but is embedded in a societal/cultural environment, and the latter exerts its pervasive influence on the organizational actors—employees and managers alike—in terms of what they bring with them to the workplace, like patterns of values, beliefs and social relationship behavioural patterns.

National culture influences organizational behaviour through personal values and ethics, attitudes, assumptions, and expectations, demonstrated in various behavioural issues. Managerial attitudes and behaviours are the product of the culture that managers are brought up in. Similarly, the perceptions and reactions of subordinates are the result of cultural conditioning. Each culture has its expectations from the roles of manager/leader and subordinate. What one culture encourages as participative manage-ment, another sees as managerial incompetence (Copeland and Griggs, 1985). It is apparent that the greatest challenge to international managers is the leadership function, because research and experience show that managers cannot assume the transferability of their leadership practices. It is in the leadership process that the effects of culture become most apparent.

Thus, in order to understand the Thai concept of effective leadership, it is necessary first to understand the Thai national culture which has been factor-analyzed in the 'Thai Nine Value Orientation' (Komin, 1991)—the foundation for understanding Thai social behaviour (see Appendix B), and Thai work behaviour (Komin, 1990; 1995b). Against the backdrop of the Thai value orientations, we focus on the leadership role, processes and patterns of the Thai manager/leader, to see what constitutes the cul-turally preferred core foundation of effective Thai leadership. From the perspective of the managerial and leadership role—to communicate, to motivate, to handle conflict, to make decisions, to solve problems, and to lead people to achieve organizational goals—we will see where foreign and Thai cultural values differ, and get a comprehensive view of Thai effective leadership.

THAI LEADER AND COMMUNICATION

Effective communication is difficult under the best of conditions, and more so when cultural factors are involved. The communication pat-tern reflects the personal and cultural backgrounds of the manager/leader (Komin, 1995b). Without going into details, it would suffice to say that Thai leaders are expected to have effective communication skills that are fitted to the Thai context and with the Thai personality and social behaviour—that is, to be 'polite' and 'considerate', with or without an authoritative overtone—the image of an all-knowing, kind, paternal figure.

THAI LEADER AND MOTIVATION

Knowledge and understanding of what motivates workers from a differ-ent culture is critical to the success of the overseas manager. In the US, individual initiative and achievement are rewarded, but in Japan, man-agers are encouraged to seek consensus before acting, and employees work as teams (Howard et al., 1984). National polls conducted by the

National Opinion Research Centre indicate that 'more than half of the work force in the United States believes that the most important characteristics of a job is that it involves work that is important and provides a sense of accomplishment' (Weaver, 1976). Meaningful work is rated 'most important' three times more frequently than 'high income' and seven times more frequently than the desire for 'shorter work hours and much free time'. A recent survey of middle-and top-level managers by the American Productivity and Quality Center found similar results (APQC, 1989). When compared to a recent study of 1,000 American employees, the Thai sample shows that they are motivated by 'good wages', 'promotion' and 'job security' (Table 16.1). The highest discrepancies between American and Thai workers consist in 'interesting work', and 'feeling of being in on things' being of higher importance for the Americans, and 'good pay' and 'promotion' being ranked higher for the Thai. Evidently, Thais value work as a means to achieve social status, signified by positions. As such, 'opportunity for promotion' has received a significant weight.

Table 16.1
Rank Order of What Workers Want from their Work: American and Thai

Work-related Factors	American	Thai	Discrepancy
Interesting work	1	6	5
Full appreciation of work done	2	4	2
Feeling of being in on things	3	7	4
Job security	4	3	1
Good wages	5	1	4
Promotion and growth in the organization	6	2	4
Good working conditions	7	5	2
Personal loyalty to employees	8	8	0
Tactful discipline	9	10	1
Sympathetic help with personal problems	10	9	1

Source: The results of the American rankings of 1,000 employees are from K.A. Kovach, 'What Motivates Employees?' *Business Horizons*, September–October, 1987: 61.

However, most current motivation theories were developed in the United States by Americans and about Americans (N.J. Adler, 1986). Maslow's (1943) need hierarchy is a case in point, to illustrate such cultural bias. The meaning of achievement, and self-actualization as the highest order of human motivation, reflects more the American cultural values of 'individualism' and 'masculinity'. A study of the People's Republic of China (Nevis, 1983) is an example to disprove the universality of Maslow's need hierarchies. The study concluded that the Chinese hierarchy of needs is arranged differently and has fewer levels than Maslow's hierarchy, with need for 'belonging' at the first level, 'physiology' second, 'safety' third, and 'self-actualization in the service of society' last. These differences are rooted in the Chinese cultural emphasis on service and loyalty to society and the American cultural emphasis on self-determination and individualism.

The determinants of work motivation in the workplace are many, including the managerial style that can affect the motivation of the employees (Komin, 1990). Is money everything in motivating Thai employees? Thai employees like money and good pay, but 'No! Money is not everything' for them. According to the Thai value orientations, a foreign manager's mishandling of Thai staff can significantly affect the morale and cost the organization expensively. A case in point occurred in an international chain hotel in Bangkok where there was a high rate of turnover after some changes in policy were initiated by the new American manager to have performance evaluation of the supervisors rated by their subordinates (critical incidents gathered by the author). An interview with the employees revealed that, even when they were paid a little less than at other hotels for the same job, they stayed and worked for years. The point here is: what makes the Thai work for even less pay?

Factors affecting employee motivation are several, and many of them are related to the manager/leader's personality and styles. Content analysis of responses to an open-ended question as to what factors they perceived as motivating and what factors they perceived as demotivating yielded interesting results. Besides the conventional motivating factors like salary, promotion and working conditions mentioned in Table 16.1, the rest of the responses mostly concerned the manager/leader's personality, personal characteristics, values, attitudes, and styles (Table 16.2). Evidently, in a relationship-oriented culture, the result reflects the Thai perception and expectation of what affects their motivation. Apart from just a rational individual task–goal contract with the organization (like in Western industrial societies), the human relations aspects related to the manager/leader were important for the Thai perception of motivation. In the Thai cultural context, motivating employees is also affected by leadership attributes and style.

Table 16.2

Perception of Motivation by Thai High-level Government Administration (N = 62)

Motivating Factors	Demotivating Factors
Good human environment: good colleagues and boss	Boss
Boss	insincere, not trusting
has '*khunathan*' (just, kind, has compassion) is capable and well accepted	does not '*hai kiat*' (i.e., give respect to employee's ego and face)
has good relationships with people	not competent, lacks knowledge
shows good understanding and concerns	lacks '*khunathan*'
is a good example or model person (good, capable, and just)	lacks vision
gives advice	selfish, and self-centred
should refrain from playing office politics (as it causes conflicts and affects employee morale)	comments but does not advice
recognition for work well done from boss in public	blames unreasonably
good reputation of the organization	by-passes authority line
	plays favouritism for 'clique', his '*phakphuak*' or entourage
	serving interests of selfclique rather than organization
	uses patron–client relationship for salary increase and promotion
	reward/acknowledgements are not performance based
	promotion based on seniority is fine, but the person has to be capable
	too much competition among colleagues over power positions
	vague and ever-changing policy

THAI LEADER AND CONFLICT MANAGEMENT

Over the 1970s and 1980s we have witnessed the rise of conflict management into a major area of organizational behaviour. Is there cultural difference in the perception of conflict as well as in the management of conflict? It is important for foreign managers to know how the Thai employees see conflict, and how they handle it or how Thai managers/leaders handle it.

Given the Thai value system which places high priority on 'ego' and good and 'smooth interpersonal relationship', the Thai in general is more likely to dislike conflict, feel uneasy about it, tend to avoid conflict, and find ways to indirectly handle it. This is clearly indicated by the response to the statement that 'most organizations would be better off if conflict could be eliminated forever' (Table 16.3). The Thai showed the highest

Table 16.3
Agreement to the Statement: 'Most Organizations would be
Better Off if Conflict could be Eliminated Forever'

Country	Percentage of Agreeing
Thailand:	
Government officials (N = 86)	96.4
Business (middle managers) (N = 138)	85
Italy	41
Belgium	27
France	24
Denmark	19
Switzerland	18
The Netherlands	17
Germany	16
USA	6
Sweden	4

Source: Results of countries other than Thailand are based on A. Laurent, 'The Cultural Diversity of Western Conceptions of Management', *International Studies of Management and Organization*, 1983, 13(1–2): 75–96.

percentage of agreeing, when compared to the response of 817 managers from various countries reported by Laurent (1983). This personal conflict avoidance clearly explains Thai employees' reluctance to criticize and make opposing comments against other persons in meetings or at the workplace, and the reluctance of Thai managers to make negative reports of subordinates to his expatriate executive boss.

Given the Thai conflict avoidance value, one might wonder to what extent Thai organizations are conflict-free. The present research has used a brief checklist for assessing conflict in organizations in order to identify three conflict stages: 'daily events', 'challenges' and 'battles'. In stage I conflict is normal, the least threatening and easiest to manage. Stage-II conflict is characterized by the 'win–lose' and 'cover your hind-end' attitudes. For people who are tied to conflict issues with self-interest, such behaviour becomes very important. There is behaviour like keeping track of verbal victories and recording mistakes, as well as taking sides. Stage-III conflict shifts from 'wanting to win' toward 'winning to hurt'. The motivation is to 'get rid' of the other party. When conflict escalates to this level, it is an all-out war, with the relationship reaching the point of deadly personal vengeance (physical violence included), as manifested in numerous cases. Given the Thai value

Table 16.4
Percentage of Conflict in Various Stages in Thai Organizations

Three Stages of Conflict	Government Officials (N = 37)	State Enterprise (N = 31)
Stage I: Daily events	13.5	41.9
Stage II: Challenges	21.6	32.9
Stage III: Battles	64.9	25.8

system which is sensitive to ego and relationship, coupled with the usually high degree of office politics in government circles, it is not surprising to find that a high degree of conflict exists (Table 16.4). The data indicate that Stage-III conflict is prevalent particularly among government officials, with 64.9 per cent perceiving their offices as having conflicts at the 'battles' level. Stories are told, at high-level government official meetings, about conflicting senior administrators who do not look at each other, let alone talk to each other, and would do anything (i.e., pretending to be so engrossed in reading the newspaper) just to avoid acknowledging the presence of the other. For the Thai, most conflicts are personal (see Komin, 1990; 1991, for details). The situation in the business sector needs to be explored. One can, however, hypothesize that the same pattern will emerge, but with a lesser degree of intensity.

People tend to handle conflict in patterned ways referred to as 'styles'. There are five different styles developed by Rahim (1983; 1985) within a 2 × 2 grid on the two axes of 'concern for self' and 'concern for others'. These five styles are Integrating (Collaboration), Obliging (Accommodation), Dominating (Competition), Avoiding and Compromising.

According to Hofstede's findings, people in countries low on uncertainty avoidance would feel secure and relatively free from threats of uncertainty, and their organizations, would be more open and flexible. Countries high in masculinity would emphasize assertiveness. The cultural climate of low uncertainty avoidance and high masculinity would foster a society that is open, direct, and competitive. It would also generate in individuals competition and collaboration for handling conflicts. Likewise, persons from Scandinavian countries which rate high on feminity would prefer avoidance or accommodation behaviours. Japan, Greece, or other countries which rate high on uncertainty avoidance would have extensive use of formal rules and employment guarantees to minimize conflicts and encourage cooperation.

Table 16.5
Conflict Handling Styles of Thai Educated Employees (by Ranking of Score)
Compared to the Australian Comparative Study (N = 69)

Styles	1	2	3	4	5	Median	Rank[1]			
							Rank	Thai	Aust	
Collaboration	48	12	5	3	1	1.2	1	3	1	+[2]
Accommodation	0	11	18	34	8	3.7	5	1	1	=[3]
Forcing	6	11	29	15	6	3.1	3	2	3	=
Avoiding	10	8	19	15	17	3.4	4	4	4	−[4]
Compromising	22	31	14	2	0	1.9	2	5	5	−

[1] Results of Negotiation Styles reported in Chau, *Australia–Thailand: A Cross-cultural Survey of Business Practices*, 1991, unpublished.
[2] Australians do more than Thai.
[3] About equal.
[4] Thai a lot more than Australian.

Using the short form of Rahim's instrument on a sample of educated Thai employees and Thai government officials, it was found that the Thai's prominent conflict handling style was 'Integrating' or Collaboration, followed by 'Compromising', 'Avoiding', and 'Dominating' (Competition or Forcing). The data show that nobody used 'Obliging' (Accommodation) as his/her dominant style (Table 16.5). It seems that the high rate on feminity of the Thai, according to Hofstede's findings, does not lead to the prediction of Avoidance and Accommodation conflict handling styles as was expected. However, an Australian study of Thai–Australian business practices reported that Thai were highest on 'Obliging' or differing only in degree. This study found that the Thai were much higher in 'Avoiding' and 'Compromising' than the Australian, with the Australian a little higher in 'Collaboration' (Chau, 1991). The small size of the sample makes the findings tentative. However, in view of the high relationship orientation of the Thai, the difference is not unexpected.

THAI LEADER IN DECISION-MAKING AND PROBLEM-SOLVING

Role expectations for managers and subordinates are culturally determined. What is perceived as participative management in one culture is seen as managerial incompetence in another (Copeland and Griggs, 1985). In fact, who makes the decision and when it is made, seem to vary in organizations around the world (N.J. Adler, 1986). Our knowledge

Table 16.6

Percentage of Agreement to the Statement: 'It is Important for a Manager to Have at Hand Precise Answers to Most of the Questions that his Subordinates May Raise about their Work'

Country	Percentage of Agreeing
Japan	78
Indonesia	73
Italy	66
France	53
Germany	46
Belgium	44
Switzerland	38
Britain	27
Denmark	23
United States	18
Holland	17
Sweden	10
Thailand:	
Government officials (high level) (N = 41)	82.9
Government officials (middle level) (N = 62)	91.9
State enterprise (TG) (N = 43)	86.0
Business employees (CP) (N = 87)	74.7
Educated Thai managers (N = 10)	100.0
Overall Thai	84.5
TG Asian managers (N = 17)	94.1
Western managers:	
(Mobil Oil, Redd Barna, TG) (N = 19)	0.0

Source: Results of countries other than Thailand are based on A. Laurent, 'The Cultural Diversity of Western Conceptions of Management', *International Studies of Management and Organization*, 1983, 13(1–2): 75–96.

of power distance difference tells us that low ranking employees in low power-distance cultures like Sweden, expect to make most of their own decisions about day-to-day operations, while in high power distance cultures, only senior-level managers make decisions.

In the survey conducted at INSEAD, an international management school in France, 817 managers from various countries were asked whether they agreed to the statement: 'It is important for a manager to have at hand precise answers to most of the questions that his subordinates may raise about their work'. Responses indicated that managers in Italy, France and Indonesia, for example, were seen as experts who were expected to have the answers (Table 16.6). Managers in America and Holland were regarded as participative problem-solvers. Japan had 78 per cent agreeing to the statement. A sample of the Thai managers (from public and private sectors) revealed the highest percentage agreeing, with an overall average of 84.6 per cent—91.9 per cent from middle-level government officials (Thai International), 74.7 per cent from middle managers of a big Thai business firm (C.P.), and 100 per cent from the Thai staff of a foreign organization in Bangkok. In contrast, all the Western managers in these companies did not agree to the statement.

With large power distance among the Thais and their cultural system valuing hierarchical structure with acceptance of unequal personalized power and status, the finding is not unexpected. It was expected of the managers by the subordinates and constituted an essential attribute of leadership (see Komin, 1995a, for Thai decision-making behaviour). Because of differing expectations, when a Thai staff member tells his Western boss of certain problems he has encountered, both are unhappy and frustrated. The Western boss is annoyed, and complains that 'The Thai lack sense of responsibility. Don't they know they should be accountable for what they are doing?' On the other hand, the usual complaint of the Thai staff is 'It's terrible. When I told my boss what happened, he said 'It's your problem.' He doesn't seem to care [about what will happen to the organization].' And it seems to be just *tua khrai tua man* (each taking care of his own skin). The Thai who perceives and expects the manager/leader to make decisions and solve problems, interprets the boss' comment and attitude as being selfish, uninvolved, and even incompetent.

ON POWER AND AUTHORITY

Related to this is the issue of power and authority as influenced by culture. Laurent (1983) in his research on the cultural diversity of Western conceptions of management, questioned 817 managers of different cultures on various managerial concepts. Three statements are pertinent in the present context: 'Most managers seem to be more motivated by obtaining power than by achieving objectives'; 'The main reason for having a hierarchical structure is to make everyone know who has authority over whom'; and 'Today there seems to be an authority crisis in organizations.' Responses to these statements indicate (Table 16.7) that in countries like Italy and France, managers emphasize the importance of power motivation within the organization, more than managers in the United Kingdom, United States, Germany and the Netherlands. The same pattern is observed for perceptions of organizational structure, where managers in Italy and France see it more as power and authority, and perceive the authority

Table 16.7
Percentage of Agreement to Statements Regarding Perception
of Power and Authority

Country	Statements		
	1 (On Power)	2 (On Authority)	3 (Authority Crisis)
Italy	63	50	69
France	56	45	64
Belgium	42	36	64
Sweden	42	26	46
United Kingdom	32	38	43
Denmark	25	35	40
The Netherlands	26	38	38
Switzerland	51	25	29
Germany	29	24	26
United States	36	18	22
Thailand government middle managers	67.9	57.1	92.9

Source: Results of countries other than Thailand are based on A. Laurent, 'The Cultural Diversity of Western Conceptions of Management', *International Studies of Management and Organization*, 1983, 13(1–2): 75–96.

crisis threat, more than managers in countries like Switzerland, Germany and United States. Laurent concludes that French, Italian and Belgian managers display a more personal and social concept of authority that regulates relationships among individuals in organizations. American, Swiss and German managers have a more rational and instrumental view of authority that regulates interaction among tasks or functions. For the former, authority appears to be more a property of the individual; for the latter, it appears to be more an attribute of the role or function (Laurent, 1983). The author's study on middle-level Thai government officials indicated a pattern similar to Italy with the highest percentage agreeing to these statements. According to the Thai Value Study (Komin, 1990; 1991), power and authority are personalized matters for the Thai.

BARAMEE: THE CULTURALLY PREFERRED CORE FOUNDATION OF THAI EFFECTIVE LEADERSHIP

National culture influences the preference for certain personality characteristics. The Thai Value Study reveals that the non-aggressive personality, which the researcher sums up in a well-known Thai phrase, *on*

Table 16.8
Ideal Leader Characteristics Perceived and Expected by Thai
Middle/High Managers (N = 123)

Characteristics	Frequency Count
Decisive, courageous	68
Fair and kind	49
Knowledgeable, competent	40
Honest, 'clean'	37
Self-confident	29
Good human relations	27
Vision	24
Intelligent, sharp	23
Has *baramee*	19
Cautious, calm, not gullible	18
Polite and non-aggressive	14
Has the art of managing people	13
Good speaker	13
Clear working principle	11
Responsible	10
Has public interest in mind	9
Sincere	8
Listens to others' opinions	7
Good background, record	4
Helps subordinates solve problems	3

nork khaeng nai (meaning literally 'soft outside, firm and tough inside'), describes the competent yet polite and successful personality as well as leadership in the Thai context (Komin, 1990; 1991).

To ascertain the Thai perception of effective leadership, a number of middle- and high-level Thai administrators were asked: 'What do you think are the characteristics of a leader?' Content analysis of responses revealed 'decisiveness' to be the most significant trait expected from a manager, followed by 'fairness', and 'kind' (Table 16.8). While most of these leadership traits are universal, some are culture-specific, expected only in some cultural groups. For example, the expectation that a leader is 'polite and non-aggressive' (which is a highly valued personality quality) and to expect an effective and truly respected leader to have acquired *baramee* (given true respect and love from the followers) are characteristics particularly expected in the Thai culture. A person who has *baramee* 'can command respect, love, loyalty, and sacrifice from others'. The Thai term *baramee* has no English equivalent. The closest meaning would be 'charisma' plus 'goodness' and *med taa* ('loving-kindness')—the inherent goodness that the person has acquired as a result of years of good, respectable and warm interactions with people. It is something that cannot be bought, cannot be demanded, but one has to earn it on a continuous basis. For example, a frustrated and mismanaging Western manager asked his Thai executive: 'Why do the employees come to you, but not come to me?' The Thai executive, as usual, did not reply frankly, and gave a situational excuse for the employees. But he told his Thai friend that it was 'because he never "wins the heart" of his subordinates in his daily dealing with them'. If one starts to behave like a good leader, he is gradually building his *baramee*, and one day he will be a well-respected and well-loved leader.

The study further revealed that the concept of *baramee* as a form of personal power was at the core of the culturally preferred ideal leadership. A leader who is regarded as a person of *baramee* is one who consistently and over time displays meritorious acts of selfless behaviour, is honest, fair and kind, and in the process gains full acceptance (*kaan yomrap*), respect, devotion (*khwaam sattaa*) and love, and thus unlimited cooperation from people. Further analysis revealed five distinct characteristics of *baramee*:

1. *Baramee* spreads its influence naturally, without force or control, as people learn of it, respond to it, and relate the goodness of its possessor to others. It is not only perceived and appreciated by those directly benefiting from its actions, but also by those indirectly observing such effects.
2. *Baramee* is 'built up' (*saang*) or accrued gradually over a long period of time.
3. *Baramee* has no temporal limits. It is not bound by position and can last one's entire lifetime.
4. A *baramee* leader does not expect compensation for services or goodness rendered, does not play favourites or seek to control others. *Baramee* is seen as working for the common good, not self-seeking for its own benefits. Moreover, the person possessing it is not personally corrupt.
5. As a foundation for leadership and leadership formation, *baramee* is always viewed positively.

The formation and parameter of *baramee* can be illustrated in the 'concept map of *baramee*' (Conner, 1996) (see Figure 16.1). As people commonly confuse *baramee* with *amnaat* (authority) and *ittiphon* (influence), Conner (1996) has clearly distinguished them as *amnaat* (authority) meaning position power, and *ittiphon* (influence) meaning power to control

Figure 16.1
Concept Map of *Baramee* Leadership and Formation

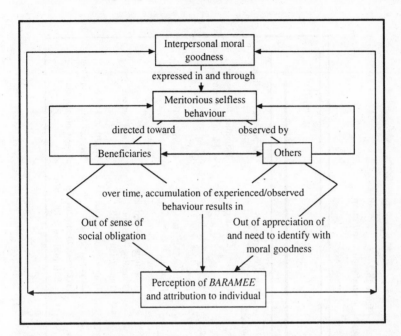

others. He further distinguishes these three basic concepts from the perspective of their origins on a continuum ranging from the moral character of the individual leader (*baramee*) to the ability to control others maintained by the individual leader (*ittiphon*). The origin of *baramee* is internal to the individual leader (being socially acceptable), while that of *amnaat* and *ittiphon* are both external to the individual leader. The difference between the latter two is that one is socially established and socially acceptable, while the other is individually established and socially unacceptable. In the light of these 'origins', there seems to exist a continuous relationship among these three foundations, moving from what is socially unacceptable (*ittiphon*) to that which is socially acceptable (*amnaat* and *baramee*), as depicted in Figure 16.2. The concept of *baramee* leader provides an insight into many successful managers/leaders who exist in Thai society at the present time, from political public figures like former Prime Ministers Prem Tinsulanon and Anand Panyarachun, to successful businessmen like Bangkok Bank tycoon Chin Sophonpanich and C.P. multibillionaire Thanin Chairavanon, and many others.

Figure 16.2
Thai Leadership Foundation Continuum

	BARAMEE	AMNAAT	ITTIPHON
1. Originates from:	Interpersonal Moral Goodness of Individual	Legal/Institutional Code	Means of Controlling Others
2. Resides in:	Others' Perceptions of Individual	Position of Authority	Individual Possessing Means of Control
3. Characterized by:			
Lifespan	Infinite	Finite	Finite
Growth/Expansion	Unlimited/Natural	Limited/Depletable	Unlimited/Force
Measurability	Possible	Possible	Possible
Compensation Expectation	None	Officially—None (Unofficially—Perhaps)	Definite
Focus of Benefits	Others	Officially—Others (Unofficially—Self)	Self and Retinue
4. Evidenced by:	Attributions of Others	Trappings of Position	Wealth and Power
5. Used as a Means to:	Serve Others	Carry out Duties	Increase Means of Control
6. Elicits Response of:	Admiration, Honour, Respect	Protective, Destructive or Self-protective Response	Fear, Compliance

Source: Adapted from Conner, 1996: 268.

Figure 16.3
Thai Cultural Leadership Model

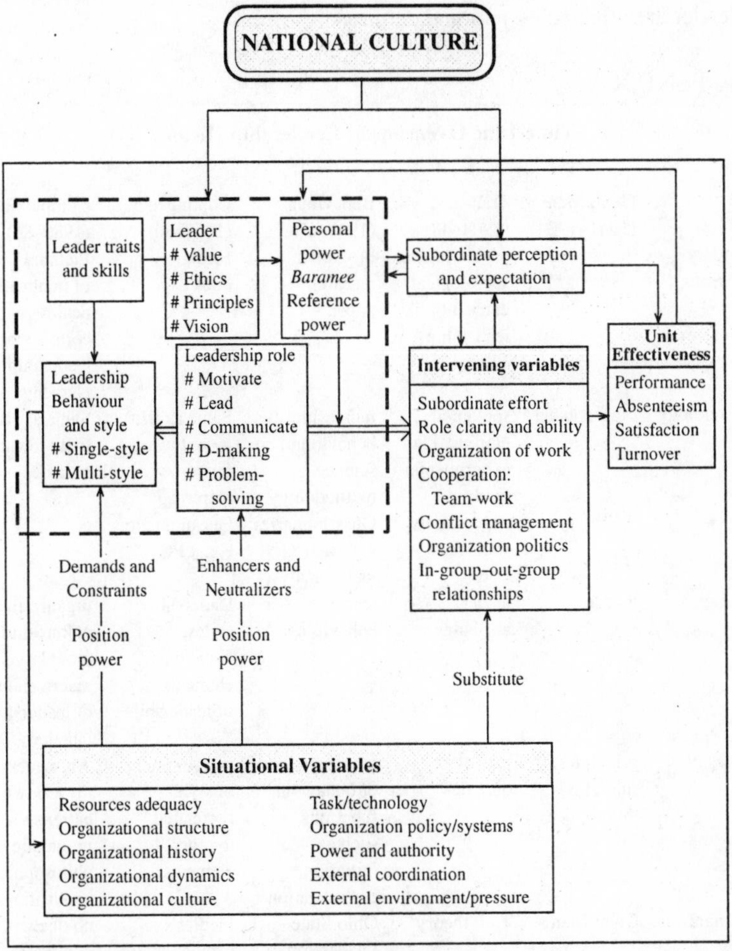

NATIONAL CULTURE

Leader traits and skills	Leader # Value # Ethics # Principles # Vision	Personal power *Baramee* Reference power		Subordinate perception and expectation			

Leadership Behaviour and style
Single-style
Multi-style

Leadership role
Motivate
Lead
Communicate
D-making
Problem-solving

Intervening variables

Subordinate effort
Role clarity and ability
Organization of work
Cooperation:
   Team-work
Conflict management
Organization politics
In-group–out-group
   relationships

Unit Effectiveness

Performance
Absenteeism
Satisfaction
Turnover

Demands and Constraints

Position power

Enhancers and Neutralizers

Position power

Substitute

Situational Variables

Resources adequacy	Task/technology
Organizational structure	Organization policy/systems
Organizational history	Power and authority
Organizational dynamics	External coordination
Organizational culture	External environment/pressure

THAI CULTURAL LEADERSHIP MODEL

Given all the empirical evidence and pertinent information with regard to cross-cultural differences pertaining to leadership studies, be it traits, behaviour, role, styles, and management styles, particularly in the Thai cultural context, the author finds the existing Western frameworks inadequate to help explain effective leadership. Therefore, the Thai model of leadership (Figure 16.3) is proposed (Komin, 1994). It looks at leadership process as spelled out by Yukl (1989), and adds the component of subordinate perception and expectation, through which culture plays a major influencing role. These and other components within the leader are affected by national culture.

APPENDIX A

Time-Line Overview of Leadership History

Phase	I	II	III	IV	V
	Great Man (1841–1904)	Trait (1904–48)	Behaviour (1948–67)	Contingency (1967–80)	Complexity (1980–86)
Boundary conditions		psychological sociological entry into leadership	Stogdill's research paper	Fiedler's book	Plethora of publications dealing with complexity of leadership elements
Methodology	biographical	sociometry, empirical lab experiments, field experiments, statistics	increasingly behavioural science methodology, Questionnaires e.g., LBDG factor analysis	Same as III, more toward micro/ empirical Questionnaires e.g. LPC	Same as III, trend toward macro
Focus on	leader	leader attributes	leader behaviour	leadership styles, situational elements of leadership	organizational culture and other larger macro elements of leadership labelled
End result	principles, rule of thumb ideas	lists of qualities	measurements of behaviour functions such as initiation, consideration	measurements of style correlated to other elements	? my guess toward two extremes: pragmatic, and philosophical applications
Dominant theory	Great Man	Trait theory	Ohio State Leadership Theory	Fiedler's Contingency Model; Other situational theories # Hollander # Hersey and # Blanchard House's Path-Goal	no one will dominate; multiple theories

APPENDIX B

UNDERSTANDING THE THAI NATIONAL CULTURE

Despite Hofstede's significant contribution to the study of national culture with his four universal dimensions, the extent to which it is sufficient and effective in explaining the local culture depends on in-depth analysis of each culture. For instance, the Thai profile is identical with all other Asian countries in the region except Japan. Although Hofstede and Bond (1988) have added a fifth dimension called Confucian Dynamism, which identified four Asian countries, namely, Hong Kong, Taiwan, Korea and Japan, the fact remains that intuitively, one feels that there are differences between Thai, Indian, Indonesian, Malayasian and Singaporean subjects. This is where the large-scale national surveys of the Thai Value Study over the last ten years would be useful, with a more in-depth picture of the Thai 'mental programming' which will serve as the foundation for understanding and explaining Thai work-related behaviours as well as for reflecting on effective leadership as perceived and practised in the Thai cultural context.

THE NINE THAI VALUE ORIENTATIONS

To understand the Thai way of thinking, feeling and acting, one needs to look at the nine Thai value orientations which underlie much of the Thai personality and social behaviours. With a carefully constructed, less Western-biased value measurement instrument ('The Thai Value Survey'), two nation-wide surveys were conducted during the 1980s, and resulted in the identification of nine Thai Value Orientations for explaining the Thai national character (Komin, 1990; 1991). These nine value orientations, or the 'mental programming' of the Thai, are placed on a continuum of psychological importance from high to low. The higher one is up the order, the more likely it is to be activated for action. The nine Thai value orientations in their positions of relative importance in the Thai cognitive system are as follows:

1. *Ego orientation:* This orientation explains the highly sensitive 'ego' and 'face' value of the Thai, the criticism avoidance, the stressing of 'feelings' above other issues (even money), and the personalization of conflict.
2. *Grateful relationship orientation:* This orientation explains the 'gratitude reciprocity' behaviour, long-term relationship orientation and compassion.
3. *Smooth interpersonal relationship orientation:* This orientation explains the preference for non-aggressive, friendly 'harmonious relation' in social interactions.
4. *Flexibility and adjustment orientation:* This orientation explains the penchant of the Thai for flexible 'means', ever-adjustable to 'situation', 'person' and 'clique' values. The Thai are in general not ideological or principle-oriented, unless it is linked with 'person'.

5. *Religio-psychical orientation:* This orientation explains the general belief in spiritual things, in *Bun-kam* (good and bad *karma* predetermined by one's past lives), in the acceptance of unequal power status, including the attitude of tolerance.

6. *Education and competence orientation:* This orientation explains the emphasis on education and competence as 'means' to achieve the 'end' of higher social status; the preference for 'materials' possession and 'form' over 'content' value.

7. *Interdependence orientation:* This orientation explains the mutual help-fulness and collaboration spirit among villagers, the peaceful coexistence of people, and the successful cultural assimilation of different ethnic groups in Thailand.

8. *Fun–pleasure orientation:* This orientation explains the 'light', humour-ous, fun-oriented social interactions and atmosphere.

9. *Achievement–task orientation:* This orientation explains the pheno-menon where task-achievement is often subjected to maintaining good relationships—the social element in the achievement value.

From this 'mental programming' or the inner logic of Thai social behaviour, several implications of a general nature pertaining to motivation and management at the workplace can be derived, whereas specific examples will be illustrated under various organizational and management issues:

1. In a culture which values 'ego' and 'face', straightforward negative perform-ance feedback, strong criticism and face-to-face confrontation techniques should be avoided. When necessary, indirect means are used. 'Face-saving' is a key criterion in handling all person-related decisions, particularly neg-ative ones. In addition, compromise is often used as an effective means of saving face, and to keep the 'surface harmony'.

2. As a culture with relatively tight hierarchical social systems, accepted exis-tential inequality and a strong value on 'relationships', Thai employees can be motivated to work devotedly for the leader they like and respect. Reasonable authority and special privileges are accepted. An impersonal, cut-and-dried type of system-oriented managerial style is not as effective as the benevolent paternalistic leadership style. Straightforward, ambitious and aggressive personalities like those of the West, although highly capa-ble, are not tolerated and are hardly ever successful. But personalism with a 'soft' and polite approach often guarantees cooperation. Although the concept of participative democracy is attractive and legitimate, the 'form' is accepted but the 'substance' is still lacking in the basic value systems of the Thai

3. As a culture loosely committed to any ideology, any new system approach can be indoctrinated, but not without a relation-oriented leadership style, and not overlooking the above two implications.

17

SOME BEHAVIOURAL DIMENSIONS OF EFFECTIVE MANAGERIAL STYLE IN THE INDIAN CONTEXT

Satish Kumar Kalra and Rajen K.Gupta

Economic liberalization and globalization have opened the doors to the world economy and, in the process, to many foreign investors who are coming to India either for joint ventures or to start independent operations. While this has led to tremendous business opportunities and potential for economic growth, it has also led to a cross-cultural flux of managerial manpower across nations. Making these 'cross-cultural marriages' successful requires effective running of organizations in different cultures. Among other things, it requires enhancing the effectiveness of the managers manning these organizations. One of the important dimensions of organizational effectiveness is managerial style. In today's changing context, a manager has to be culturally sensitive in order to be effective. This is, however, a recent concern. For a long time it was believed that leadership/managerial styles developed in the West were universally applicable. It was the success of Japan, and later of some other Eastern countries which achieved success through the application of culturally rooted indigenous styles of management, that made researchers and practitioners all over the world think and reflect on developing indigenous styles of management (D. Sinha, 1995).

In the Indian context, as in many Asian countries, researchers had started questioning the applicability of Western managerial leadership practices like participative management as early as the mid-1970s (Kalra, 1975; J.B.P. Sinha, 1974). In fact, Kalra (1975) also questioned the applicability of Management by Objectives (MBO) in the Indian context, based as it is on employee-oriented participative decision-making. On the whole, the studies have yielded conflicting results. Some studies using the questionnaire method showed that respondents preferred the democratic style of leadership (J.L. Gupta, 1985; Kakar, 1971; 1974). However, other studies, which used either business simulations or project-ive/experimental methodology, showed the acceptance of authoritarian leaders (Casico, 1974; Kalra, 1988; Thiagarajan and Deep, 1970). Kumar and Singh (1976) have also reported that 'authoritarian leadership was no less preferred than the participants style'.

It is to be noted that the questionnaire-based studies showed preferred styles of leadership, whereas the studies using experimental business simulation/projective methodology showed what was actually accepted (Casico, 1974; Kalra, 1988; Meade, 1967). In fact, Kalra (1988) observed that 13.6 per cent of his respondents rejected the authoritarian boss, and 38.9 per cent showed tentative acceptance of such a boss (i.e., they questioned him before accepting him). Combining the responses, it was indicated that 52.5 per cent of the respondents tended to question an authoritarian boss. Commenting on this, Kalra reports that 'This in a way does indicate that if given a choice, people do tend to show less preference for an authoritarian boss but, at the same time, they may not strongly oppose or reject him.' Kalra (1988) also makes a distinction between preferred style and actually accepted style, wherein acceptance may not really imply liking.

In contrast, studies by J.B.P. Sinha (1980) and his associates conducted over a period of five years developed the concept of Nurturant Task (NT) leader, which Sinha found was more relevant and characteristic of effect-ive leaders/managers in the Indian context. Describing the NT leader he writes:

> A NT leader is one whose primary concern is his task system. He wants to get work done. He structures his subordinates' roles clearly so that commu-nications are explicit and task-relevant, subordinates understand and accept organizational goals and cultivate commitment to them, and organization aims at a climate of purposiveness and goal orientation. The task orientation has the ethos of a nurturant and benevolent guide who cares for his subordin-ates and takes a personal interest in their well being and growth. He in fact

helps them grow and mature so that they may assume greater responsibilities and may be competent to participate in decision-making. The nurturant task leader believes that it is through the task system, that a meaningful, trusting and growth-oriented inter-relationship may be developed in an organizational setting (J.B.P. Sinha, 1980: 193).

Besides these, a large number of studies on leadership have been conducted in India (see Sahay et al., 1994, for a detailed bibliography). These studies report conflicting results due to methodological reasons, and also due to the fact that most of them have been conducted basically for the purpose of research, using Western instruments, where the authenticity of the responses is likely to be affected by the lack of involvement of respondents and also by their tendency to put up a 'projected self' rather than the 'real self'. To some extent, the second aspect can be taken care of by using projective or other types of methodologies (see Casico, 1974; Kalra 1988; Meade, 1967). The involvement of the respondents is likely to increase if the respondents find the activity directly useful and beneficial to their roles and to the organization. Therefore the data collected through such activities is likely to be more authentic and true to reality. Management Development Programmes/Training and more specifically the organization-based experiential developmental programmes for managers constitute one such approach where the participants' involvement is generally high, and the responses collected through such programmes, both during the designing and conducting stages, could provide very rich and authentic data on managerial and organizational issues (see Kalra, 1991; Kalra and Gupta, 1989; Kalra et al., 1994). The present paper is based on data collected while designing and conducting 'Managerial Effectiveness Through Self Awareness' (METSA) programmes for two organizations, one of which was a private sector process organization, and the other, a large public sector financial service organization. In both organizations, the programmes were designed and the data collected using TA (Transactional Analysis) framework as developed by Pareek (1988).

PAREEK'S TA FRAMEWORK

The TA framework for understanding the human personality was originally developed by Berne (1961), and popularized by his disciple and partner Harris (1967) through his famous book *I am O.K.—You are O.K.* Later researchers and practitioners modified the concept by creating further subdivisions of 'Parent', 'Adult' and 'Child' ego states. James (1975)

noted that the psychic energy used through these ego states and their subdivisions did not have O.K. and not-O.K. dimensions. She labelled these
subdivisions as the critic, the coach, the shadow, the analyst, the paci-
fier, the fighter and the inventor. She observed that all these subdivisions
had O.K. and not-O.K. dimensions. Depending on one's personality,
individuals use O.K. or not-O.K. influencing styles in interpersonal relations. James felt that understanding this aspect of personality can help
enhance effectiveness by using the functional/O.K. dimensions of these
ego states. Using the same logic, Pareek (1988) developed his framework
of influencing styles and also developed an instrument, popularly known
as the Style Profile of Influence Roles in Organization (SPIRO), to tap
the functional and dysfunctional influencing styles of managers.
   Pareek's (1988) classification is as follows:

	Ego State	O.K./Functional Influencing Style	Not-O.K./Dysfunctional Influencing Style
P	Nurturing Parent	Supportive	Rescuing
	Controlling Parent	Normative	Prescriptive
A	Adult	Problem-solving	Task Obsessive
	Free Child	Innovative	Bohemian
C	Rebellious Child	Confronting/ Assertive	Aggressive
	Compliant Child	Resilient	Sulking

Pareek (1988; 1997: 188–90) describes these twelve styles as follows:

1. Supportive (+NP): In this style, support is provided when needed.
   Managers with this style are supportive coaches. They encourage
   their subordinates, cheer them up, and provide the necessary conditions for their continuous improvement. They help them to help
   themselves.
2. Rescuing (−NP): In this style, support is provided by almost impos-
   ing oneself on others. The belief is that the subordinate is not
   capable of taking care of himself. This style inculcates dependency-
   proneness.
3. Normative (+CP): Managers with this style are interested in developing proper norms of behaviour for their subordinates and helping
   them to understand how some norms are more important than
   others. The manager is concerned with setting appropriate norms

by involving his subordinates in evolving these norms, and also in deciding how such norms will be followed.

4. Prescriptive (−CP): People with this style are critical of others' behaviour. They impose themselves and want others to do what they think is right or wrong. Managers with this style prescribe solutions rather than helping subordinates to work out alternative solutions to the problem.

5. Problem-solving (+A): In this style the concern of the person is to solve the problem by himself working and involving others in it. He does not see the problem as being merely confined to the tasks. For him the problems have various dimensions.

6. Task obsessive (−A): The manager with this style is primarily concerned with tasks, and is so obsessed with the work to be done that he overlooks various other things. They are not concerned with feelings and, in fact, fail to recognize them, since they see them as not related to the task. They function like computers.

7. Innovative (+FC): People with this style are enthusiastic about new approaches, and take others along with them. They pay enough attention to mustering an idea so that it results in concrete action, and is internalized in a system.

8. Bohemian (+FC): Such a manager does not stay with one idea and is obsessed with new ideas all the time. He overwhelms his subordinates with new ideas. He is less concerned about the working of these new ideas, and is mainly concerned with the ideas themselves. He hardly allows an idea or a practice to stabilize. He goes from one idea to another.

9. Confronting/Assertive (+RC): In this style the person is concerned with the exploration of a problem. Perseverence is the main characteristic. Such managers confront the organization in order to get things done for their subordinates. Even when something is to be explored with the person, the focus is always a particular issue or a problem and the person is not the target.

10. Aggressive (−RC): A person with this style is likely to show his aggressiveness by in-fighting, making heavy demands, fighting or going back to issues and never allowing these to be settled. Managers with this style will help achieve results. Their aggressiveness, however, makes people ignore them and not take them seriously.

11. Resilient (+CC): This style is characterized by functional compliance. The person respectfully accepts others' ideas which appeal to him, and changes his approach when needed.

12. Sulking (−CC): A manager with this style keeps negative feelings to himself, finds it difficult to share them and avoids meeting people if he has not been able to fulfil his part of the contract. Instead of confronting problems, a person with this style avoids them, feels bad about situations but does not express himself.

METHODOLOGY

As already mentioned, the data for this study were collected as a part of the Self Awareness Oriented Managerial Effectiveness programmes in two organizations. In one of the private sector process organizations, the data were collected using SPIRO (Pareek, 1984; 1997). The SPIRO consists of thirty-six items with three items in each of the twelve categories of Pareek's framework. The respondents indicated, on a five-point scale, how frequently they behaved in a particular way indicated in the statement, from almost always to 'rarely' or 'never'. Thus the range of scores was from 3 to 15 for each category.

In the functional styles, a total score of 12 or more was considered healthy and, in the case of dysfunctional styles, a score up to 8 was acceptable. A score of 9 was acceptable only if it was made up of all 3s.

Forty-seven managerial-level participants, who attended the three-day Self Awareness Programme for Managerial Effectiveness in three batches, were asked to think of the one most effective and one least effective manager with whom they had worked, and were then asked to rate them on SPIRO. All these managers had about ten years or more of experience, and had the experience of working under three or more bosses.

In the second public sector financial service organization, the data were collected during a four-day Self Awareness Programme for the Senior Mangers (Deputy-General Managers/General Managers) of the organization. Two such programmes were conducted, one at Lucknow and the other at Mumbai. Data were collected by interviewing managers from the Lucknow, Pune, Patna and Bombay offices of the organization, and from seventy officers who were below the level of the target group (i.e., levels E and F). All these officers were in the A to D levels and they were asked to think about the most effective and the least effective bosses in their experience till then and were asked to write a brief description of each. These descriptions were then content-analyzed and categorized using Pareek's framework (Pareek, 1988).

RESULTS AND DISCUSSION

PRIVATE SECTOR PROCESS ORGANIZATION

As earlier indicated, there were forty-seven participants in the Managerial Effectiveness Programme of this organization, and they had all given ratings for the most effective and least effective manager on SPIRO. Therefore, to get an overall picture, the ratings of all the participants on all the dimensions were added and average ratings were worked out. Tables 17.1 and 17.2 give the overall average ratings of the most effective and least effective managers.

Table 17.1
Perceived Average SPIRO of the Most Effective Managers/Bosses (N = 47)

	Supportive	Normative	Problem-solving	Innovative	Confronting	Resilient
Plus(+)	12.7	13.2	12.5	12.7	11.8	12.5
	Rescuing	Pre-scriptive	Task Obsessive	Bohemian	Aggres-sive	Sulking
Minus(−)	11.5	8.9	8.3	7.6	7.8	6.6

As can be seen from Table 17.1, the most effective managers were perceived as high on all the 'functional' ego state dimensions, and they were also considered high on rescuing (patronizing). On all the other dysfunctional ego state dimensions, they were rated low. On the other hand, the least effective managers were perceived as low on all the ego state dimensions (Table 17.2).

In general, as the SPIRO ratings are given on behaviour, i.e., how an individual behaves in a particular situation as described by SPIRO items, the total overall SPIRO scores are also indicative of the activity level of the individual. The total average score for the Most Effective managers was 126.1, and for the Least Effective managers, 91.4.

PUBLIC SECTOR FINANCIAL SERVICE ORGANIZATION

As mentioned earlier, the data were collected from seventy officers in the form of descriptions of the most effective and the least effective bosses. These descriptions were then content-analyzed using Pareek's TA Framework dimensions (Pareek, 1988). In Tables 17.3 and 17.4 are given respectively the number of respondents in each ego state category, both for the most effective and the least effective managers. There were a large number of supportive and rescuing responses for the most effective managers.

Table 17.2
Perceived Average SPIRO Scores of the Least Effective Managers/Bosses (N = 47)

	Supportive	Normative	Problem-solving	Innovative	Confronting	Resilient
Plus(+)	8.6	7.7	8.3	7.5	6.8	8.6

	Rescuing	Pre-scriptive	Task Obsessive	Bohemian	Aggressive	Sulking
Minus(−)	7.5	6.8	7.8	7.3	7.2	9.3

Table 17.3
Ego State Category-wise Distribution of Responses for the Most Effective Manager/Bosses as Given in the Descriptions (N = 70)

Supportive	Normative	Problem-solving	Innovative	Confronting	Resilient
56	27	51	11	14	11

Rescuing	Pre-scriptive	Task Obsessive	Bohemian	Aggressive	Sulking
44	7	8	2	0	0

Besides being supportive and rescuing (patronizing), many of the respondents also perceived their most effective bosses as problem-solving-oriented as well as normative. Other dimensions did not emerge clearly.

On the other hand, it is interesting to observe that in the case of the least effective bosses, none of the descriptions given by the respondents were positive. A very large number of them perceived their least effective bosses as prescriptive, Bohemian, aggressive and avoidant (Table 17.4).

Taking the results of both the organizations together, one notices some interesting similarities and differences. Differences are more noticeable in the case of the profiles of least effective managers (Tables 17.2 and

Table 17.4

Ego State Category-wise Distribution of Responses for the Least Effective Managers/Bosses as Given in their Descriptions (N = 70)

Supportive	Normative	Problem-solving	Innovative	Confronting	Resilient
0	0	0	0	0	0

Rescuing	Prescriptive	Task Obsessive	Bohemian	Aggressive	Sulking
10	49	9	32	25	28

17.4). It can be observed that none of the least effective bosses is seen to exhibit any functional behaviours, whereas in SPIRO-based data (Table 17.2) they do show some but very few functional behaviours. The differences are more striking in the case of dysfunctional behaviours. Whereas SPIRO-based data (Table 17.2) show low dysfunctional behaviours also, the descriptions (Table 17.4) are full of only dysfunctional behaviours. This means that either the ineffective managers are seen to be those who are not active in any way or those who are very active in dysfunctional ways.

In general, in both types of organizations, respondents perceived the most effective managers as rescuing (patronizing) as well as supportive, normative, and problem-solving-oriented. On SPIRO data, they were innovative, confronting/assertive and resilient. In a way, this indicates that Indian subordinates do not see patronizing as an ineffective managerial style, provided it is not clubbed with prescriptive, task obsessive, Bohemian, aggressive and (avoidant) managerial behaviours. In other words, if the boss is supportive and patronizing along with other functional ego state styles, he is likely to be seen as effective by subordinates. In this context it is to be noted that studies on childhood socialization and child-rearing practices in India indicate that patronizing is associated with taking care and is generally perceived positively. Individuals reared in such an atmosphere are likely to expect patronizing from their bosses and may feel good about it. This finding is in a way consonant with J.B.P. Sinha's (1980) Nurturant Task Leadership Style where nurturance includes both supportive and patronizing dimensions.

The study being exploratory needs to be backed up with more systematic and elaborate investigations conducted on larger samples and in different types of organizations. The managerial role being highly complex, its effectiveness is not dependent on one or two stylistic dimensions, but is the outcome of the interplay within specific socio-cultural contexts, interactions with different dimensions, and all interacting with personality characteristics of managers.

REFERENCES AND SELECT BIBLIOGRAPHY

Abdel-Rahman, A. (1989). Haul Takwin Al-Islamia Wa Tabiatah [The Nature and Development of the Islamic State]. *Arab Studies*, 26(1): 3–24.

Adair, J.G. (1989). Indigenous Developments in Indian Psychology: A Quantitative Assessment. Paper presented at the Annual Meeting of the Canadian Psychological Association, Halifax, Nova Scotia.

Adams, J.S. (1965). Inequity in Social Exchange. In L. Berkowitz (ed.), *Advances in Experimental Social Psychology*, Vol. 2 (pp. 267–99). New York: Academic Press.

Adeji, A. (1995). Africa in Transition: The Challenge of Pluralism, Democracy, Governance and Development. *The Courier*, 150: 93–95.

Adler, N.J. (1986). *International Dimensions of Organizational Behaviour*. Boston: Kent Publishing.

Adler, N.J., R. Doktor and **S.G. Redding** (1989). From Atlantic to the Pacific Century: Cross-cultural Management Reviewed. In A.B. Chimezie and Yg Osiwegh (eds), *Organizations Abroad* (pp. 27–54). New York: Plenum.

Adler, P.A., P. Adler and **A. Fontana** (1987). Everyday Life Sociology. *Annual Review of Sociology*, 13: 217–35.

Agarwal, R. and **G. Misra** (1986). Factor Analytic Study of Achievement Goals and Means. *International Journal of Psychology*, 21: 217–31.

Ahmed, K. (1976). *Islam: Its Meaning and Message*. London: Islamic Council of Europe.

Al-Fingary, A. (9 February 1996). Al-adari Al-Muslim fi Huda Silouk Al-rasoul Wa adaritah Lashouan Al-rayeh [Muslim Administrator in the Vision and Behaviour of Prophet Mohammed and his Management of People's Affairs]. *Al-Hawadeth*, 54–55.

Ali, A. (1988). Scaling an Islamic Work Ethic. *Journal of Social Psychology*, 26(1): 13.

—— (1990). Management Theory in a Transitional Society. *International Studies of Management and Organization*, 20(3): 7–35.

—— (1992). Islamic Work Ethic in Arabia. *Journal of Psychology*, 126(5): 507–19.

Ali, A.J. and **A. Azim** (1994). Islamic Work Ethic and Organizational Development. Paper presented in the Symposium on Organizational Development: Religio-spiritual and Social-cultural Perspectives, XXIII International Congress of Applied Psychology, Madrid, Spain, 17–22 July.

Ali, I. (1989). *Nahajul Balagah* (translated and edited by F. Ebeid). Beirut: Dar Alkitab Al-labnani. (First published *c.* A.D. 990.)

Ali, M. (1977). *A Manual of Hadith*. New York: Olive Branch Press.

Ali, S. (1964). *The Spirit of Islam*. London: Chatto and Windus.

Alilto, G.S. (1987). *The Last Confucian*. Berkeley: University of California Press.

Amarah, M. (1988). *Mutazilas wa Mashkalt al-heria al-ansynah* [Mutazilas and the Problem of Human Freedom]. Beirut, Lebanon: Arab Institute for Publishing and Studies.

American Productivity and Quality Center (APQC). (1989). *What Motivates Managers? INC,* p. 115.

Auerbach, J.D. (1988). *In the Business of Child Care.* New York: Praeger.

Aurobindo, S. (1977). *The Message of the Gita.* Pondicherry: Sri Aurobindo Ashram.

Bahl, V. (1995). *The Making of the Indian Working Class: The Case of Tata Iron and Steel Co., 1880–1946.* New Delhi: Sage.

Bailyn, L. (1992). Issues of Work and Family in Different National Contexts: How the United States, Britain and Sweden Respond. *Human Resource Management,* 31(3): 201–8.

Bass, Bernard M. (1990). *Bass and Stogdill's Handbook of Leadership.* New York: Free Press.

Baviskar, B.S. (1982). In N.R. Sheth (ed.), *Industrial Sociology in India: A Book of Readings.* New Delhi: Allied.

Bernard van Leer Foundation (1986). *Parents as Prime Educators: Changing Patterns of Parenthood: Summary Report and Conclusions.* The Hague: Bernard van Leer Foundation.

Berne, E. (1961). *Transactional Analysis in Psychotherapy.* New York: Grove Press.

Berry, J.W. (1986). Multiculturalism and Psychology in Plural Societies. In L.H. Ekstrand (ed.), *Ethnic Minorities and Immigrants in a Cross-cultural Perspective.* Lisse: Swets and Zeitlinger, B.V.

Bhattacharya, K.C. (1977). 'Swaraj' in Ideas. In S.K. Ghosh (ed.), *Four Indian Essays.* Calcutta: Jijnasa.

Bi, Xiaoxiong (1988). The Comparison Mechanism and the Perspective of Fairness. *Brightness Daily,* February 11.

Bird, B.J. (1989). *Entrepreneurial Behaviour.* Glenview, Illinois: Scott, Foresman & Co.

Blau, P.M. (1964). *Exchange and Power in Social Life.* New York: Wiley.

Bles, R.J. and **J.S. Moag** (1986). International Justice: Communication Criteria of Fairness. In R.J. Lewicki, B.H. Seppand and M.H. Bazerman (eds), *Research on Denotation in Organizations.* Greenwich, CT: JAI Press.

Boase, A. (1985). The Economic System in Islam: A Model for All Men. *Islamic Quarterly,* 29(3): 129–47.

Bond, M.H. and **K.K. Hwang** (1986). The Social Psychology of Chinese People. In M.H. Bond (ed.), *The Psychology of the Chinese People.* Hong Kong: Oxford University Press.

Boserup, E. (1970). *Women's Role in Economic Development.* Geneva: International Labour Organization.

Boyacigiller, N.A. and **N.J. Adler** (1991). The Parochial Dinosaur: Organizational Science in a Global Context. *Academy of Management Review,* April: 264–65.

Brass, D.J. (1984). Being in the Right Place: A Structural Analysis of Individual Influence in an Organization. *Administrative Science Quarterly,* 29(4): 518–39.

Brewer, M.B. (1988). A Dual Process Model of Impression Formation. In T.K. Srull and R.S. Wyer, Jr (eds), *Advances in Social Cognition.* Hillsdale, NJ: Erlbaum.

Brockhaus, R.H. (1975). I-E Locus of Control Scores as Predictors of Entrepreneurial Intentions. *Proceedings of the Academy of Management,* 35: 433–35.

Brockhaus, R. H. (1982). The Psychology of the Entrepreneur. In C.A. Kent, D.L. Sexton and K.H. Vesper (eds), *Encyclopedia of Entrepreneurship* (pp. 39–71). Englewood Cliffs, NJ: Prentice Hall.

Brockhaus, R.H. and **P.S. Horwitz** (1986). The Psychology of the Entrepreneur. In D.C. Sexton and R.W. Smilor (eds), *The Art and Science of Entrepreneurship* (pp. 25–48). Cambridge, MA: Ballinger.

Bugnicourt, J., R. Ndiaye and **E.H. Sy** (1994). Clear the Streets and Start Again. *The Courier*, 143: 54–55.

Burks, Ardath W. (1981). *Japan: Profile of a Post-industrial Power.* Boulder, Colorado: Westview Press.

Busia, K.A. (1967). *Africa in Search of Democracy.* New York: Praeger.

Business India (1995). 19 June–2 July. New Delhi.

Business Week (1994). December 12, pp. 18–30.

Bygrave, W.D. and **C.W. Hofer** (1991). Theorizing about Entrepreneurship. *Entrepreneurship Theory and Practice*, Winter: 13–22.

Carland, J.W. F. Hoy, W.R. Boulton and **J.C. Carland** (1984). Differentiating Entrepreneurs from Small Business Owners. *Academy of Management Review*, 9(2): 354–59.

Carr, S.C. and **M. Maclachlan** (1994). Psychology for Developing Worlds. Paper presented at a thematic session during the 23rd International Congress of Applied Psychology, Madrid, Spain.

Casico, W.O. (1974). Functional Specialisation, Culture and Preference for Participative Management. *Personal Psychology*, 27(4): 593–603.

Central Committee of the Chinese Communist Party (1993). A Resolution of the Central Committee of CPC about a Number of Issues in Establishing the Socialist Market Economy. *Quishi*, No. 23.

Chakraborty, S.K. (1987). *Managerial Effectiveness and Quality of Work Life: Indian Insight.* New Delhi: Tata McGraw-Hill.

—— (1989). *Foundations of Managerial Work.* Bombay: Himalaya.

—— (1991). *Management by Values: Towards Cultural Consequence.* Delhi: Oxford University Press.

—— (1993). *Management Transformation by Values: A Corporate Piligrimage.* New Delhi: Sage.

—— (1995a) (ed.), *Human Values and Managers.* New Delhi: Wheeler Publishing.

—— (1995b). *Ethics in Management: Vedantic Perspectives.* New Delhi: Oxford University Press.

Chandler, A.D. (1977). *The Visible Hand: The Managerial Revolution in American Business.* Boston: Harvard University Press.

Chang, H.F. (1995). The Determinants of the Leader's Trust in Subordinate and its Effect on Subordinate Behaviour (Chinese text). Unpublished Master's thesis, National Taiwan University.

Chao, Y.T. (1990). Culture and Work Organization: The Chinese Case. *International Journal of Psychology*, 25(4): 583–92.

—— (1994). Culture and Work Organization: The Chinese Case. In H.S.R. Kao, D. Sinha and Ng Sek-Hong (eds), *Effective Organizations and Social Values* (pp. 34–55). New Delhi: Sage.

Chaturvedi, A. (1987). *Achieving Harmonious Industrial Relations: Successful Experiments and Experiences.* Pune: The Times Research Foundation.

Chau, R. (1991). Australia–Thailand: A Cross-cultural Survey of Business Practices. (Unpublished manuscript).

Chauvin, M. (1993). Three Decades of Development: Failure, but No Grounds for Despair. *The Courier*, 137: 59–61.

Chen, C.N. (1986). Traditional Family System and Business Enterprise (Chinese text). In C.N. Chen (ed.), *Marriage, Family and Society*. Taipei: Yuanchen.

Chen, M.C. (1984). Family Culture and Business Administration. In K.S. Yang, K.K. Hwang and C.J. Chuang (eds), *The Proceedings of Chinese Management Conference*. Taipei: Department of Psychology, National Taiwan University.

Chen, S.M., C.C. Lin, C.I. Chu, C.S. Chuang C.C. Hsi and **C.T. Liu** (1991). *Disintegrating KMT-State Capitalism* (Chinese text). Taipei: Taipei Society.

Cheng, B.S. (1988). Familism and Leadership (Chinese text). In C.F. Yang and H.S.R. Kao (eds), *Chinese and Chinese Psychology*. Taipei: Yuanliu.

—— (1993). *Paternalistic Authority and Leadership: A Case Study of a Taiwanese CEO* (Chinese text). Technical Report for National Science Council. Taipei: National Science Council.

—— (1995). The Relationship between Hierarchical Fit in Organizational Value and Employee Effectiveness (Chinese text). *Chinese Journal of Psychology*, 37(1): 25–44.

Chi, S.C. (1995). *An Empirical Study on Roles of Chin-shins in Corporate Organizations*. Research report sponsored by National Science Foundation in Taiwan.

Chi, S.C. and **H.Y. Lin** (1994). An Investigation on the Chin-shin Relations of Business Top Executives. *Journal of Management Science*, 11(2): 281–312.

Chiao, C. (1982). *Guanxi*: A Preliminary Conceptualization (Chinese text). In K.S. Yang and C.I. Wem (eds), *The Sinicization of Social and Behavioural Science Research*. Taipei: The Institute of Ethnology, Academia Sinica.

Chie (1988). Hierarchy in Japanese Society. In D.I. Okimoto and T.P. Rohlen (eds), *Inside the Japanese System* (pp. 8–14). Stanford: Stanford University Press.

Chin-Ning Chu. (1995). *Thick Face, Black Heart*. Australia: Allen and Unwin.

Chiu, C. (1988). The Notion of Justice and Pattern of Justice Behavior in Chinese Culture. Unpublished Master's thesis, Hong Kong University.

Chou, Y.H. (1984). The Planning and Control Activities in the Large-scale Taiwanese Enterprises (Chinese text). Ph.D. dissertation, National Chengchi University.

Chuang, H.C. and **Y.C. Ku** (1987). Gift-giving in Hospitals: An Open Secret, an Unwritten Ethical Rule. In Living Psychology Editorial Board (ed.), *The Social Games of the Chinese: Renqing and Shigu* (pp. 14–19) (Chinese text). Taipei. Living Psychology Publications.

Clark, R. (1988). The Company as Family: Historical Background. In D.I. Okimoto and T.P. Rohlen (eds), *Inside the Japanese System* (pp. 103–5). Stanford: Stanford University Press.

Clinton, J.R. (1985). *A Short History of Leadership Theory: A Paradigmatic Overview of the Leadership Field from 1841–1986*. Altadena, CA: Barnabas Resources.

Coates, N. (1988). Determinants of Japan's Business Success: Some Japanese Executives' Views. *Academy of Management Executive*, February: 69–72.

Cochran, T.C. (1949). Approaches to Entrepreneurial Personality. In *Change and the Entrepreneur* (pp. 97–112). Prepared by the Research Center in Entrepreneurial History. Cambridge, MA: Harvard University Press.

Cohen, N. (1980). The Five Stages of the Entrepreneur. *Venture*, July: 40–43.

Cole, A.H. (1949). Entrepreneurship and Entrepreneurial History. In *Change and the Entrepreneur* (pp. 85–107). Prepared by the Research Center in Entrepreneurial History. Cambridge, MA: Harvard University Press.

Collins, O.F. and **D.G. Moore** (1970). *The Organization Makers*. New York: Appleton–Century–Crofts.

Confucius (n.d.). The Analects of Confucius. Chapter 16, *Ji Shi, annotation on analects of Confucius*. Chengdu, China: Bashu Press. 1993.

Conger, J.A. and **R.N. Kanungo** (1994). Charismatic Leadership in Organizations: Perceived Behavioural Attributes and their Measurement. *Journal of Organizational Behaviour*, 15(5): 439–52.

Conner, D.W. (1996). Personal Power, Authority, and Influence: Cultural Founda-tions for Leadership and Leadership Formation in Northeast Thailand and Implications for Adult Leadership Training. Doctoral dissertation, Northern Illinois University.

Copeland, L. and **L. Griggs** (1985). *Going International*. New York: Random House.

Corporate Governance (1993). Vol. 1, No. 1–4.

—— (1994). Vol. 2, No. 1–4.

Crocker, D.A. (1993). Toward an Ethic for Development. *The Courier*, 137: 62–63.

Cummings, R.J. (1986). Africa between the Ages. *African Studies Review*, 29(2): 1–26.

Cusumano, M.A. (1985). *The Japanese Automobile Industry: Technology and Management at Nissan and Toyota*. Cambridge, Mass.: Harvard University Press.

Dalton, M. (1959). *Men who Manage*. New York: John Wiley.

Dansereau, F. Jr, G. Grean and **W.J. Haga** (1975). A Vertical Dyad Linkage Approach to Leadership within Formal Organizations: A Longitudinal Investigation of the Role Making Process. *Organizational Behavior and Human Performance*, 13(1): 46–78.

David, D. (1994). Fighting Poverty and Exclusion. *The Courier*, 143: 40.

—— (1994). Poverty in the Developing World: "The Main Trends". *The Courier*, 143: 43–44.

Dayal, I. (1976). *Cultural Factors in Designing Performance Appraisal Systems*. New Delhi: SRC Industrial Relations & Human Resources.

Deal, Terrence E. and **Allan A. Kennedy** (1982). *Corporate Culture: The Rites and Rituals of Corporate Life*. Reading, Mass.: Addison Wesley Publishing Co.

Deci, E.L. (1972). The Effects of Contingent and Noncontingent Rewards and Controls on Extrinsic Motivation. *Organizational Behavior and Human Performance*, 8: 217–29.

Dessler, G. (1986). *Organization Theory: Integrating Structure and Behavior*. Englewood Cliffs, NJ: Prentice-Hall Inc.

Deutsch, M. (1975). Equity, Equality and Need: What Determines Which Values Will be Used as the Basis of Distributive Justice. *Journal of Social Issues*, 31: 137–49.

—— (1985). *Distributive Justice*. New Haven, CT: Yale University Press.

Diduk, S. (1989). Women's Agricultural Production and Political Action in the Cameroon Grassfields. *Africa*, 59(3): 338–55.

Dom, C. (1994). Combating Poverty and Exclusion: Women and Banking: A Case Study from Southern Mali. *The Courier*, 143: 70–73.

Dore, Ronald P. (1973). *British Factory, Japanese Factory: The Origins of National Diversity in Industrial Relations*. Berkeley: University of California Press.

Drucker, D. (1986). Ask a Silly Question, Get a Silly Answer. In D.C. Korten (ed.), *Community Management: Asian Experience and Perspectives* (pp. 162–63). Kumarian Press.

Drucker, P. (1989). *The New Reality*. New York: Harper and Row.

Dunphy, D.C. (1986). A Historical Review of the Literature on the Japanese Enterprise and its Management. In S.R. Clegg, D.C. Dunphy and S.G. Redding (eds), *Enterprise and Management in East Asia* (pp. 343–68). Hong Kong: Center of Asian Studies.

Eisenhardt, K.M. and **C.B. Schoonhoven** (1990). Organizational Growth: Linking Founding Team, Strategy, Environment, and Growth among U.S. Semiconductor Ventures, 1978–1988. *Administrative Science Quarterly*, 35: 504–29.

Ekeh, P.P. (1974). *Social Exchange Theory: The Two Traditions*. Cambridge, MA: Harvard University Press.

Ellis, J. (ed.) (1978). *West African Families in Britain*. London: Routledge and Kegan Paul.

Emerson, R. (1962). Power Dependence Relations. *American Sociological Review*, 27: 31–40.

England, G.W. (1975). *The Manager and his Values: An International Perspective from the United States, Japan, Korea, India and Australia*. Cambridge, MA: Ballinger.

Ernst, C. and **J. Angst** (1983). *Birth Order: Its Influence on Personality*. New York: Springer-Verlag.

Etizioni, Amitai (1964). *Modern Organizations*. Englewood Cliffs, N.J.: Prentice-Hall.

Farmer, R.N. and **R.M. Richman** (1964). A Model for Research in Comparative Management. *California Management Review*, 4(2): 55–68.

—— (1965). *Comparative Management and Economic Progress*. Homewood, IL: Richard D. Dorwin.

Fei, H.T. (1948). *Peasant Life in China*. London: Routledge and Kegan Paul.

—— (1994). A Scholarly Autobiography (Chinese text). *Hong Kong Journal of Social Sciences*, 3: 1–22.

Fei, X.T. (1948). *Rural China*. Shanghai: Guancha She.

Fiedler, F.E. (1967). *A Theory of Leadership Effectiveness*. New York: McGraw-Hill.

Fleishman, E.A. (1967). Performance Assessment Based on an Empirically Derived Task Economy. *Human Factors*, 9: 349–66.

Foa, E.B. and **U.G. Foa** (1974). *Societal Structures of the Mind*. Springfield, IL: Charles C. Thomas.

Foa, E.B. and **U.G. Foa** (1980). Resource Theory of Social Exchange. In K.J. Gergen, M.S. Greenberg and R.H. Willis (eds), *Social Exchange: Advances in Theory and Research*. New York: Plenum.

Fox, Alan (1974). *Beyond Contract: Work Power and Trust Relations*. London: Faber and Faber.

Fukuda, K.J. (1996). Japanese in the Mind of Chinese. Working Paper, Chinese University of Hong Kong, September 1996.

Gartner, W.B. (1988). "Who is an Entrepreneur" is the Wrong Question. *American Journal of Small Business*, 13(Spring): 11–32.

—— (1989). Some Suggestions for Research on Entrepreneurial Traits and Characteristics. *Entrepreneurial Theory and Practice* (Fall): 27–37.

Gasse, Y. (1985). A Strategy for the Promotion and Identification of Potential Entrepreneurs at the Secondary School Level. In J.A. Hornaday, B. Shills, J.A. Timmons and K.H. Vesper (eds), *Frontiers of Entrepreneurial Research* (pp. 538–59). Wellesley, MA: Babson College.

Gergen, K.J., M.S. Greenberg and **R.H. Willis** (eds) (1980). *Social Exchange: Advances in Theory and Research* (pp. 189–96). New York: Plenum Press.

Gergen, K.J., S.J. Morse and **M.M. Gergen** (1979). Behaviour Exchange in Cross-cultural Perspective. In H.C. Triandis (ed.), *Handbook of Cross-cultural Psychology*. New York: Allyn and Bacon.

Giddens, A. (1984). *The Constitution of Society: Outline of the Theory of Structure*. Berkeley, CA: University of California Press.

Gilder, G. (1984). *The Spirit of Enterprise*. New York: Simon and Schuster.

Goffman, E. (1955). On Face-work: An Analysis of Ritual Elements in Social Interaction. *Psychiatry*, 18: 213–31.

Goheen, M. (1989). The Ideology and Political Economy of Gender: Women and Land in Nso, Cameroon. In C. Gladwin (ed.), *Women and Structural Adjustment in Africa* (Carter Lecture Series). Florida: University of Florida.

Gonyea, J.G. and B.K. Googins (1992). Linking the Worlds of Work and Family: Beyond the Productivity Trap. *Human Resource Management*, 31(3): 20–226.

Gopakumar, K. (1995). Entrepreneurship in Economic Thought: A Thematic View. *Journal of Entrepreneurship*, 4(1): 1.

Gopal, S. (1989). *Radhakrishnan: A Biography*. New Delhi: Oxford University Press.

Gouldner, A.W. (1960). The Norm of Reciprocity: A Preliminary Statement. *American Sociological Review*, 25(2): 161–78.

Graen, G. (1976). Role Making Processes within Complex Organizations. In M.D. Dunnette (ed.), *Handbook of Industrial and Organizational Psychology* (pp. 1201–45). Chicago: Rand McNally.

Graen, G. and J.F. Cashman (1975). A Role Making Model of Leadership in Formal Organizations: A Developmental Approach. In J.G. Hungt and L.L. Larson (eds), *Leadership Frontiers* (pp. 143–65). Kent, OH: Kent State University Press.

Graen, G.B. and T.A. Scandura (1987). Toward a Psychology of Dyadic Organizing. *Research in Organizational Behaviour*, 9: 175–208.

Granovetter, M. (1985). Economic Action and Social Structure: The Problem of Embeddedness. *American Journal of Sociology*, 91(3): 481–510.

Graves, D. (1972). Cultural Determinism and Management Behaviour. *Organizational Dynamics*, 1: 46–49.

Greenberg, M.S. (1980). A Theory of Indebtedness. In K.J. Gergen, M.S. Greenberg and R.H. Wills (eds), *Social Exchange: Advances in Theory and Research* (pp. 3–26). New York: Plenum Press.

Gregory, F.W. and I.D. Neu (1952). The American Industrial Elite in the 1870s—Their Social Origins. In Miller (ed.), *Men in Business*. Cambridge (MA): Harvard University Press.

Greshenkron, A. (1968). The Entrepreneur. *American Economic Review* (Papers and Proceedings), 58(2): 99.

Gupta, J.L. (1985). *Leadership Styles and Power Sharing in Business Enterprises*. Bombay: Himalaya Publishing House.

Gupta, R.K. (1991). Employees and Organization in India: Need for Moving beyond American and Japanese Models. *Economic and Political Weekly*, 26(21): M-68–M-76.

Hagen, E.E. (1962). *On the Theory of Social Change: How Economic Growth Begins*. London: Tavistock Publications.

Haire, M., E.F. Ghiselli and L.W. Porter (1966). *Managerial Thinking: An International Study*. New York, NY: John Wiley.

Hall, D. (1990). Promoting Work/Family Balance: An Organization Change Approach. *Organizational Dynamics*, Winter: 5–18.

Hambrick, D.C. and D.L. Brandon (1988). Executive Values. In D.C. Hambrick (ed.), *Executive Effect: Concept and Methods for Studying Top Managers*. Greenwich, CT: JAI Press.

Hamilton, G.G. (1984). Patriarchalism in Imperial China and Western Europe: A Revision of Weber's Sociology of Domination. *Theory and Society*, 13: 393–426.

Hamilton, G.G. and **M.W. Biggart** (1989). Market, Culture and Authority: A Comparative Analysis of Management and Organization in the Far East. *American Journal of Sociology*, 94 (Supplement): 52–94.

Han, Zhiguo (1987). On the Perspectives of Fairness and Efficiency in a Commodity Economy. *Brightness Daily*, December 14.'

Hannan, M.T. and **J. Freeman** (1977). The Population Ecology of Organizations. *American Journal of Sociology*, 82(5): 929–64.

Harbison, F. (1959). Management in Japan. In F. Harbison and C.A. Myers (eds), *The Industrial World: An International Analysis* (pp. 259–64). New York: McGraw-Hill.

Harbison, Frederick and **Charles A. Myers** (1959). *Management in the Industrial World.* New York: McGraw-Hill.

Hareven, T.K. (1982). *Family Time and Industrial Time: The Relationship between the Family and Work in a New England Industrial Community.* Cambridge: Cambridge University Press.

Harris, T.A. (1967). *I am O.K.—You are O.K.* New York: Avon Publishers.

Harrison, P. (1987). Africa: Food and Environment. Part III of *World Resources*, unpublished manuscript in preparation for World Resource Institute, Washington D.C.

Hassan, A. and **S.K. Singh** (eds) (1990). *Organizational Research in Indian Perspective.* New Delhi: Commonwealth Publishers.

Hay, M.J. and **S. Stichter** (1984). Introduction. In M.J. Hay and S. Stichter (eds), *African Women South of the Sahara* (pp. ix–xiv). London: Longman.

Hebert, R.F. and **A.N. Link** (1982). *The Entrepreneur: Mainstream Views and Radical Critiques.* New York: Praeger Publishers, CDS Inc.

Heller, F.A. and **B. Wilpert** (1981). *Competence and Power in Managerial Decision Making.* Chichester: Wiley.

Henn, J.K. (1984). Women in the Rural Economy: Past, Present and Future. In M.J. Hay and S. Stichter (eds), *African Women South of the Sahara* (pp. 1–18). London: Longman.

Herzberg, F. (1966). *Work and Nature of Man.* Cleveland: World Publishing.

Herzberg, F., B. Mausner and **B. Snyderman** (1959). *The Motivation to Work* (2nd edn). New York, NY: Wiley.

Hickson, D.J., C.R. Hinings, C.J. McMillan and **J.P. Schwitter** (1977). The Culture Free Context of Organizational Structure: A Tri-national Comparison. In T.D. Weinshall (ed.), *Cultural and Management* (pp. 354–82). Harmondsworth: Penguin.

Hill, P. (1978). Food-farming and Migration from Fante Villages. *Africa*, 48(3): 220–30.

Hisrich, R.D. (1986). The Woman Entrepreneur: Characteristics, Skills, Problems and Prescriptions for Success. In D.L, Sexton and R.W. Smilor (eds), *The Art and Science of Entrepreneurship* (pp. 61–81). Cambridge, MA: Ballinger.

——— (1990). Entrepreneurship/Intrapreneurship. *American Psychologist*, 45(2): 209–22.

Ho, D.Y., S.C. Chen and **C.I. Chiao** (1991). *Guanxi* Orientation: An Alternative to Explain Chinese Social Behavior (Chinese text). In K.S. Yang and K.K. Hwang (eds), *Chinese Psychology and Behavior* (1989). Taipei: Laureate.

Hofstede, G. (1980a). *Culture's Consequences: International Differences in Work-related Values.* London and Beverly Hills: Sage.

——— (1980b). Motivation, Leadership, and Organization: Do American Theories Apply Abroad? *Organizational Dynamics*, Summer: 42–63.

Hofstede, G. (1983). The Cultural Relativity of Organizational Practices and Theories. *Journal of International Business Studies,* Fall: 75–89.

—— (1988). McGregor in Southeast Asia? In D. Sinha and H.S.R. Kao (eds), *Social Values and Development: Asian Perspectives* (pp. 304–14). New Delhi: Sage.

—— (1991). *Cultures and Organizations: Software of the Mind.* London: McGraw-Hill.

Hofstede, G. and **M.H. Bond** (1988). The Confucius Connection: From Cultural Roots to Economic Growth. *Organizational Dynamics,* 16(4): 5–21.

Hollander, E.P. (1980). Leadership and Social Exchange Process. In K.J. Gergen, M.S. Greenberg and R.H. Wills (eds), *Social Exchange: Advances in Theory and Research* (pp. 103–18). New York: Plenum Press.

Holy Quran (1981). Arabic text and English translation (translated by M. Sarwari). Elmhurst, NY: Islamic Seminary.

Homans, G.C. (1958). Social Behaviour as Exchange. *American Journal of Sociology,* 63(6): 597–606.

Hornaday, J.A. and **J. Aboud** (1971). Characteristics of Successful Entrepreneurs. *Personnel Psychology,* 24(2): 141–53.

Hornaday, R.H. (1987). Small Business Managerial Types and Financial Performance: Further Evaluation of the Filley and Aldag Instrument. Paper presented at the 1987 National Academy of Management meeting, August, New Orleans, Louisiana.

Hornaday, R.H. and **B.H. Nunnally** (1987). *Decision Styles of Black Small Business Owners: A Replication.* Paper presented at the 1987 National Academy of Management meeting, August, New Orleans, Louisiana.

Hoselitz, B.F. (1960). The Early History of Entrepreneurial Theory. In J. Spengler (ed.), *Essays in Economic Thought* (pp. 234–57). Chicago: Rand McNally & Co.

Howard, A., K. Shudo and **M. Umeshima** (1984). Motivation and Values among Japanese and American Managers. *Personnel Psychology,* 36(4): 883–98.

Howell, J.P., P.W. Dorfman and **S. Kerr** (1986). Leadership and Substitutes for Leadership. *Journal of Applied Behavioral Science,* 22(1): 29–46.

Hsu, F.L.K. (1971). Eros, Affect and Bao. In F.L.K. Hsu (ed.), *Kinship and Culture.* Chicago, IL: Aldine Publishing.

Hsu, S.C. (1993). Don't Underestimate Taiwanese Family Enterprise (Chinese text). *Wealth Journal,* March: 267–70.

Hsung, R.M. and **Y.C. Hwang** (1992). Social Resources and Petty Bourgeoisie (Chinese text). *The Workship on Taiwanese Small-sized Home Workshop.* Taipei: Institute of Ethnology, Academia Sinica.

Huang, K.K. (1985). Face and Favour: Chinese Power Games. In K.S. Yang (ed.), *Modernization and Chinese Culture* (pp. 125–54). Taipei: Guey-Guann Publishing Company.

Hubbard, D. (1985). Economic Trends in Africa—1985. *Africa South of the Sahara* (15th edn). London: Europa Publications.

Hui, C.H. (1990). Work Attitudes, Leadership Styles, and Managerial Behaviours in Different Cultures. In R.W. Brislin (ed.), *Applied Cross-cultural Psychology* (pp. 186–208). Newbury Park: Sage.

Hunt, J.G. and **C. Michael** (1983). Mentorship: A Career Training and Development Tool. *Academy of Management Review,* 8: 475–85.

Hwang, F.S. (1977). *The Woman Worker and Taiwan Industrialization* (Chinese text). Taipei: Mutom.

Hwang, K.K. (1987). Face and Favor: The Chinese Power Game. *American Journal of Sociology*, 97(4): 944–74.

—— (1988). The Modernization of Chinese Family Enterprises (Chinese text). In K.K. Hwang (ed.), *The Chinese Power Game*. Taipei: Chiliu.

—— (1990a). The Individual and the Collective in *Bao*. In Living Psychology Editorial Board (ed.), *The Social Games of the Chinese: Renquing and Shigu* (pp. 20–27) (Chinese text). Taipei: Living Psychology Publications.

—— (1990b). Discussing the Chinese Concept of *Bao*. In Living Psychology editorial Board (ed.), *The Social Games of the Chinese: Renquing and Shigu* (Chinese text). Taipei: Living Psychology Publications.

—— (1995). Modernization of the Chinese Family Business. In H.S.R. Kao, D. Sinha and N. Sek-Hong (eds), *Effective Organizations and Social Values* (pp. 37–62). New Delhi: Sage.

Imai, Masaaki (1982). Quality Control and Small Group Activities: The Key to Improved Productivity. In *When in Japan: An Introduction for doing Business in and with Japan*, Vol. 3. Tokyo: Planning and Promotion Division, Hotel Okura, April 20, 1982.

India Today (1995). 15 June. New Delhi.

Inkeles, A. and **D.H. Smith** (1974). *On Becoming Modern*. London: Heinemann.

Izzeddin, N. (1953). *The Arab World*. Chicago, IL: Henry Regnery Co.

Jacobs, G. and **R. MacFarlane** (1990). *The Vital Corporation*. New Jersey: Prentice-Hall.

James, M. (1975). *The O.K. Boss*. Reading, Mass.: Addison-Wesley Publishing Co.

Japanese External Trade Organization (JETRO) (1982). *Japanese Corporate Decision Making*. JETRO, Business Information Series 9, Tokyo: JETRO.

Jaycox, E.V.K. (1993). Capacity Building: The Missing Link in African Development. *The Courier*, 141: 73–75.

Jenks, L.K. (1949). Approaches to Entrepreneurial Personality. In *Change and the Entrepreneur* (pp. 80–96). Prepared by the Research Center in Entrepreneurial History. Cambridge, MA: Harvard University Press.

Jin, Pei (1986). To Promote Productivity via Fairness and to Realize Fairness via Efficiency. *Economic Studies*, No. 7.

Kakar, S. (1971). Authority Patterns and Subordinate Behaviour in Indian Organizations. *Administrative Science Quarterly*, 16: 298–307.

—— (1974). *Personality and Authority in Work*. Bombay: Somaiya Publications.

—— (1978). *The Inner Experience: A Psychoanalytic Study of Childhood and Society in India*. New Delhi: Oxford University Press.

Kalra, S.K. (1975). Are We Ripe for Participative Management? *ISTD Review*, 5(3): 12–13.

—— (1981). Family Life of High Achievers—A Study in a Business Organization. *Indian Journal of Social Work*, 42(3): 252–63.

—— (1988). Reaction to Authoritarian Leadership: A Projective Study. *Indian Journal of Social Work*, 39(1): 27–43.

—— (1991). Perceived Self-improvement among Post-graduate Management Students after the Self-development Course. *Indian Journal of Training and Development*, 21(4): 34–39.

Kalra, S.K. and **R.K. Gupta** (1989). Reinforcing Self-development Training for the Branch Staff of a Large Engineering Company. *Indian Journal of Training and Development*, 19(1): 18–23.

Kalra, S.K., R.K. Gupta and **R. Raina** (1994). Higher Education Teachers' Perceptions and Feelings about their Community and Institutions: A Study of the Culture of Educational Institutions. *Indian Journal of Social Work*, 55(2).

Kamata, S. (1982). *Japan in the Passing Lane: An Insider's Account of Life in a Japanese Auto Factory*. London: Unwin Paperbacks.

Kamerman, S.B. (1983). *Meeting Family Needs: The Corporate Response*. New York: Pergamon Press.

Kanter, R.M. (1992). *The Change Masters: Corporate Entrepreneurs at Work*. London: Routledge.

Kanungo, R.N. (1980). *Biculturalism and Management*. Toronto: Butterworth.

—— (1990). Work Alienation in Developing Countries. In A.M. Jaeger and R.N. Kanungo (eds), *Management in Developing countries* (pp. 193–208). London: Routledge.

Kanungo, R.N. and **J. Bhatnagar** (1978). Achievement Orientation and Occupational Values: A Comparative Study of Young French and English Canadians. *Canadian Journal of Behavioural Science*, 10(3): 202–13.

Kanungo, R.N. and **J.A. Conger** (1995). Modal Orientation in Leadership Research and their Implications for Developing Countries. In R.N. Kanungo (ed.), *New Approaches to Employee Management*, Vol. 3: *Employee Management in Developing Countries* (pp. 155–70). Greenwich, Conn.: JAI Press.

Kanungo, R.N. and **A.M. Jaeger** (1990). Introduction: Need for Indigenous Management in Developing Countries. In A.M. Jaeger and R.N. Kanungo (eds), *Management in Developing Countries* (pp. 1–19). London: Routledge.

Kanungo, R.N. and **M. Mendonca** (1994). *Fundamentals of Organizational Behaviour*. Iowa: Kendall/Hunt Pub. Company.

Kanungo, R.N. and **S. Misra** (1992). Managerial Resourcefulness: A Reconceptualization of Managerial Skills. *Human Relations*, 45(12): 1311–32.

Kao, C.H.C. and **J.S. Lee** (1991). *The Taiwan Experience, 1949–1989* (Chinese text). Taipei: Commonwealth.

Kao, C.S. (1990). The Role of Personal Trust in Large Businesses in Taiwan: In G.G. Hamilton (ed.), *Business Group and Economic Development in East Asia*. Hong Kong: Center of Asian Studies.

Kao, C.S. and **C.S. Chen** (1989). The Social Order of Business Operation in Taiwan: *Renchin Guanxi* and Law (Chinese text). *Society and Economy*, 3 and 4: 151–65

Kao, H.S.R. (1994). *Emerging Trends in Asian Applied Psychology*. Keynote address presented at the 23rd International Congress of Applied Psychology, Madrid, Spain.

Kao, H.S.R. and **Ng Sek-Hong** (1988). Minimal Self and Chinese Work Behaviour: Psychology of the Grass-roots. In D. Sinha and H.S.R. Kao (eds), *Social Values and Development: Asian Perspectives* (pp. 254–72). New Delhi: Sage.

—— (1993). Organizational Commitment: From Trust to Altruism at Work? *Psychology and Developing Society*, 5(1): 47–60.

Kao, H.S.R., D. Sinha and **N. Sek-Hong** (eds) (1994). *Effective Organizations and Social Values*. New Delhi: Sage.

Kaplan, R. (1987). Entrepreneurship Reconsidered: The Anti-management Bias. *Harvard Business Review*, 84–85.

Kapp, W.K. (1963). *Hindu Culture, Economic Development and Economic Planning in India*. Bombay: Asia Publishing House.

Kassire, N.D. (1994). Which Should Come First—Tackling Poverty or Building Democracy? *The Courier*, 146: 34–36.

Katz, D. and **R.L. Kahn** (1978). *The Social Psychology of Organization* (2nd edn). New York: Wiley.

Kebzabo, S. (1994). An Opposition Overview: Our Programme and Our Ideas have to be Convincing. *The Courier*, 146: 40–42.

Kelley, L. and **R. Worthley** (1981). The Role of Culture in Comparative Management: A Cross-cultural Perspective. *Academy of Management Journal*, 24(1): 164–73.

Keys, J.B. and **T.R. Miller** (1984). The Japanese Management Theory Jungle. *Academy of Management Review*, 9: 342–53.

Khadra, B. (1990). The Prophetic-Caliphal Model of Leadership: An Empirical Study. *International Studies of Management and Organization*, 20: 37–52.

Khandwalla, P.N. (1980). Management in Our Backyard. *Vikalpa*, 5: 173–84.

—— (1994). The PI Motive: A Resource for Socio-economic Transformation of Developing Societies. In R.N. Kanungo and M. Mendonca (eds), *Work Motivation: Models of Developing Countries* (pp. 114–34). New Delhi: Sage.

Khare, A. (1997). Strategic Advantages of Good Supplier Relations in the Indian Automobile Industry. *Technovation*, 17(10): 17.

King, A.Y.C. (1980). An Analysis of *Renqing* in Interpersonal Relationships: A Preliminary Inquiry. In *Proceedings of the International Conference on Sinology* (pp. 423–28) (Chinese text). Taipei: Academia Sinica.

Kingma, K. (1993). Can Development be Measured? *The Courier*, 137: 70–72.

Kirzner, I.M. (1973). *Perception, Opportunity and Profit: Studies in the Theory of Entrepreneurship*. Chicago: University of Chicago Press.

Kobayashi, Yoko (1996). Outlook for Jobless Stays Grim. *Eastern Express*, p. 21, 2 March.

Komin, S. (1990). Culture and Work-related Values in Thai Organizations. *International Journal of Psychology*, 25(4): 681–704.

—— (1991). *Psychology of the Thai People: Values and Behavioral Patterns*. Bangkok: Research Center, NIDA.

—— (1994). Value-added Perception of Effective Thai Leadership. Paper presented at the Symposium of Perception of Leadership and Cultural Values at the 23rd International Congress of Applied Psychology. The International Association of Applied Psychology (IAAP), 17–22 July 1994, Madrid, Spain.

—— (1995a). *National Decision-making Behavior in Thailand*. Paper presented for Stockholm International Peace Research Institute (SIPRI), Research project on Arms Procurement Decision-Making, Stockholm, Sweden.

—— (1995b). Socio-cultural Influences in Managing for Productivity in Thailand. In Kwang-Kuo Hwang (ed.), *Easternization: Socio-cultural Impact on Productivity* (pp. 334–72). Tokyo: Asian Productivity Organization (APO).

Koontz, H. and **C. O'Donnell** (1964). *Principles of Management*. New York: McGraw-Hill.

Koontz, H., C. O'Donnell and **H. Weihrich** (1980). *Management*. New York: McGraw-Hill.

Korean Chamber of Commerce and Industry (KCCI) (1988). A Survey Report on the Labor–Management Relations in Korea (Korean text). Seoul: KCCI.

—— (1991). A Survey Report on the Values and Attitudes of the Industrial Workers of Korean Enterprises (Korean text). Seoul: KCCI.

—— (1992). *Corporate Culture: Toward Super Business Corporation* (Korean text). Seoul: KCCI.

Kovach, K.A. (1987). What Motivates Employees? *Business Horizons*, p. 61.

Kram, K.E. (1985). *Mentoring at Work: Development Relationships in Organizational Life*. Glenview, IL: Scott Foresman.

Kumar, Usha and **K.K. Singh** (1976). The Interpersonal Construct System of the Indian Manager: A Determinant of Organizational Behaviour. *Indian Journal of Social Psychology*, 51(4): 275–90.

Kuo, S.W.Y. (1983). *The Taiwan Economy in Transition*. New York: Westview Press.

Kuratko, D.F. and **R.M. Hodgetts** (1989). *Entrepreneurship: A Contemporary Approach*. New York: Dryden.

Lamb, R.K. (1952). Entrepreneur and Community. In W. Miller (ed.), *Men in Business* (pp. 91–119). Cambridge, MA: Harvard University Press.

Lan, Xinliang (1987). The Guiding Principle on Adjusting the Values of the Relationship between Fairness and Efficiency. *Brightness Daily*, May 21.

Laurent, A. (1983). The Cultural Diversity of Western Conceptions of Management. *International Studies of Management and Organization*, 13(1–2): 75–96.

Lee, Bong-Jin (1992). *The Korean Management Style: The Maeil Kyongje Shinmunsa* (Korean text).

Leibenstein, H. (1968). Entrepreneurship and Development. *American Economic Review* (Papers and Proceedings), 58(2): 75.

Li, Chunqiu (1984). *Popular Ethics*. Changchun, Jilin, China: Jilin People's Press.

Likert, R. (1967a). *New Pattern of Management* (2nd edn). New York, NY: McGraw-Hill.

——— (1967b). *The Human Organization*. New York: McGraw-Hill.

Lin, C.H. (1993). *The Formation of Leader's In-group Bias in a Taiwanese Enterprise* (Chinese text). Unpublished Master's thesis, Fujen Catholic University.

Lin, Jianchu and **Chufu Zhao** (1986). *A Course in Ethics*. Changchun, Jilin, China: Jilin People's Press.

Lin, K.T. (1987). The Career Development of Second-generation Enterprise Leader (Chinese text). *Modern Management Journal*, 126: 34–36.

Lin, S.I. (1993). An Investigation on the *Chin-shin* relations of Top Executives and the Roles of *Chin-shin* (Chinese text). Unpublished Master's thesis, National Taiwan University.

Liu, C.C. (1975). *An Analysis of Taiwan Economy after Postwar Era* (Japanese text). Tokyo: Tokyo University Press.

Liu, C.M. (1992). The Development of Theories on Work Motivation. *Chinese Journal of Applied Psychology* (Chinese text), 1: 39–51.

Liu, C.M. (1993a). The Development of an Integrated Work Motivation Theory: A Preliminary Empirical Study. *Chinese Journal of Applied Psychology* (Chinese text), 2: 1–24.

——— (1993b). Building a Foundation for a Deeper Indigenous Psychology: A Systematic Process. *Indigenous Psychological Research in Chinese Society* (Chinese text). 1: 201–7.

——— (1994). *Bao and Job Motivation* (Chinese text). Technical Report for National Science Council. Taipei: National Science Council.

Liu, C.M. (1995). *Bao* and Work Motivation: A Strategy for Qualitative Data Analysis (Chinese text). Papers presented at the Chinese Psychologist's Academic Symposium. Taipei: Department of Psychology, National Taiwan University.

Liu, C.Y. (1982). Public and Private: The Ethical Implications of Loyalty (Chinese text). In C.J. Hwang (ed.), *Heaven Way and Human Way*. Taipei: Lenchin.

Locke, E.A. and **D. Henne** (1986). Work Motivation Theories. In C.L. Cooper and I. Robertson (eds), *International Review of I/O Psychology* (pp. 1–35). Chichester: John Wiley & Sons.

Lopezllera, L. (1993). Development and Poverty: The Case of Latin America. *The Courier*, 137: 73–74.

Lorriman, John and **Kenjo Takashi** (1994). *Japan's Winning Margins*. Oxford: Oxford University Press.

Luckham, R. (1985). Political and Social Problems of Development. In *Africa South of the Sahara* (15th edn). London: Europa Publications.

Mamkoottam, K. (1982). *Trade Unionism Myth and Reality: Unionism in the Tata Iron and Steel Company*. Delhi: Oxford University Press.

Mao, Zedong (1963). Where Do Correct Ideas Come From? (first pocket edn). Beijing: People's Press.

—— (1964a). Struggle in the Chingkang Mountains. *Selected works of Mao Zedong*, Vol. 1 (1st edn). Beijing: Foreign Language Press. (First Published in 1928.)

—— (1964b). On Correcting Mistaken Ideas in the Party. *Selected works of Mao Zedong*, Vol. 1 (1st edn). Beijing: Foreign Language Press. (First Published in 1929.)

Mappa, S. (1994). Exclusion in North and South. *The Courier*, 143: 74.

Maquet, J. (1972). *Africanity*. New York: Oxford University Press.

Marx, K. (1970). Critique of the Gotha Program—Marginal to the Program of German Worker's Party. In S.K. Padovov (ed.), *Karl Marx on Revolution*, Vol. 1. New York, NY: McGraw-Hill. (First published in 1875.)

Maslow, A.H. (1943). A Theory of Human Motivation. *Psychological Review*, 80(50): 370–96.

Mauss, M. (1925). *The Gift*. Glencoe, IL: Free Press.

Mazrui, A.A. (1986). *The Africans*. New York: Praeger.

McClelland, D.C. (1961). *The Achieving Society*. Princeton: Van Nostrand.

—— (1975). *Power: The Inner Experience*. New York: Free Press.

—— (1987). Characteristics of Successful Entrepreneurs. *Journal of Creative Behaviour*, 21(3): 219–33.

McClelland, D.C. and **D.G. Winter** (1969). *Motivating Economic Achievement*. New York: Free Press.

McGregor, D. (1960). *The Human Side of Enterprise*. New York: McGraw-Hill.

—— (1967). *The Human Side of Enterprise*. New York, NY: McGraw-Hill.

Meade, R.D. (1967). An Experimental Study of Leadership in India. *Journal of Social Psychology*, 72: 35–73.

Mehta, P. (1994). Empowering the People for Social Achievement. In R.N. Kanungo and M. Mendonca (eds), *Work Motivation: Models for Developing Countries* (pp. 161–83). New Delhi: Sage.

Meindl, J.R., K.C. Yu and **J. Lu** (1987). Distributive Justice in the Workplace: Preliminary Data on Managerial Preferences in the PRC. In J.B. Beak (ed.), *Proceedings of the International Conference on Personnel and Human Resources Management*. Hong Kong.

Mendonca, M. and **R.N. Kanungo** (1990). Performance Management in Developing Countries. In A.M. Jaeger and R.N. Kanungo (eds), *Management in Developing Countries*. London: Routledge.

Mendonca, M. and **R.N. Kanungo** (1994). Conclusions: The Issue of Culture Fit. In R.N. Kanungo and M. Mendonca (eds), *Work Motivation: Models for Developing Countries* (pp. 49–83) New Delhi: Sage.

Menon, Sanjay T. (1994). Designing Work in Developing Countries. In R.N. Kanungo and M. Mendonca (eds), *Work Motivation: Models for Developing Countries* (pp. 84–113). New Delhi: Sage.

Mintzberg, H. (1973). *The Nature of Managerial Work.* New York: Harper and Row.

—— (1983). *Structure in Fives: Designing Effective Organisations* (pp. 293–97). Englewood Cliffs, New Jersey: Prentice-Hall.

—— (1989). *Minzberg on Management.* New York: Free Press.

Mishra, R. (1967). A Study of Role Clarity Efficiency and Job-satisfaction. Ph.D. thesis, Patna University, Patna.

Misra, G. and **R. Agarwal** (1985). The Meaning of Achievement: Implications for a Cross-cultural Theory of Achievement. In A.R. Lagunes and Y.H. Poortinga (eds), *From Different Perspectives: Studies of Behaviour Across Cultures* (pp. 250–66). Lisse: Swets and Zeitlinger.

Misra, S., R. Ghosh and **R.N. Kanungo** (1990). Measurement of Family Involvement— A Cross-national Study of Managers. *Journal of Cross-cultural Psychology,* 21(3): 232–48.

Misumi, J. (1983). Decision-making in Japanese Groups and Organizations. In B. Wilpert and A. Sorge (eds), *International Yearbook of Organizational Democracy* (pp. 525–39). London: John Wiley & Sons.

—— (1985). *The Behavioral Science in Leadership.* Ann Arbor: Michigan University Press.

Mitton, D.G. (1989). The Complete Entrepreneur. *Entrepreneurship Theory and Practice,* 13(3): 9–20.

Miyamoto, Musashi (1982). *The Book of Five Rings* (English edition). New York: Bantam Books.

Moghaddam, P.M., D.M. Taylor and **S.C. Wright** (1993). *Social Psychology in Cross-cultural Perspective.* New York: Freeman.

Morita, A. and **S. Ishihara** (1989). NO to ieru Nihon [Japan that can Say "NO"]. Tokyo: Kobunsha.

Morrow, L. (1992). Japan in the Mind of America. *Time,* p. 11, 10 February.

Naisbitt, John (1995). *Megatrends Asia.* London: Nicholas Brealey Publishing.

Negandhi, R.N. (1975). Comparative Management and Organization Theory: A Marriage Needed. *Academy of Management Journal,* 8(2): 334–44.

Nevis, E.C. (1983). Using an American Perspective in Understanding Another Culture: Toward a Hierarchy of Needs for the People's Republic of China. *The Journal of Applied Behavioral Science,* 19(3): 256.

Newsweek (1996). A Plea from the Bad Guys, p. 56, 19 February.

Nitobe, Inazo (1969). Bushido: *The Soul of Japan* (English edition). Tokyo: Charles E. Tuttle Company.

Nnoli, O. (1981). Introduction. In O. Nnoli (ed.), *Path to Nigerian Development* (pp. 1–20). Dakar, Senegal: Codesria Book Series.

Nohria, N. and **R.G. Eccles** (1992). *Networks and Organizations: Structure, Form and Action.* Boston: Harvard Business School Press.

Nord, W.R. (1980). The Study of Organizations through a Resource-exchange Paradigm. In K.J. Gergen, M.S. Greenberg and R.H. Willis (eds), *Social Exchange: Advances in Theory and Research* (pp. 119–39). New York: Plenum Press.

Nsamenang, A.B. (1992). *Human Development in Cultural Context.* Newbury Park, CA: Sage.

Nsingo, K. (1994). Africa's Population: The Paradox of Natural Wealth and Poverty. *The Courier,* 144: 72–73.

Oppong, C. (ed.) (1983). *Female and Male in West Africa.* London: Allen and Unwin.

Ouchi, W.G. (1981). *Theory Z: How American Business can Meet the Japanese Challenge.* Reading, Mass.: Addison-Wesley Publishing Company.

Oza, A.N. (1988). Integrated Entrepreneurship Development Programmes: The Indian Experience. *Economic and Political Weekly,* 23(22): M-73–M-79.

Padaki, O. (1988). Job Attitudes. In J. Pandey (ed.), *Psychology in India: The State of the Art,* Vol. 3. New Delhi: Sage.

Palmer, M. (1971). The Application of Psychological Testing to Entrepreneurial Potential. *California Management Review,* 13(3): 32–38.

Pan, W.C. (1989). The "Guanxi Networks" of Entrepreneurs in Taiwan and its Transformation: A Sociological Perspective (Chinese text). Ph.D. dissertation, Tunghai University.

Pandey, J. (1981). Ingratiation as a Social Behaviour. In J. Pandey (ed.), *Perspectives on Experimental Social Psychology in India* (pp. 157–87). New Delhi: Concept Publishing Co.

Pandey, S.N. (1989). *Human Side of Tata Steel.* New Delhi: Tata McGraw-Hill.

—— (1991). *Social Side of Tata Steel.* New Delhi: Tata McGraw-Hill.

Pareek, U. (1984). Interpersonal Styles: The SPIRO Instrument. *Developing Human Resources: The 1984 Annual* (pp. 119–30). San Diego, California: University Associates.

—— (1988). *Organizational Behaviour Processes.* Jaipur: Rawat Publications.

—— (1997). *Training Instruments for Human Resource Development.* New Delhi: Tata McGraw-Hill.

Perrow, C. (1992). Small-firm Networks. In N. Nohria and R.G. Eccles (eds), *Networks and Organizations: Structure, Form and Action.* Boston: Harvard Business School Press.

Petit, B. (1993). Democracy and Structural Adjustment in Africa. *The Courier,* 138: 74–75.

Pfeffer, J. (1981). *Power in Organization.* Marshfield, MA: Pitman.

Pfeffer, J. and **G.R. Salancik** (1978). The External Control of Organizations. New York: Harper and Row.

Powell, W.W. (1990). Neither Market nor Hierarchy: Network Forms of Organization. *Research in Organizational Behaviour,* 12: 295–336.

Prakash, K. (1995). Establishing Linkages between End-state Values and Core-values. In S.K. Chakraborty (ed.), *Human Values for Managers.* New Delhi: Wheeler Publishing.

Price, James L. (1972). *Handbook of Organizational Measurement.* Lexington, MA: Heath and Company.

Pryor, F.R. and **N.H.H. Graburn** (1980). The Myth of Reciprocity. In K.J. Gergen, M.S. Greenberg and R.H. Wills (eds), *Social Change: Advances in Theory and Research* (pp. 215–37). New York: Plenum Press.

Rahim, M.A. (1983). A Measure of Styles of Handling Interpersonal Conflict. *Academy of Management Journal*, pp. 368–76.

——— (1985). A Strategy for Managing Conflict in Complex Organizations. *Human Relations*, 38(1), January.

Ramaswamy, U. (1983). *Work, Union and Community: Industrial Man in South India.* Delhi: Oxford University Press.

Randon, Michel (1987). *Japan: Strategy of the Unseen.* Northamptonshire: Aquarian Press.

Redding, G. and **G.Y. Wong** (1986). The Psychology of Chinese Organizational Behavior. In M.H. Bond (ed.), *The Psychology of the Chinese People* (pp. 267–95). Hong Kong: Oxford University Press.

Redding, S.G. (1990). *The Spirit of Chinese Capitalism.* Berlin: Walter de Gruyter.

Redding, S.G., A. Norman and **A. Schlander** (1994). The Nature of Individual Attachment to the Organization: A Review of East Asian Variations. In H.C. Triandis, M.D. Dunnette and L.M. Hough (eds), *Handbook of Industrial and Organizational Psychology*, Vol. 4 (pp. 647–88). Palo Alto, CA: Consulting Psychologists Press.

Reitz, H.J. (1977). *Behavior in Organizations.* Homewood, IL: Irwin.

Reynolds, P.D. (1991). Sociology and Entrepreneurship: Concepts and Contributions. *Entrepreneurship Theory and Practice*, Winter: 47–70.

Riddell, J.C. and **D.J. Campbell** (1986). Agricultural Intensification and Rural Development: The Mandara Mountain of North Cameroon. *African Studies Review*, 29(3): 89–106.

Robinson, M. (1974). *Islam and Capitalism.* London: Allen Lane.

Robinson, P.B., D.V. Stimpson, J.C. Huefner and **H.K. Hunt** (1991). An Attitude Approach to Prediction of Entrepreneurship. *Entrepreneurship Theory and Practice* Summer: 13–31.

Rohlen, Thomas P. (1992). Learning: The Mobilization of Knowledge in the Japanese Political Economy. In S. Kumon and H. Rosovsky (eds), *The Political Economy of Japan*, Vol. 3 (pp. 321–63). Stanford: Stanford University Press.

Roland, A. (1984). The Self in India and America. In V. Kavolis (ed.), *Design of Selfhood.* New Jersey: Associated University Press.

——— (1988). *In Search of Self in India and Japan—Towards a Cross-cultural Psychology.* Princeton: Princeton University Press.

Rozman, G. (1991). The East Asian Region in Comparative Perspective. In G. Rozman (ed.), *The East Asian Region.* Princeton, NJ: Princeton University Press.

Rychlak, J.F. (1981). *Introduction to Personality and Psychotherapy: A Theory Construction Approach.* Boston: Houghton and Mifflin.

Sahay, A., S.K. Kalra and **R.K. Gupta** (1994). A Bibliography of Managerial Leadership in Indian Context: 1985 to Early 1992. *Indian Journal of Training and Development*, 24(2).

Sahlins, M.D. (1965). On the Sociology of Primitive Exchange. In *The Relevance of Models for Social Anthropology* (pp. 139–238). Association of Social Anthropologists of the Commonwealth, Monograph 1. New York: Praeger.

Sakaiya, T. (1993). *Soshiki No Seisui.* PHP Institute Inc.

Sato, Y. (1993). The Determinants and Implications of Export-oriented Industrialization: Beyond Trading Policy Approach (Japanese text). Unpublished manuscript. Tokyo: Institute of Asia Economy, Tokyo University.

Saul, J.S. and **R. Woods** (1981). African Peasantries. In D.L. Cohen and J. Daniel (eds), *Political Economy of Africa* (pp. 112–18). London: Longman.

Say, J.B. (1967). *A Catechism on Political Economy* (translated by John Richter). New York: Augustus M. Kelley. (Originally published in 1967.)

Schatz, S.P. (1971). n-Achievement and Economic Growth: A Critical Appraisal. In P. Kilby (ed.), *Entrepreneurship and Economic Development*. New York: Free Press.

Schein, E.H. (1985). *Organizational Culture and Leadership*. San Francisco: Jossey-Bass.

—— (1990). Organizational Culture. *American Psychology*, 45(2): 109–19.

Schein, H.E. (1984). Coming to New Awareness of Organizational Culture. *Sloan Management Review*, 25(2): 3.

Schultheis, M.J. (1989). Refugees in Africa: The Geopolitics of Forced Displacement and Repatriation. *African Studies Review*, 32(1): 3–29.

Schumpeter, J.A. (1934). *The Theory of Economic Development*. Cambridge, MA: Harvard Economic Studies.

—— (1949). *The Theory of Economic Development*. Cambridge, MA: Harvard University Press.

Senege, P.M., C. Roberts, R.B. Ross, B.J. Smith and **A. Kliner** (1994). *The Fifth Discipline Fieldbook: Strategies and Tools for Building a Learning Organization*. New York: Currency and Doubleday.

Servan-Schreiber, J.J. (1967). *Le défi Americain*. Paris: Danoel.

Sexton, D.L. and **P.V. Auken** (1982). Characteristics of Successful and Unsuccessful Entrepreneurs. *Texas Business Review*, September–October: 236–39.

Shapero, A. (1975). The Displaced Uncomfortable Entrepreneur. *Psychology Today*, November: 83–86.

Shaver, K.G. & **L.R. Scott** (1991). Person, Process, Choice: The Psychology of New Venture Creation. *Entrepreneurship Theory & Practice*, Winter: 23–45.

Sheth, N.R. (1968). *The Social Framework of an Indian Factory*. Bombay: Oxford University Press.

Shin, Yoo-Gen (1992). *The Management of Korean Business Organizations: Characteristics and Perspective* (Korean text). Seoul: Parkyoungsa Publishing Co.

Silin, R.F. (1976). *Leadership and Values*. Cambridge, MA: Harvard University Press.

Singh, N.K. (1990). *The Dialogue with Yeti: Insight on Man and Organization*. New Delhi: Foundation for Organizational Research and Education.

Sinha, D. (1988). Basic Indian Values and Behaviour Disposition in the Context of National Development: An Appraisal. In D. Sinha and H.S.R. Kao (eds), *Social Values and Development: Asian Perspectives* (pp. 31–55). New Delhi: Sage.

—— (1995). Towards Indigenisation of Management: The Asian Scenario. *Abhigyan*, Spring: 7–13.

—— (1997). Indigenizing Psychology. In J.W. Berry, Y.H. Poostinga and J. Pandey (eds), *Handbook of Cross-cultural Psychology*, Vol. 1 (2nd edn) (pp. 129–69) Boston: Allyn and Bacon.

Sinha, D. and **H.S.R. Kao** (1988). Value-development Congruence. In D. Sinha and H.S.R. Kao (eds), *Social Values and Development: Asian Perspectives* (pp. 10–27). New Delhi: Sage.

Sinha D. and **M. Sinha** (1990). Dissonance in Work Culture in India. In A.D. Moddie (ed.), *The Concept of Work in Indian Society* (pp. 206–19). New Delhi: Manohar Publications.

Sinha, D. and **R.C. Tripathi** (1994). Individualism in a Collective Culture: A Case of Coexistence of Opposites. In U. Kim, H.C. Triandis, C. Kagitcibasi, S.C. Choi and

G. Yoon. (eds), *Individualism and Collectivism: Theory, Method and Application* (pp. 123–36). Thousand Oaks, CA: Sage.

Sinha, Dhauni P. (1996). For a Home Space Work Ethos. *The Hindu Business Line*, 9 March, Madras.

Sinha, J.B.P. (1974). A Case of Reversal in Participative Management. *Indian Journal of Industrial Relations*, 10(2): 179–87.

—— (1980). *The Nurturant Task Leader: A Model of the Effective Executive*. New Delhi: Concept Publishing Co.

—— (1990). *Work Culture in the Indian Context*. New Delhi: Sage.

—— (1993a). Cultural Embeddedness and Developmental Role in Industrial Organizations in India. In M.V. Dunnette (ed.), *Handbook of Industrial and Organizational Psychology*, Vol. 4 (pp. 727–64). Palo Alto, CA: Consulting Psychologists Press.

—— (1993b). A Model for Effective Leadership Style in India. In A.M. Jaeger and R.N. Kanungo (eds), *Management in Developing Countries* (pp. 253–63). London: Routledge.

Sinha, J.B.P. and D. Sinha (1990). Role of Social Values in Indian Organizations. *International Journal of Psychology*, 25: 705–14.

—— (1994). Role of Social Values in Indian Organizations. In H.S.R. Kao, D. Sinha and N. Sek-Hong (eds), *Effective Organizations and Social Values* (pp. 164–73). New Delhi: Sage.

Smelser, N.J. (1976). *The Sociology of Economic Life*. Englewood Cliffs, NJ: Prentice Hall.

Smith, Adam (1976). *An Inquiry into the Nature and Causes of the Wealth of Nations*. R.H. Campbell and A.S. Skinner (eds). Oxford: Oxford University Press. (First Published in 1776.)

Smith, Charles (1995). Excess Labor Burdens Corporate Japan. *South China Morning Post*, p. B1, 10 November.

Smith P.C., L.M. Kendall and C.L. Hulin (1969). *The Measurement of Satisfaction in Work and Retirement*. Chicago: Rand-McNally.

Smith, R.J. (1983). *Japanese Society: Tradition, Self and the Social Order*. Cambridge: Cambridge University Press.

Snow, C.C. and R.E. Miles (1992). Managing 21st Century Network Organizations. *Organizational Dynamics*, Winter: 5–20.

Snyder, M. (1987). *Public Appearances/Private Realities: The Psychology of Self-monitoring*. New York: W.H. Freeman.

Solo, C. (1951). Innovation in the Capitalist Process: A Critique of Schumpeterian Theory. *Quarterly Journal of Economics*, 65(3): 57.

Srinivas, Kalburgi M. (1994). Organization Development: Maya or Moksha. In R.N. Kanungo and M. Mendonca (eds), *Work Motivation: Models for Development Countries* (pp. 248–82). New Delhi: Sage.

Staehle, W.H. (1996). *Management*. München: Franz Vahlen.

Staudt, K. (1986). Stratification, Implications for Women's Politics. In C. Robertson and I. Berger (eds), *Women and Class in Africa* (pp. 197–215). New York: Holmes and Meier.

Stewart, I.N. and P.L. Peregoy (1983). Catastrophe Theory Modeling in Psychology. *Psychological Bulletin*, 94: 336–62.

Swayer, J.E. (1952). Entrepreneur in Social Order. In W. Miller (ed.), *Men in Business* (pp. 7–22). Cambridge, MA: Harvard University Press.

Swayne, C.B. and **W.R. Tucker** (1973). *The Effective Entrepreneur.* Morristown, NJ: General Learning Press.

Szterenfeld, A. (1994). Emerging Markets: Latin America. *Crossborder,* Winter: 6–9.

Tagore, Rabindranath (1988). *Lectures and Addresses.* New Delhi: Macmillan.

Takayama, Hideo (1996). The New Corporate Culture. *Newsweek,* pp. 40–42, 25 March.

Tang, C.Y. (ed.) (1980). *Sickness: Its State of Affairs* (pp. 103–13) (Chinese text). Taipei: Swanlake Monthly Publications.

Taylor, F.W. (1911). *Principles of Scientific Management.* New York: Harper and Row.

Tedeschi, J. (1981). *Impression Management Theory and Social Psychological Research.* Orlando, Fla: Academic Press.

Tetlock, P.E. and **A. Manstead** (1985). Impression Management Versus Intrapsychic Explanations in Social Psychology: A Useful Dichotomy? *Psychological Review,* 93: (1) 59–77.

The Hindustan Times (1995). p. 20, 20 May, New Delhi.

Thiagarajan, K.M. and **S.D. Deep** (1970). A Study of Supervisor Subordinate Influence on Satisfaction in Four Cultures. *Journal of Social Psychology,* 82: 173–80.

Thompson, E.P. (1963). *The Making of the English Working Class.* New York: Pantheon.

Thurow, Lester (1993). *Head to Head: The Coming Economic Battle among Japan, Europe and America.* New York: Warner Books.

Toffler, Alvin (1981). *The Third Wave.* New York: Bantam Books.

Triandis, H.C. (1973). Some Psychological Dimensions of Modernization. *Proceedings of the 17th International Congress of Applied Psychology,* Vol. 2 (pp. 60–85). Bruxelles: Editat.

—— (1988). Collectivism and Development. In D. Sinha and H.S.R. Kao (eds), *Social Values and Development: Asian Perspectives* (pp. 285–303). New Delhi: Sage.

Tripathi, R.C. (1981). Machiavellianism and Social Manipulation. In J. Pandey (ed.), *Perspectives on Experimental Social Psychology in India* (pp. 133–56). New Delhi: Concept Publishing Co.

—— (1988). Aligning Values to Development in India. In D. Sinha and H.S.R. Kao (eds), *Social Values and Development: Asian Perspectives* (pp. 315–33). New Delhi: Sage.

—— (1990). Interplay of Values in the Functioning of Indian Organizations. *International Journal of Psychology,* 25: 715–34.

—— (1994). Interplay of Values in the Functioning of Indian Organizations. In H.S.R. Kao, D. Sinha and Ng Sek-Hong (eds), *Effective Organizations and Social Values* (pp. 174–92). New Delhi: Sage.

Tsui, A.S. and **C.A. O'Reilly III** (1989). Beyond Simple Demographics Effects: The Importance of Relational Demography in Superior–Subordinate Dyads. *Academy of Management Journal,* 32(2): 402–23.

Turner, B. (1981). *Weber on Islam.* London: Routledge and Kegan Paul.

Turrittin, J. (1988). Men, Women and Market Trade in Rural Mali, West Africa. *Canadian Journal of African Studies,* 22(3): 583–604.

Udy, S.N. (1970). *Work in Traditional and Modern Society.* Englewood Cliffs, MJ: Prentice-Hall.

United Nations (1955). *Processes and Problems of Industrialisation in Undeveloped Countries.* New York: United Nations.

United Nations Development Programme (UNDP). *Human Development Report, 1996.* New York: Oxford University Press.

Van Maanen, J. and **E.H. Schein** (1979). Toward a Theory of Organizational Socialization. *Research in Organizational Behaviour,* 1: 209–64.

Verma, J. (1987). Some Observations by an Indian Visitor to the United States. *International Journal of Intercultural Relations,* 11: 327–35.

Vesper, K.H. (1980). *New Venture Strategies.* Englewood Cliffs, NJ: Prentice-Hall.

Virmani, B.R. and **S. Guptan** (1991). *Indian Management.* New Delhi: Vision Books.

Vivekananda, S. (1958). *Collected Works,* Vol. II. Calcutta: Advaita Ashrama.

—— (1976). *India and her Problems* (Swami Nirvedananda, ed.). Calcutta: Advaita Ashrama.

Vogel, E.F. (1989). *One Step Ahead in China: Guangdong under Reform.* Cambridge, MA: Harvard University Press.

Vroom, V.H. (1964). *Work and Motivation.* New York: Wiley.

Walder, A.G. (1983). Organized Dependency and Culture of Authority in Chinese Industry. *Journal of Asian Studies,* 63(1): 51–76.

Watanabe, Takao (1991). *Demystifying Japanese Management.* Tokyo: Gakuseisha Publishing Co.

Weaver, C.N. (1976). What Workers Want from their Jobs. *Personnel,* May–June: 49.

Weber, M. (1930). *The Protestant Ethic and the Spirit of Capitalism* (translated by Talcòtt Parsons). New York: Charles Scribner's Sons.

—— (1947). *The Theory of Social and Economic Organization* (translated by T. Parsons). New York: Free Press.

Weekly Post (1996). Research and Development (Japanese text). 19 April: 31–42.

Wei, C.T. (1987). The Concept of *Bao,* its Past and its Present. In Living Psychology Editorial Board (ed.), *The Social Games of the Chinese: Renqing and Shigu* (pp. 5–13) (Chinese text). Taipei: Living Psychology Publications.

Wen, C.I. (1982). Repay and Revenge: An Analysis of Social Exchange Behavior. In K.S. Yang and C.I. Wen (eds), *The Sinicization of Social and Behavioural Science Research* (pp. 311–44) (Chinese text). Taipei: Academia Sinica.

—— (1987). Alternation and Changes in *Bao.* In Living Psychology Editorial Board (ed.), *The Social Games of the Chinese: Renqing and Shigu* (pp. 14–19) (Chinese text), Taipei: Living Psychology Publications.

Whitley, R. (1992). *Business Systems in East Asia: Firms, Market and Societies.* London: Sage.

Wilder, D.A. (1986). Social Categorization: Implications for Creation and Reduction of Intergroup Bias. In L. Berkowitz (ed.), *Advance in Experimental Social Psychology* (pp. 291–355). New York: Academic Press.

Williamson, H.F. (1966). Business History, Economic History. *Journal of Economic History,* 26(4): 407–17.

Wilpert, B. and **S.Y. Scharpf** (1990). Chinese–German Joint Venture Management. *International Journal of Psychology,* 25: 643–56.

Wilson, D. (1986). *The Sun at Noon: An Anatomy of Modern Japan.* London: Hamish Hamilton.

Wipper, A. (1982). Riot and Rebellion among African Women: Three Examples of Women's Political Clout. In J. O'Brian (ed.), *Perspectives on Power: Women in Africa, Asia and Latin America* (pp. 50–72). Durham, NC: Duke University Center for International Studies.

Wong, S.L. (1988). *Emigrant Entrepreneurs: Shanghai Industrialists in Hong Kong.* Hong Kong: Oxford University Press.

—— (1990). The Chinese Culture and Hongkong Modernization (Chinese text). In S.L. Wong (ed.), *Chinese Religion Ethics and Modernization.* Taipei: Sanwu.

World Bank (1984). *Toward Sustained Development in Sub-Saharan Africa*. Washington, DC: World Bank.

Wu, Liangliang (1991). New Exploration on Equity Theory. *Behavioral Sciences*, No. 3.

Xin, Changxing (1987). Problems of Fairness and Efficiency in the Reform of Distribution System. *Brightness Daily*.

Xu, Chang and **Wei Sun** (1987). Why People Still Complain When Meat in their Bowl has been Becoming More? *People's Daily*, August 16.

Yang, C.F. (1988a). Familism and Development: An Examination of the Role of Family in Contemporary China Mainland, Hong Kong and Taiwan. In D. Sinha and H.S.R. Kao (eds), *Social Values and Development: Asian Perspectives* (pp. 93–123). New Delhi: Sage.

—— (1988b). Gift-giving and Changes in Sense of Values. In K.S. Yang (ed.), *The Psychology of the Chinese People* (pp. 383–413) (Chinese text). Taipei: Kuikauan Book Company.

Yang, K.S. (1981). The Chinese Character and Behavior: Formation and Transformation. *Chinese Journal of Psychology*, 23(1): 39–55.

—— (1988). The Relationship between Chinese and Nature, Others and Self (Chinese text). In C.I. Wen and M.H.H. Hsiao (eds), *Chinese: The Concept and Behavior*. Taipei: Chiliu.

Yang, L.S. (1957). The Concept of *"Bao"* as a Basis for Social Relations in China. In J.K. Fairbank (ed.), *Chinese Thought and Institutions* (pp. 291–309). Chicago, IL: University of Chicago Press.

—— (1987). *Repayment, Protection and Forbearance in Chinese Culture* (Chinese text). Hong Kong: Chinese University Press.

Yen, C.C. (1987). *A Theory of Head of State*. Taipei: Yuen-Liu Publishing Company.

Yoshino, M.Y. (1968). *Japan's Managerial System: Tradition and Innovation*. Cambridge, MA: MIT Press.

Young, C.F. and **C.H. Hui** (1986). Equal Distribution and Sense of Unfairness. *Journal of Chinese Psychology*, 28(2).

Young, S. (1994a). CDI Transformation Supported by the Private Sector: Industrialists Prepare for Lome IV Mid-term Review. *The Courier*, 143: 10–11.

—— (1994b). Saving Biodiversity. *The Courier*, 143: 83–84.

Yu, K.C., D.R. Bunker and **C.P.M. Wilderom** (1989). Employee Values Related to Rewards and the Operation of Reward Systems in Contemporary Chinese Enterprises. Proceedings of the Third International Conference of Management, Eastern Academy of Management.

Yu, K.C., C.P.M. Wilderom and **R.G. Hunt** (1989). Reward Allocation Norms of Employees in the People's Republic of China. *Proceedings of the Third International Conference of Management*. Eastern Academy of Management.

Yu, P.C. (1993). Instrumental *Ren-chyng* and Affective *Ren-chyng*: A Case Study of a Governmental Enterprise. *The Journal of Social Science*, Vol. 41, November: College of Law, National Taiwan University, Taipei, Taiwan.

Yu, Wenzhao (1991). Threshold of Fairness Gaps and Fair Distribution. *Behavioral Sciences*, No. 1.

Yukl, G.A. (1989). *Leadership in Organizations*. Englewood Cliffs: Prentice-Hall.

—— (1994). *Leadership in Organizations* (3rd edn). Englewood Cliffs, New Jersey: Prentice-Hall.

Zelikoff, S.B. (1969). On the Obsolescence and Retraining of Engineering Personnel. *Training and Development Journal*, 23(5): 3–14.

Zhang, Chunqiao (1958). Do Away with Bourgeois Right Ideology. *People's Daily*, 13 October.

—— (1975). On the All-round Dictatorship Over Bourgeois. *People's Daily*, 1 April.

Zhou, Weimin and **Zhongyuan Lu** (1985). Give Priority to Efficiency while Paying Consideration to Justice—A Trade-off for Forwarding towards Prosperity. *Economic Studies*, No. 2.

NOTES ON CONTRIBUTORS

Abbas J. Ali is Professor of Management at Indiana University, USA. His research interests include global business leadership, foreign policy, comparative management and organizational politics. He is Editor of *International Journal of Commerce and Management* and *Advances in Competitiveness Research*, and Executive Editor of *Competitiveness Review*.

Suresh Balakrishnan is Research Coordinator at the Public Affairs Centre, Bangalore. He received his Ph.D. in organizational behaviour from the Indian Institute of Management (Ahmedabad). Besides a variety of training and research experiences in the areas of organizational redesign, entrepreneurial development and participatory methodologies, he has been active as an advisor and consultant to the UN and other international agencies, NGOs and self-help groups. Recently, he was Visiting Fellow at the Institute of Development Studies, Sussex, UK.

S.K. Chakraborty is on the faculty of the Indian Institute of Management, Calcutta, and is also Convenor of the Management Centre for Human Values there. His areas of interest include finance and control, and human values and ethos. He is the convenor of an annual workshop on Management by Values at IIM, Calcutta. He has taught at the Stockholm Business School and the Melbourne Institute of Technology. In 1994, he received the 'Best Management Teacher' award from the Association of Indian Management Schools. Apart from numerous publications on human resource management, he is the editor of the Journal of Human Values.

Borshiuan Cheng is Professor at the Department of Psychology, National Taiwan University, from where he also received his Ph.D. An industrial and organizational psychologist, he has been Visiting Fellow at the Universities of California and Cambridge. He has published widely in the fields of leadership, organizational culture and Chinese organization studies.

Shu-Cheng Chi is Associate Professor of Organizational Behaviour and Human Resources Management at National Taiwan University. His research interests include leadership behaviour and corporate culture in Chinese organizations. He has published widely (in Mandarin Chinese).

John Fukuda is Professor at the Department of International Business, Chinese University of Hong Kong. He received his Ph.D. from the University of Hong Kong, and holds degrees in economics and journalism, and has also attended the Advanced International Certificate Programme on Conflict Resolution from the European University Centre for Peace Studies in Austria.

K. Gopakumar is Research Officer at the Public Affairs Centre, Bangalore. He is writing his doctoral dissertation on entrepreneurship, with a special focus on entrepreneurial behaviour among small and micro enterprises. A scholar with varied interests, he holds degrees in economics and journalism, and has also attended the Advanced International Certificate Programme on Conflict Resolution from the European University Centre for Peace Studies, Austria.

Rajen K. Gupta is on the faculty of the Management Development Institute, Gurgaon. An electrical engineer from the Indian Institute of Technology, Kanpur, he received his Ph.D. in management studies from IIM, Ahmedabad. He is a founding member of the National Human Resource Development Network, and a member of the Indian Society for Applied Behavioural Science. In 1993–94 he was Visiting Professor at the Rotterdam School of Management. His publications include *Implementing Human Resources Development*.

He Wei is Associate Professor of Organizational Behaviour and Human Resource Management at the School of Management, Dalian University of Technology, Liaoning, PRC. His research interests include motivation and values, cross-cultural management and organizational management.

Satish Kumar Kalra is on the faculty of the Management Development Institute, Gurgaon. He received his Ph.D. from the Tata Institute of Social Sciences, Mumbai, and has been Professor of Organizational Behaviour and Head of the General Management Group at the National Institute for Training in Industrial Engineering, Mumbai. He was also on the faculty of the Indian Institute of Management (Lucknow). His areas of interest include self-oriented human resource development interventions, leadership and team-building. He is also Co-Chairman of the editorial board of the *Indian Journal for Training and Development*.

Rabindra N. Kanungo is Professor of Organizational Behaviour, and presently holds the Faculty Management Chair at McGill University, Canada. He has published widely in both basic and applied areas of psychology and management. His published works include *Compen- sation: Effective Reward Management* (co-authored); *Ethical Dimen- sions of Leadership* (co-authored); and *Entrepreneurship and Innovation: Models of Development* (edited). For his contribution to psychology and management, Professor Kanungo was elected Fellow of the Canadian Psychological Association and awarded the Commonwealth and Seagram Senior Faculty Fellowships and Best Paper Awards.

Henry S.R. Kao is Chair Professor of Psychology at the University of Hong Kong. He has earlier taught at Purdue University, and did research at the University of Michigan, Ann Arbor, both in the US, and at National Chengchi University in Taipei. He is President of the Division of Psychology and National Development, International Association of Applied Psychology. Apart from contributing many papers to journals worldwide, he has authored *Psychology of Chinese Calligraphy*; (co- authored with Ng Sek-Hong) *Organizational Behaviour* (in Chinese); (co-edited with Durganand Sinha) *Social Values and Development* and (co-edited with C.S. Yang) *Chinese and the Chinese Mind* (in Chinese).

Anshuman Khare is Research Scientist at the Motilal Nehru Institute of Research and Business Administration (MONIRBA) at Allahabad. His areas of interest include operations management with special reference to the Just-in-Time approach to manufacturing, and strategic management and manufacturing. He received a Japanese Government scholarship to do post-doctoral research at Ryukoku University in Kyoto, Japan.

Son-Ung Kim is Professor of Psychology at Hanyang University, Seoul. He received his Ph.D. from Iowa State University in the US. His research interests focus on social change and development. From 1975 to 1981 he was Senior Fellow at the Korean Development Institute. He has co- authored *Economic Development, Population Policy and Demographic Transition in Kerala*.

Suntaree Komin is Associate Professor of Cross-cultural Industrial/ Organizational Psychology at the National Institute of Development Administration (NIDA) in Bangkok. She obtained her doctoral degree from the University of Hawaii, and has been engaged in the psychological study of and research in Thai values and value systems, and various related cross-cultural management studies, from motivation and decision-making to leadership. Dr Komin is the author of *Psychology of the Thai People: Values and Behavioural Patterns*, and *Social Dimensions of Industrialization in Thailand*.

Chaoming Liu is Associate Professor in the Department of Applied Psychology at the Fu-Jen Catholic University in Taipei. He received his Ph.D. from Purdue University, USA, and is interested in work motivation, leadership, organizational culture and indigenous studies.

Ng Sek-Hong is Reader in the School of Business, University of Hong Kong. He is engaged in teaching and research in the areas of human resource management and industrial relations, organizational behaviour and labour law. His publications include (co-authored, in Chinese) *Organizational Behaviour*; (co-authored) *Beyond Two Societies: Hong Kong Labour in Transition*; and (co-edited) *Effective Organizations and Social Values*.

The late **Durganand Sinha** began his distinguished career as Lecturer in Applied Psychology at Patna University. He went on to hold various academic positions including Assistant Professor of Humanities and Social Sciences, IIT (Kharagpur); Professor and Head of the Department of Psychology, Allahabad University; Director of the A.N. Sinha Institute of Social Studies in Patna, and ICSSR National Fellow. Recipient of numerous awards and fellowships, Prof. Sinha's principal interests included memory transformations, social perceptions, industrial psychology, anxiety and rural psychology. Among his published works are *Indian Villages in Transition: A Motivational Analysis; Motivation and Rural Development*; (co-edited with H.S.R. Kao) *Social Values and Development: Asian Perspectives*; and (co-edited with H.S.R. Kao and Ng Sek-Hong) *Effective Organizations and Social Values*.

Mala Sinha teaches at the Faculty of Management Studies, University of Delhi (South Campus). She received her Ph.D. from Allahabad University. Her research interests include cross-cultural management and development of educational technology from the school level onwards.

Her organizational development interventions deal with revitalization of Asian cultural values culled from Vedantic, Buddhist, Tao and Folk traditions in the context of globalization.

Bernhard Wilpert is University Professor at the Institute of Psychology, Berlin University of Technology. He received his Ph.D. from the University of Tübingen in 1965, and has since held several important positions including President of the International Association of Applied Psychology (1994–98), Director of the Research Center System Safety (since 1990) and Member of the German Reactor Safety Commission (1993–1998). His research interests include the safety and reliability of complex socio-technical systems with high hazard potential. Prof. Wilpert has published extensively in German and English. Among his previous publications are *Deutch-chinesische Joint Ventures: Wirtschaft–Recht–Kultur* (co-edited); *Reliability and Safety in Hazardous Work Systems* (co-edited); and *Nuclear Safety: A Human Factors Perspective* (co-edited).

Yu Kai-cheng's long and distinguished career includes being Instructor in the Eighth Aviation School, PLA; Engineer and Trainer at Tongling Non-ferrous Metal Company and Professor at the School of Management, Dalian University of Technology, Liaoning, PRC. His interests include organizational behaviour and contemporary human resource management. Among his publications are *Preliminary Exploration in Mainland China's Enterprises: Employees' Sense of Distributive Fairness* and *Indigenous Psychological Research in Chinese Societies.*

INDEX

About the Editors

Henry S.R. Kao is Chair Professor of Psychology at the University of Hong Kong. Former Head at the same department, he has earlier taught at Purdue University and undertaken research at the University of Michigan, Ann Arbor, both in the US, and at the National Chengchi University in Taipei. He has also been Visiting Professor at East China Normal University in Shanghai, Shaanxi Teachers University in Xian, and South China Normal University in Guangzhou, China. In addition, Professor Kao has been President of the Division of Psychology and National Development, International Association of Applied Psychology. A prolific writer, his previous publications include *Psychology and Chinese Calligraphy; Organizational Behaviour* (co-author, in Chinese); *Social Values and Development* (co-edited); and *Effective Organizations and Social Values* (co-edited).

The late **Durganand Sinha,** one of the foremost Indian psychologists, began his distinguished career in 1951 as Lecturer in Applied Psychology at Patna University from where he went to IIT, Kharagpur as Assistant Professor in Humanities and Social Sciences. From 1961, till his retirement in 1982, he was Professor and Head of the Department of Psychology, Allahabad University. He also served as the Director of the A.N. Sinha Institute of Social Studies in Patna. During his illustrious career, Durganand Sinha was conferred many distinctions including the UGC National Lecturer's Award (1969–70), the UGC National Fellowship (1973–76), the ICSSR National Fellowship (1987–89), Fellowship of the International Association for Cross-cultural Psychology (1988), and the Wilhelm Wundt Centenary Medallion of the National Academy of Psychology (1994). A prolific writer on memory transformations, social perceptions, anxiety, industrial psychology, and rural psychology, his most recent publications included *Psychology in a Developing Country:*

The Indian Experience (1986); *Social Values and Development: Asian Perspectives* (co-edited) (1988); *Effective Organizations and Social Values* (co-edited) (1994); *Ecology, Acculturation and Psychological Adaptation* (co-authored) (1995); and *Asian Perspectives on Psychology* (co-edited), (1995).

Bernhard Wilpert is currently University Professor at the Institute of Psychology, Berlin University of Technology. Prior to that he was a Research Fellow at the Science Centre Berlin. During his rich and distinguished career, Professor Wilpert has received numerous awards and held various positions including an Honorary Doctorate from the University of Ghent for his contribution to comparative international organization research; and President of the International Association of Applied Psychology (1994–98). He is also the Director of the Research Center System Safety (since 1990) and Member of the German Reactor Safety Commission (1993–1998). He has previously published a large number of books both in English and German including *Nuclear Safety: A Human Factors Perspective* (co-edited); *Deutsch-chinesische Joint Ventures: Wirtschaft–Recht–Kultur* (co-edited); and *Industrial Democracy in Europe Revisited.*